EXTRATERRESTRIAL INTELLIGENCE
and the
CATHOLIC FAITH

EXTRATERRESTRIAL INTELLIGENCE
and the
CATHOLIC FAITH

*Are We Alone in the Universe
with God and the Angels?*

PAUL THIGPEN

TAN Books
Gastonia, North Carolina

Cover design by David Ferris—www.davidferrisdesign.com.

Cover image: Old church in Sarja (Belarus) under the starry sky, © Viktar Malyshchyts, Shutterstock.com

Library of Congress Control Number: 2022934854

ISBN: 978-1-5051-2013-4
Kindle ISBN: 978-1-5051-2014-1
ePUB ISBN: 978-1-5051-2015-8

Published in the United States by
TAN Books
PO Box 269
Gastonia, NC 28053
www.TANBooks.com

For my dear friend and esteemed colleague
Conor Gallagher,
who in so many ways
has made this book possible,
and in memory of
John Moorehouse,
beloved editor and friend.

He, who thro' vast immensity can pierce,
See worlds on worlds compose one universe,
Observe how system into system runs,
What other planets circle other suns,
What vary'd Being peoples ev'ry star,
May tell why Heaven has made us as we are.
ALEXANDER POPE, *An Essay on Man*

Contents

Acknowledgments

I wish to thank . . .

- Conor Gallagher, my dear friend and publisher at TAN Books, who invited me years ago to write this book, and who had the courage and foresight to publish it.
- My dear friends Brian Kennelly, Mara Persic, Caroline Green, Nick Vari, and all the wonderful folks at TAN who have been so patient with me and worked hard to see this book become a reality.
- Taynia-Renee Franche d. Laframboise, a faithful Catholic scholar with interests similar to mine who has encouraged me in this study and who has important things to say about this subject.
- Marie I. George, PhD, another faithful Catholic scholar who kindly sent me a copy of her book *Christianity and Extraterrestrials* some years ago when I expressed interest in it; her work has made an enormous contribution to my study.
- Daniel Hynes and Stephen Dunbar, who each helped me find quickly the source of an important quote from Saint Augustine.
- So many friends, especially Christian young adults, who have encouraged me by their enthusiastic interest in this topic and have waited excitedly to

read what I have to say; I trust they will not be disappointed.

- My wife, Leisa, for her patience as I worked endless hours on my most challenging writing project since my doctoral dissertation.
- Last but not least, Saint Anthony, whom I called upon often to help this aging brain remember where to find something I had read. He never fails to assist me.

"Do You Know the Ordinances of the Heavens?"

An Introduction to the Conversation

"Then the Lord answered Job out of the whirlwind: . . . 'Where were you . . . when the morning stars sang together, and all the sons of God shouted for joy? . . . Can you bind the chains of the Pleiades or loose the cords of Orion? . . . Can you guide the Bear with its children? Do you know the ordinances of the heavens?'"

—Job 38:1, 7, 31, 33

MY MATERNAL GRANDPARENTS once farmed the humble red clay in a remote part of rural central Georgia. When I was young, they would host me for a weeklong visit from the city each summer. I still remember vividly, now more than half a century later, one moonless, wildly starry night when I walked outside the farmhouse to lie alone on the ground. There were no street lights, few artificial lights of any kind, allowing a spectacular view of the heavens rarely found these days.

For what seemed like hours, the twinkling of countless stars, the steady radiance of the planets, the immense shining path of the Milky Way, all captivated me and sparked my curiosity. I knew enough science even then to suppose that only angels could fly the astronomical distances between me and those heavenly bodies. And yet I dreamed . . .

What if I could travel to those shining worlds? What would I find there? Whom *might I find there?*

Suddenly the questions took an unsettling direction. *What if* they *could travel to* my *world? Right here? Right now?*

I ran back into the farmhouse and jumped in bed, eyes wide open all night.

An Ancient Debate

Of course, I was not at all alone in pondering such things. As we'll see in the chapters to come, the possibility of intelligent life beyond earth has been debated since ancient times, both in Christian and in non-Christian cultures. (We will use a common shorthand term to refer to such life: the abbreviation "ETI," for "ExtraTerrestrial Intelligence.")

I was warned that certain segments of our contemporary society, particularly the academic world, might label me eccentric for writing about this topic. Yet those who hand out such labels must not be aware that in the light of history, such a dismissive attitude is itself revealed to be eccentric, an aberration, an anomaly. In fact, some of the best minds of the last twenty-five centuries in Western civilization—philosophers, theologians, scientists, literary figures—have energetically and sincerely engaged this subject.

To those who would award me a tinfoil hat, I simply reply that you will need many more such hats: for Democritus, Plato, and Aristotle; Origen, Athanasius, and Augustine; Albert, Aquinas, and Bonaventure; Copernicus, Galileo, and Kepler; Descartes and Pascal, Voltaire and Leibniz and

Kant; Milton, Wordsworth, Tennyson, Dostoevsky; Thomas Paine, Benjamin Franklin, John Adams; and countless more.

Humility: Key to Wisdom

From the very outset of my study, I have been convinced that in this endeavor as in every endeavor, *humility* is the key to wisdom.

We need humility in making claims about what is scientifically possible. The history of science is one long story of surprising discoveries that reveal the limited vision of our assumptions about what can or cannot exist with regard to both natural phenomena and technology.

We need humility in making theological and philosophical claims about what is "probable" or "fitting" or other admittedly subjective designations, especially with regard to what God has done or might have done. "For my thoughts are not your thoughts, neither are your ways my ways, says the LORD. For as the heavens are higher than the earth, so are my ways higher than your ways and my thoughts than your thoughts" (Is 55:8–9).

We need humility in considering our place in this vast universe that God has created. "Then Job answered the LORD: 'Behold, I am of small account'" (Job 40:3–4). And for Catholics, if the Church's Magisterium (teaching office) should make a definitive pronouncement about the subject of ETI, we need humility to accept what the Church will teach us.

God's rebuke to Job so long ago rings down through the centuries to our own time: *"Do you know the ordinances of the heavens?"* (Job 38:33, emphasis added). Given the meaning of the Hebrew word translated here as "ordinances," God is challenging us as he did Job: Do we know all the bounds, the laws, the measures, the decrees He Himself has appointed for the universe?

Quite simply, we do not. The Creator of the cosmos holds in His hands more mysteries than we can ever fathom.

What Difference Would It Make?

Some might ask, "What difference would it make for Christians if we knew for sure that ETI exists?" First, as the history of the ETI conversation demonstrates, Christians would hear the misguided claim from two types of ideological adversaries that extraterrestrial intelligence disproves their faith.

On the one hand would be those with a general skepticism toward religion, who would insist that the Christian (and especially the biblical) account of the universe cannot account for or accommodate the existence of nonhuman intelligent beings (other than angels). As we shall see, this is an unfounded claim that we have heard for centuries now.

On the other hand would be those religious (or, as they might prefer to say it, "spiritual") souls who have rejected traditional Christian faith but still seek transcendent ideas and mystical experiences in various New Age or other occult spiritual traditions. Some such traditions have already incorporated messianic notions of ETI into their mythology, looking to our superior, more advanced "space brothers" (they go by many names) as the source of enlightenment and salvation for humankind. Such believers would welcome any disclosure of ETI existence as vindication of their beliefs—and proof that the Christian faith is false. Again,

ETI proponents of this sort have been around for centuries, though they may be more numerous today.

The present work should put to rest the claims of both these groups that the public discovery or disclosure of ETI somehow disproves the Christian faith. Catholics and other Christians need not be disturbed by the possibility that intelligent extraterrestrial races could exist. As we shall see, though a public encounter with ETI would raise many questions to be answered about their spiritual and moral status, the Catholic faith could accommodate their existence as it has so many scientific discoveries over the centuries.

A second important consequence following a public, officially announced discovery or disclosure of the existence of extraterrestrial intelligence would be this: Some Catholics and other Christians, adopting for themselves the misguided notion that their faith is incompatible with the idea of extraterrestrial intelligence, would not deny their faith. Instead, they would deny the reality of ETI. To clarify, they would not deny that nonhuman intelligences exist and interact with humans; rather, they would conclude that all ETI experiences are actually deceptions perpetrated by demons.

As we will see, some claims of alien abduction or other interaction do seem to manifest the classical traits of demonic activity and deception. But it would be implausible to attribute (for example) retrieved alien spacecraft to demons who have no need of physical transport. In addition, there are countless reports of UFOs that seem to lack any demonic characteristics. The truth, Our Lord declared, will set us free (see Jn 8:32), so a false belief that any evidence of ETI is a demonic deception would ultimately bind and mislead us in important ways.

Other Reasons for Reflection

Still other reasons for reflecting on the possibility of ETI in light of the Christian faith become evident when we ponder seriously its many implications. First, the existence of ETI would demonstrate to us in new ways the greatness of God, the vastness of His wisdom and power, creativity and love. It would unveil one more rich meaning of the psalmist's cry, "The heavens are telling the glory of God; and the firmament proclaims his handiwork!" (Ps 19:1).

Second, the knowledge of ETI could at once both humble us and exalt us: "When I look at your heavens, the work of your fingers, the moon and the stars which you have established, what is man that you are mindful of him, or the son of man that you care for him? Yet you have made him little less than the angels, and you have crowned him with glory and honor" (Ps 8:3–5).

We could learn humility if we were to discover that God has many other beloved sons and daughters across this vast cosmos. Meanwhile, it would reveal to us in a new and profound way how great is our dignity—not just because we have been made in the image of God, but also because He Himself has visited this tiny planet, one among billions, to become One of us and redeem us.

In scriptural studies, the ETI conversation raises important issues in the interpretation of certain biblical texts, and for Catholics, the interpretation of magisterial texts as well. Can we reasonably conclude that these texts are intended to address only the human situation on earth and in heaven, without having intended implications for intelligent life forms beyond human beings and angels?

In Christian theology, the issues raised have potential implications first of all for *Christology*—that is, our understanding of the person and work of Jesus Christ. How would ETI relate to the human incarnation of the eternal Son of God, the Second Person of the Blessed Trinity?

This question then leads to specific issues in *soteriology*—that is, our understanding of salvation. Could there be a race of ETI that has never fallen and needs no special divine act of redemption? On the other hand, if an ETI race is fallen, as we are, would God necessarily offer them redemption, and if so, how might He redeem them?

Issues in *eschatology* are raised here as well—that is, our understanding of "the Last Things." What would be the ultimate destiny of ETI, and how would that destiny be related to our own destiny as human beings? What role would they play, what position would they occupy, in the final consummation of all things?

Finally, a discussion of alien natures inevitably has implications as well for Christian *anthropology*—that is, our understanding of what it means to be human, seen in the light of faith. The English word *define* has a Latin root that means "to mark the limit of," to determine not only what something *is* but also what it is *not*. The existence of an intelligent species not descended from Adam on earth would press us to reflect more deeply on the Christian understanding of not only what it means to be human but also what it means to be fallen, and what it means to be redeemed. Learning more about creatures who are like us in certain ways but fundamentally different in others would be a path to better understanding of ourselves.

Questions and Issues to Address

A book on this topic could take the discussion in countless directions. In light of the concerns we have noted, we will seek to focus on addressing these questions:

- What have Catholic and other Christian thinkers throughout history had to say about the possibility of ETI?
- Which passages in Scripture and in the magisterial teaching of the Catholic Church might shed light on the topic?
- Are alleged human encounters with ETI simply a form of demonic deception and manipulation?
- Is belief in ETI compatible with the teaching of the Catholic Church?
- What would be the possibilities for the spiritual and moral status of an extraterrestrial intelligent race?
- What relationship might these possible forms of ETI have to Jesus Christ, His incarnation, His redemptive work, and His final appearance in glory as Lord and Judge?
- Would a public ETI discovery, disclosure, or encounter be a threat to the faith of Catholics, or would it have the potential to clarify and confirm our faith?
- How should the Church prepare for the possibility of public ETI discovery, disclosure, or encounter, and how should the Church respond to such an event?

- If we were to experience a public encounter with ETI, with an ongoing conversation, what relevant questions, with theological implications, would need to be answered about their nature, their moral status, and their intentions toward us?

Many Catholics and other Christians may never have considered these questions to be important. They may never have considered them at all. Yet they do have significant implications, as we have noted.

Scope and Approach

Some authors have examined the topic of Christian thought about ETI primarily as historians, without proposing theological conclusions. Others have approached the subject as Christian philosophers. Still others have engaged in lively theological debate but with scant reference to specific scriptural and doctrinal texts that have an important bearing on the topic for Christians and for Catholics in particular.[1]

---

[1] For historical surveys and primary texts of the theological conversation about ETI, see Steven J. Dick, *Plurality of Worlds: The Extraterrestrial Life Debate from Democritus to Kant* (Cambridge: Cambridge University Press, 1982); Michael J. Crowe, *The Extraterrestrial Life Debate, 1750–1900: The Idea of a Plurality of Worlds from Kant to Lowell* (Cambridge: Cambridge University Press, 1986; new ed., Mineola, N.Y.: Dover Publications, 1999); Michael J. Crowe, ed., *The Extraterrestrial Life Debate: Antiquity to 1915: A Source Book* (Notre Dame, Ind.: University of Notre Dame Press, 2008); Steven J. Dick, *The Biological Universe: The Twentieth-Century Extraterrestrial Life Debate and the Limits of Science* (Cambridge: Cambridge University Press, 1996). For a Thomist philosophical approach, see *Marie I. George, Christianity and Extraterrestrials? A Catholic Perspective* (New York: iUniverse, 2005). For primarily theological discussions, see the works noted in later chapters of this work.

My academic training and experience are as an historical theologian and student of Scripture in the Catholic tradition. For this reason, my work will focus on the subject of ETI in light of Scripture, the teaching of the Catholic Church, and the debates among Christians and other thinkers throughout the history of the Church.

A number of theological studies have spent considerable time surveying the scientific debates related to extraterrestrial intelligence. These debates tend to focus on two concerns: The first is whether ETI is more likely to be common throughout the universe or extremely rare (perhaps even unique to planet Earth). The second is whether contact between multiple forms of ETI would be technologically possible, given the vast chasms of time and distance between habitable planets.

Though I have read deeply in the scientific literature with regard to extraterrestrial intelligence, I have decided not to spend much time discussing the scientific context in this book, for several reasons. First, I am not a scientist, and other writers have already done an admirable job of presenting the strengths and weaknesses of the opposing scientific positions. I recommend especially David Wilkinson's *Science, Religion, and the Search for Extraterrestrial Intelligence* (Oxford University Press, 2013). Wilkinson holds a PhD in Theoretical Astrophysics as well as one in Systematic Theology, so he is immanently qualified to address these issues.

Second, the various scientific arguments proposed appear to me thoroughly speculative and the evidence inconclusive, given the uncertainties of the subject matter. So much of what we know, or think we know, about the fundamental nature of the cosmos and the laws of physics has been challenged in recent times, and basic scientific paradigms may be shifting, as they have in the past. We do well not to make theological arguments based on current scientific assumptions about what is or is not possible with regard to the existence of ETI. And we cannot simply rule out the possibility of interstellar travel as long as our knowledge of fundamental cosmology and physics is so limited.

In any case, my goal is not to make claims about the likelihood of ETI's existence or the possibility of making contact with it. The primary concern of this book is to show that the Christian faith as traditionally held by the Catholic Church would not be contradicted by the public discovery or disclosure of extraterrestrial intelligence.

I do have opinions about what are popularly called UFOs or "Unidentified Flying Objects." (The more current designation is UAP: "Unidentified Aerial Phenomena.") But the historical and theological arguments I make here do not rest on the credibility of claims regarding such phenomena, nor even on the nature of what is being observed—whether they might actually be of extraterrestrial origin or might represent something more astounding. For this reason, I bring UAP into my analysis only when needed to explain an historically eccentric trait of our contemporary culture: the widespread failure to take the ETI issue seriously.

Even so, I consider UAP an important subject in its own right, and my guess is that most people who choose to read a book about ETI will reasonably expect that at least a few pages will be devoted to the topic. With this in mind, I have included an appendix entitled "What About UFOs?"

The public discovery or disclosure of extraterrestrial intelligence would of course raise questions about how best to interpret certain biblical passages and Church doctrines. But new scientific knowledge of this sort could be accommodated with integrity within the doctrinal and devotional framework of this ancient faith. For this reason, whichever scientific position on these matters turns out to be the true one (if we should find out this side of heaven), the Catholic Church can embrace the truth, and the Catholic faith will serve to illuminate and interpret what science or experience will teach.

One author to whom I owe a great deal (in the study of this subject as in so many others) is the celebrated and inimitable Christian writer C. S. Lewis. A Cambridge professor of Medieval and Renaissance English, he was formally trained neither as a scientist nor as a theologian. Yet he had much of value to say about this topic because of an acute clarity in analysis, a startlingly wide range of interests, a phenomenal breadth and depth of study, and a marvelously rich imagination.

In writing about ETI, Lewis tends to take one of two approaches, both appropriate for a popular rather than scholarly audience. In essays such as "Religion and Rocketry," he reasons in prose at a simple, common-sense level. In novels such as *Perelandra,* he weaves a richly speculative tale that opens to the reader's imagination a wide horizon of possibilities. In both approaches, he demonstrates a brilliant and exemplary humility. I trust that I have learned from him in crafting my approach.[2]

---

[2] "Religion and Rocketry" appears in C. S. Lewis, *The World's Last Night and Other Essays* (New York: Harcourt Brace, 1952); *Out of the Silent Planet, Perelandra,* and *That Hideous Strength* are a trilogy

Curiosity and Wonder

My fervent hope is that this study can in some way make a contribution to the fascinating, age-old conversation about ETI and the Christian, specifically Catholic, faith. My goal is to embrace the attitude of inquiry once described by Alistair Cooke: "Curiosity endows the people who have it with a generosity in argument and a serenity in their own mode of life which springs from their cheerful willingness to let life take the form it will"—even, we might add, extraterrestrial life.[3]

If we are to have any chance at understanding these things, we must maintain a sense of *wonder*—an attitude of humility in the face of mystery. As usual, Shakespeare says it best. His title character in *Hamlet* sets the stage for our conversation when he tells Horatio: "There are more things in heaven and Earth . . . than are dreamt of in your philosophy."[4]

Paul Thigpen, PhD
November 15, 2021
Feast of St. Albert the Great, OP
Theologian, philosopher, scientist, mediator
Patron saint of philosophers and scientists
Doctor of the Church

---

of science fiction novels, now available together in a 2011 edition by Simon & Schuster.

[3]   Quoted in David Wilkinson, *Science, Religion, and the Search for Extraterrestrial Intelligence* (Oxford: Oxford University Press, 2013), 3.

[4]   *Hamlet* (1.5.167–8).

I

A History of the ETI Conversation

"Worlds without Number"

A Lively Debate since Ancient Times

"With God it is easy to make worlds without number and end. As it is easy for you to conceive a city and worlds without bound, unto God it is easy to make them; or rather again, it is easier by far."

—Saint John Chrysostom[1]

ARE WE ON Earth the lone intelligent inhabitants of this vast universe? The angels, both fallen and unfallen, act upon it without physical bodies in the fulfillment of their assigned missions, whether heavenly or infernal. But do we humans share the cosmos with any other *embodied* intelligent forms of life created by God?

Today, speculation about the existence of extraterrestrial intelligence (ETI) is livelier than ever. A growing number of science fiction novels and films about alien life continue to find a wide and enthusiastic audience. Scientists look for evidence of life beyond earth through multiple means:

---

[1] St. John Chrysostom, *Homilies on First Corinthians, vol. 12, Nicene and Post-Nicene Fathers,* First Series, ed. Philip Schaff (Grand Rapids, Mich.: Eerdmans, 1988), Homily XVII, [3], 239–40.

interplanetary explorations by NASA;[2] studying unidentified aerial phenomena (UAP) and searching beyond Earth for evidence of extraterrestrial technological artifacts (such as possible ETI space probes);[3] monitoring electromagnetic radiations from the heavens for potential signs of transmissions from extraterrestrial civilizations;[4] and transmitting interstellar messages in an attempt to contact such civilizations.[5]

Civil and military authorities in the United States and other nations have established formal agencies to examine continuing reports of UAP that cannot be explained by conventional, or even cutting-edge, technology. Elected officials are demanding more government transparency about these matters, with concerns about national security.

Meanwhile, stories of alien abductions or other close encounters have multiplied. Even new religious traditions have emerged, such as Scientology, whose novel mythologies claim to be based on revelations from or about ETI. Some have concluded that ancient pagan myths about the gods, and even biblical accounts of angelic beings, actually refer to creatures who visited Earth from other planets. Others now look for alien saviors to descend from the heavens, enlightening us and rescuing us from the miserable state we have created for ourselves on this planet. Many non-Christians

---

[2] "Astrobiology at NASA," NASA, updated January 13, 2022, https://astrobiology.nasa.gov/.
[3] See the goals of the Galileo Project: https://projects.iq.harvard.edu/galileo/home.
[4] See the goals of SETI: https://www.seti.org/.
[5] See the goals of METI: http://meti.org/.

insist that any public revelations of ETI would disprove the Christian faith.[6]

Even so, many who contribute to this intensifying interest in ETI fail to realize that such contemporary discussion is only the most recent portion of a debate that stretches back at least twenty-six centuries. How can we hope to come in on the tail of such a lengthy conversation and make a useful contribution if we have no idea what has already been said? To do justice to this complex topic, we must begin an exploration of ETI and the Catholic faith with an historical overview.

Though I am convinced that the historical aspect is essential for understanding our subject, I recognize that some readers may be less interested in history and more eager to read my theological analysis in light of that history. Those who find themselves in that category should proceed to the second section of the book, "A Contribution to the ETI Conversation." They will nevertheless at times find themselves, I suspect, referring back to previous historical chapters for important background information.

Ancient Greek Debates

Fathers and Doctors of the Catholic Church, Catholic philosophers and theologians, popes and bishops, friars and priests, scientists and saints have all taken part in the ETI

---

[6] For more on these religious movements and the challenges they pose to uninformed Catholics and other Christians, see T. Franche d. Laframboise, *"ALIEN JESUS": exogenesis, posthumanism, and the rise of the A.I. gods* (Dalton, Penn.: Mount Thabor Press, forthcoming).

conversation. But the conceptual foundations for their discussion were laid in the centuries before Christ.

In the long history of Western thought, the earliest surviving records of debate with implications for ETI come from
ancient Greek philosophers in the sixth, fifth, and fourth
centuries BC. The question of intelligent life beyond earth
was at that time part of a larger discussion about what came
to be known as "the plurality of worlds." This notion originally referred, not so much to multiple heavenly bodies in
our universe (the stars, planets, their moons, and other features of the cosmos), but rather to multiple *entire universes*,
all coexisting independently of one another, each cosmos
with its own earth and celestial bodies.[7]

Thinkers in the Greek philosophical tradition known as
atomism concluded that there is indeed a plurality of such
worlds. They reached this conclusion on the basis of several
assumptions about all that exists: First, all things come into
existence, they taught, not by some action of the gods, but by
the constant movement and coalition of particles they called
atoms. Second, the laws of nature governing these atoms and
their movement are universal. Third, there is nothing special
about our planet Earth. Fourth, nature tends to realize all
possibilities. What is potential eventually becomes actual.[8]

Some atomists, such as Leucippus (fifth century BC) and
Democritus (d. 361 BC) insisted that these multiple worlds
are "innumerable." Epicurus (d. c. 270 BC) taught that
"there are infinite worlds both like and unlike this world

---

[7] For an excellent historical overview of the early "plural worlds"
debate, see Dick, *Plurality of Worlds*.
[8] See Wilkinson, *Search for Extraterrestrial Intelligence*, 17.

of ours," and since all possibilities are realized, in all these worlds there are living creatures.[9] Under the influence of these Greek philosophers, this plurality of worlds idea eventually gained a following among certain Roman thinkers as well, such as the poet Lucretius (99–55 BC).

Plato, Aristotle, Plutarch

Meanwhile, the celebrated Greek philosopher Plato (427–347 BC) taught that the universe was organized by the "Demiurge." This figure was a kind of divine craftsman—not like the omnipotent God of the ancient Hebrews Who spoke the universe into existence out of nothing, but rather a universal architect and builder who organized eternally existing matter and brought order out of the chaos. The Demiurge, Plato insisted, distributed souls to the stars (the stars, he believed, were living creatures), inserting one soul into each star.[10] In this way, he conceived of ETI in the form of living stars who moved across the sky.

Aristotle, Plato's most famous pupil, rejected the atomist teaching that there could be more than one cosmos. The philosophical position he developed would become extremely influential in the medieval Christian world. His geocentric—that is, earth-centered—model of the universe led him to conclude that all things in existence have a single circumference and a single center, and that center is the Earth. For this reason, there is no possibility of another universe. Aristotle presented other arguments against plural universes as well, but this one was primary.

---

[9] Quoted in Crowe, *Extraterrestrial Life Debate: Antiquity to 1915*, 4.
[10] See Wilkinson, *Search for Extraterrestrial Intelligence*, 17.

Aside from the debate over multiple worlds, with at least some of those worlds inhabited, a few Greek philosophers speculated about extraterrestrial life in a much closer setting: the Moon. Followers of the ancient sixth-century philosopher and mathematician Pythagoras claimed that the Moon was much like the Earth, with plants and animals and intelligent creatures vastly superior to humans. Rather than insisting on either an infinity of worlds or a single world, this speculation took a kind of middle ground: Within the single universe that we ourselves inhabit, the Moon is a second inhabited "world," though not its own cosmos.[11]

Plutarch was a Greek philosopher, biographer, and essayist who lived about the time of the writing of the New Testament (AD 46–c. 120). His treatise *De facie in orbi lunae* ("On the Face Appearing in the Orb of the Moon") was more literary than scientific, but it provided an extended speculation about possible lunar inhabitants. The *True History* of the Assyrian satirist Lucian of Samasota (c. 115–200), Plutarch's younger contemporary, was even more fanciful. It described an imaginary voyage to the inhabited moon, which he deemed quite earthlike.

Aristotle, for his part, actually suggested on one occasion that living creatures of a kind unknown to us might inhabit the Moon. But this speculation seems to contradict his larger philosophical understanding of the cosmos. Life on the Moon would entail change (birth, death, movement, growth, and more), yet he insisted that the Moon was an unchangeable region.[12]

---

[11] Wilkinson, 18.

[12] Aristotle, *De Generatione Animalium,* 761b, lines 21–23.

Early Christian Thinkers

The theologians of the early Church were often familiar with the ideas of Greek and Roman philosophers, including the ongoing discussions about a plurality of worlds. These Christian thinkers reported and sometimes debated the ideas themselves.

We should note that when most early Christian writers affirmed the reality of multiple "worlds," they were not speaking of multiple universes, as the atomists had posited. Typically, they were echoing Scripture, which speaks of "this world" and "the world to come." These biblical passages refer to the present *age* and the *age* to come, when the present heavens and earth will find their final consummation in "new heavens and a new earth in which righteousness dwells" (2 Pt 3:13; see also Is 65:17; 66:22).

This meaning of "world" or "age" seems to be the sense as well of the declaration by the fathers of the Council of Constantinople (381), reaffirmed by the Council of Chalcedon (451): "We believe . . . in one Lord, Jesus Christ . . . begotten of His Father before all worlds [ages]." That is, the relationship of God the Son and God the Father existed before time itself began; indeed, outside of time, in eternity. We have no record of any debate in these councils about plurality of worlds, but we do know that in the popular Arian heresy of the period, the coeternal nature of the Father and the Son had been challenged. So this truth had to be firmly and repeatedly declared.

The second-century "Divine Liturgy of the Holy Apostle and Evangelist Mark" used similar language to refer to God the Father. It invoked Him as "God of light, Father of Life, Author of grace, *Creator of worlds* [ages]."[13]

One possible exception to this common meaning, however, is found in a letter written by Pope Saint Clement of Rome (first century), a Church Father who, according to ancient tradition, knew Saint Peter and other Apostles. He spoke of "the ocean, impassable to man, and the worlds beyond it," which are regulated by God's laws. This statement was made in the context of surveying various ways in which the elements of God's creation are placed in the service of men and the other living creatures. "All these the great Creator and Lord of all has appointed to exist in peace and harmony, while he does good to all."[14]

One third-century Christian commentator suggested two possible interpretations for these words. Saint Clement, he explained, might be referring to other parts of the earth that we cannot reach because the ocean prevents such a journey. In this sense, "worlds" would be parallel to the expression used by later, ocean-crossing explorers when they referred to Europe and Asia as the "Old World" and the Americas as the "New World."

A second interpretation suggested by the commentator was that Saint Clement thought "the whole universe of

---

[13] "Second Ecumenical Council (381)" in *The Seven Ecumenical Councils,* vol. 14, eds. Philip Schaff and Henry Wace (Grand Rapids, Mich.: Eerdmans, 1986), 184; "The Divine Liturgy of the Holy Apostle and Evangelist Mark, the Disciple of the Holy Peter, in *The Ante-Nicene Fathers,* vol. 7, ed. A. Cleveland Coxe (Eerdmans, 1985), 558. The Greek words most often translated in all these ancient texts as "world" or "age" are *cosmos* and *aion.*

[14] St. Clement, *The First Epistle of Clement to the Corinthians in The Ante-Nicene Fathers,* vol. 1, ed. Alexander Roberts and James Donaldson (Grand Rapids, Mich.: Eerdmans, 1987), [20], 10–11.

existing things" contained "other worlds"; he "wished the globe of the sun or moon, and of the other bodies called planets, to each be termed 'worlds.'" If this is the correct interpretation, then we have here what might well be the earliest surviving Christian reference to other worlds within our universe, and even to worlds whose natural features serve as God's gifts to their inhabitants.[15]

Some would argue, of course, that an affirmation of ETI has been part of the Christian tradition from the very beginning, because we could place angels in the category of "extraterrestrial intelligence." Others would respond that angels, pure spiritual beings who do not possess bodies or occupy space, are a different kind of creature altogether; and the age-old debates we will be considering had implications for the existence, not of angels (which were a given for Christians), but of intelligent extraterrestrial creatures with physical bodies.

Even so, some ancient and medieval Christian writers thought that angels are in fact embodied in the sense that they have matter, but their bodies are made of a more "subtle" matter than ours—a kind of "aerial body" made of refined "spiritual matter." With regard to those Christians, we might consider: Since they believed in extraterrestrial angelic intelligences moving through space with physical bodies different from our own, how much of a stretch would it have been for them to believe as well in the kinds of ETI envisioned by our popular culture today?

---

[15] Origen, *De Principiis,* Bk. II, ch. 3, para. 6, 273–47; trans. and quoted in George, *Christianity,* 221. George notes: "The Latin is taken from *Vier Bücher von den Prinzipien*, ed. Herwig Görgemanns and Heinrich Karpp (Darmstadt: Wissenschaftliche Buchgesellschaft, 1976), 318."

In this light, Fr. Roch Kereszty, OCist, has suggested that the "omission of the angels' role in salvation history [by modern theologians who ignore or deny their existence] . . . makes it more difficult for [them] to create space for the role of possible extraterrestrial intelligent beings in God's universal plan."[16]

The Speculations of Origen

The commentator who offered the alternative interpretations of Saint Clement's letter was Origen (185–254), one of the most influential, prolific theologians of the early Christian centuries—and also one of the most controversial. His personal holiness is undoubted, and he heroically endured imprisonment and barbarous torture for his Christian faith in one of the Roman imperial persecutions. He sought to elaborate faithfully the Church's tradition as he understood it; many passages of his homilies, scriptural commentaries, and theological treatises still yield important insights today.

Even so, Origen's intellectual brilliance and fertile imagination often led him to speculations that were later rejected by the Church as incompatible with the apostolic tradition she had received. Among those ideas was his distinctive notion of a plurality of worlds—not simultaneous, spatially separated ones, as Epicurus and others had claimed, but rather multiple universes in succession through time. This speculation had its roots in the Greek philosophical tradition called Stoicism.

---

[16] See Roch A. Kereszty, *Jesus Christ: Fundamentals of Theology*, rev. ed. (New York: St. Paul's, 2002), 445.

Origen supported his idea in part by citing the scriptural passages just noted that speak of this world and the world to come. But he took the idea to a different level altogether, asserting that God has created and dissolved, and will continue to create and dissolve, an infinite series of universes, including inhabited earthlike planets.

Origen's speculations about successive worlds involved startling notions of a kind of reincarnation that were contrary to Catholic teaching as it developed from the apostolic deposit of faith. Saint Jerome (343–420) reported that, according to Origen, successive worlds come into being through sin; that humans in one world may become demons in another; that demons in one world may become incarnate as humans in another; and that an archangel in one world can become a devil in the next and then be changed back into an archangel in a later world.[17]

We should not be surprised, then, that such teaching was condemned by Saint Jerome. Saint Augustine also opposed it, in part because of "the fact of the eternal life of the saints."[18] That is, the Church's teaching that after their earthly life, the glorified saints live forever with God in heaven contradicts Origen's notions of reincarnation. As the book of Hebrews declares: "It is appointed for men to die once, and after that comes judgment" (Heb 9:27).

Nevertheless, we must note that these writers were not objecting specifically to the idea of intelligent life beyond

---

[17] St. Jerome, Letter 124, "To Avitus," in *The Principal Works of St. Jerome,* vol. 6, *Nicene and Post-Nicene Fathers,* Second Series, ed. Philip Schaff and Henry Wace (Grand Rapids, Mich.: Eerdmans, 1983), [3–5], 239–40.

[18] St. Augustine, *City of God,* 12:19.

this earth. They were opposed to Origen's entire system of successive worlds, with the unorthodox conclusions he drew from a misguided premise.

Other passages from Origen have been cited by ETI advocates to suggest that he considered the benefits of Christ's redemption to extend to all the creatures of the universe. A similar claim is made for several Eastern Church Fathers with regard to certain of their comments about the universal scope of the merits of the Incarnation and the Holy Sacrifice of the Mass. Though these remarks from ancient Christian sources may at least in principle allow for the possibility of salvation for intelligent extraterrestrials, as we shall see in a later chapter, they do not explicitly refer to ETI as we would understand the term today.[19]

Atomism Rejected

Meanwhile, the earlier Greek notion of an infinite plurality of simultaneous, spatially separated worlds was explicitly rejected by the third-century Christian theologian Saint Hippolytus of Rome in his treatise *Refutation of All Heresies*. In the following century, Saint Philastrius, bishop of Brescia, also wrote of the "heresy that says there are infinite and innumerable worlds, according to the empty opinion of certain philosophers" such as Democritus, "who proclaimed this [teaching] as proceeding from his own wisdom."[20] To

---

[19] Comte Joseph de Maistre, *Soirées de Saint-Pétersbourg*, vol. II (Paris, n.d.), 318–19; trans. Eugene Lynch, "On Sacrifices," in *The United States Catholic Magazine and Monthly Review* (1845, vol. 4), 300–5.
[20] George, *Christianity*, 66; the Philastrius quote is from a passage translated by George.

clarify, Saint Hippolytus and Saint Philastrius were rejecting the idea of multiple universes, not of multiple worlds in the sense of inhabited planets in our universe.

At the same time, we should note that several Church Fathers freely confessed that because God is all-powerful, he could certainly create multiple worlds if he wished. Saint John Chrysostom, patriarch of Constantinople and a Father and Doctor of the Church (345–407), declared: "For with God, nothing is difficult: but as the painter who has made one likeness will make ten thousand with ease, so also with God it is easy to make worlds without number and end. Rather, as it is easy for you to conceive a city and worlds without bound, unto God it is easy to make them; or rather again, it is easier by far."[21]

The fourth-century bishop theologians Saint Athanasius (297–373) and Saint Basil (329–379), also Fathers and Doctors of the Church, agreed that God is all-powerful in this way. The former wrote that "God might have made other [Universes]," and the latter that divine "creative power is capable of bringing a greater number of heavens into existence." Saint Athanasius went on to say that, nevertheless, "the Universe that has been made is one."[22]

---

[21] St. John Chrysostom, *Homilies on First Corinthians,* vol. 12, *Nicene and Post-Nicene Fathers,* First Series, ed. Philip Schaff (Grand Rapids, Mich.: Eerdmans, 1988), Homily XVII, [3], 239–40.
[22] Athanasius, *Epistola ad Adelphium,* 25; St. Basil, *Exegetical Homilies,* trans. Agnes Clare Way, CDP (Washington, D.C.: Catholic University Press, 1963), Homily 3, 40.

The Antipodes

An interesting related debate in the ancient world, about another kind of intelligent creature beyond those we know, involved the notion of the "Antipodes." These were humans that walk on the other side of the earth (which is presumably spherical) with their feet turned toward our feet. Thus they were not so much extraterrestrials as what we might call "other terrestrials."

Of course, we now know that the Earth is indeed spherical, and there are human beings walking the sphere opposite us, with their feet turned toward our feet. But such knowledge was only speculative and seemed far-fetched in the ancient world; Saint Augustine spoke of the idea as merely a "fable." We cannot know this to be the case, he said, because the other side of a spherical earth, if it is in fact a sphere (he was open to the idea), might be uninhabitable, covered with ocean or inhospitable desert.

More importantly, Saint Augustine was concerned that claims of the Antipodes' existence were contrary to Christian faith in this way: The Church teaches that all human beings are descended from Adam. Because of his fall, his descendants are all subject to original sin and need the salvation offered by Jesus Christ.

Given the presumed limits of sea-going vessels in Saint Augustine's day, and the ignorance of a prehistoric land bridge between what we now call the Eastern and Western Hemispheres, we can appreciate his conclusion: It is "absurd," he reasoned, to assume that some of Adam's descendants had been able to journey from this side of the world across the vast ocean to the other side (if it exists). This means that any

Antipodes, if they existed, would have to be humans who were not descended from Adam.[23]

Even though it is not really part of the ancient debate over ETI, we note this particular subject of discussion for two reasons. First, Saint Augustine's comments have been taken by some to mean that he rejected the notion of ETI. But it should be clear that he was instead objecting to the idea that the human race is not all one family, descended from the same first parents.

The significance of this belief, still firmly maintained by the Catholic Church today, became especially obvious in the twentieth century. In Germany, within the National Socialist (Nazi) movement, a myth emerged that not all humans have the same ultimate origins—in fact, that some racial groups are actually subhuman. The consequences of that belief, of course, were catastrophic.[24]

A second reason to note this particular debate is that it foreshadows later theological conversations in history about the possibility of ETI. As we will see, much of the more recent religious discussion about these matters has revolved around this essential issue: If an intelligent extraterrestrial species exists and is not human (descended from Adam), what role would it have in God's redemptive plan?

To sum up: Early Christian thinkers were aware of the ancient discussion among pagan philosophers about the plurality of worlds. They continued the conversation, adding their insights derived from the apostolic tradition of the

---

[23] St. Augustine, *The City of God*, Bk. XVI, ch. 9.
[24] See the encyclical of Pope Pius XII *Humani generis* (1950), especially par. 37.

Church. But they were concerned primarily with speculations about entire multiple universes, presumably inhabited. The notion of ETI in the sense of inhabited planets or even moons within our universe received little if any attention.

In the centuries to come, however, Christian writers of the Medieval and Renaissance periods would eventually turn their attention to that more specific issue—with fascinating results.

2

"One of the Most Wondrous and Noble Questions"

The Medieval and Early Renaissance Debates

"Since one of the most wondrous and noble questions about Nature is whether there is one world or many, a question that the human mind desires to understand per se, it seems desirable for us to inquire about it."

—Saint Albert the Great[1]

WITH THE DECLINE and fall of the Western Roman Empire, theological, philosophical, and scientific inquiry languished. But even in the first centuries that followed, before medieval theology, philosophy, and science came to flourish, we find indications that the debate about a plurality of worlds continued.

A brief and curious comment appears in a surviving letter of Pope Saint Zachary (d. 752) to Saint Boniface, archbishop of Mainz, known as "the Apostle of Germany" (c. 680–754),

---

[1] *Alberti Magni opera omnia,* vol. V, pt. 1, as quoted and translated by Dick, *Plurality of Worlds,* 23.

in 752. The epistle is mostly focused on questions about Baptism, but one particular passage seems relevant to the question of ETI. It refers to the "perverse and contrary teaching" of a priest named Vergilius (also spelled "Virgelius"), "which he spoke against God and his soul."

"If it will have become clear that he professes that there exists another world [Latin *alius mundus*], and other men [*alii homines*] under the earth [*sub terra*], or the sun and the moon [*seu sol et luna*], he, when counsel has been taken, is to be ejected from the Church, and deprived of [priestly] honor."[2] The exact meaning of these words has been disputed.

The notion of "other men under the earth" seems to refer to speculation about the so-called Antipodes that Saint Augustine had talked about centuries before. If so, Saint Zachary was probably rejecting the idea on the same grounds as his predecessor: There cannot be any human beings on the underside of the earth, he reasoned, because to be human, they would have to be descended from Adam, and so would have had to arrive at their present place by crossing what was considered an impassible ocean.

What is meant here by "the sun and the moon"? In the original Latin text, these words are serving as a grammatical subject, not the object of the preposition "under." Did Vergilius teach that there was another sun and moon, and the pope rejected that idea as an unreasonable speculation? Or was Vergilius claiming that there are human inhabitants of the sun and moon? In that case, the pope would have

---

[2] *Epistola XI Zacharia Papae ad Bonifacium Archiepiscopum* in the *Patrologia Latina*, vol. 89, 946–47; quoted in George, *Christianity,* 222, n. 41.

rejected such a notion for the same reason he rejected the notion of the Antipodes.

Still another ambiguity in the text: When the pope says "another world," did he mean another *planet* under the earth, or another *universe*? Either meaning could have been intended. But the Catholic tradition up to that time had primarily debated "the plurality of worlds" with the assumption that "world" meant "universe." So it seems more likely that this is the sense Saint Zachary was intending.

In any case, three insights are useful here: First, the pope's statement cannot be read as a clear rejection of the possibility that other earthlike planets exist, or that such planets could be inhabited by intelligent creatures who are not humans—who are *not* of Adam's race.

Second, the pope's statement appeared in a private letter, so it does not represent a definitive teaching of the Catholic Church, even though he was a pope. Instead, it was his private belief, based on his private interpretation of the Christian tradition and the common scientific assumptions of his day. The Church has never authoritatively addressed this issue.

In fact, there is no surviving evidence that Vergilius was actually condemned formally for his teaching. There does seem to be, however, evidence that he was not, since he was later appointed archbishop of Salzburg.[3]

Finally, we can see that the philosophical and theological debate about the plurality of worlds, with its implications for the possible existence of ETI, was continuing even

---

[3] P. Delhay, "Antipodes," *New Catholic Encyclopedia* (New York: McGraw-Hill, 1967), vol. 1, 631–2.

during the so-called Dark Ages in which Saint Zachary and Saint Boniface lived.

Aristotle's Influence

The rediscovery of Aristotle's work in the West made an unparalleled contribution to the flourishing of philosophy, theology, and science in the High Middle Ages (c. 1000–1250). But that philosopher's fertile influence on medieval thinkers brought with it certain limitations in philosophical and theological thought. Nowhere are those limitations more evident than in the continuing debate about the plurality of worlds, and its implications for the idea of ETI.

Following the claims of Aristotle, the great scholastic philosopher-theologians of this period largely concluded that only one world can exist. Again, the word "world" was taken in the sense of "universe," not earthlike planets. As we have seen, Aristotle's geocentric—that is, earth-centered—model of the universe led him to conclude that all things in existence have a single circumference and a single center, and that center is the Earth. Thus there could be no possibility of another universe with a different circumference and center.

Saint Albert the Great (1193–1280), a German Dominican friar, scholar, Doctor of the Church, and bishop of Regensburg, Germany, took up the question of the plurality of worlds with great enthusiasm. "Since one of the most wondrous and noble questions about Nature is whether there is one world or many," he observed, "a question that the human mind desires to understand per se, it seems desirable for us to inquire about it."[4] He answered that question in the negative, with "world" understood as "universe," and arguments drawn mainly from Aristotle.

The English philosopher and Franciscan friar Roger Bacon (c. 1219–c. 1292) reasoned in a similar fashion. In his arguments, he even cited other elements of Aristotle's system that Aristotle himself had not used as support for his denial that plural worlds could exist. In this approach he was following the lead of such thinkers as William of Auvergne, bishop of Paris (1180/90–1249).[5]

Saint Thomas Aquinas

Saint Albert's most celebrated student, Saint Thomas Aquinas (1225–1274), worked diligently to synthesize, as far as possible, Christian theology with the newly rediscovered philosophy of Aristotle. Not surprisingly, then, Saint Thomas followed Aristotle in concluding that there could be only one cosmos. Saint Thomas also drew from Plato's thought in claiming that a singular universe resulted from a singular divine Craftsman. Because of the oneness of God, he insisted, it was fitting for Him to create only one world, mirroring His own perfection.[6]

The philosopher cited a Gospel passage to buttress this claim: "It is said [Jn 1:10]: *The world was made by him [God],*

[4] *Alberti Magni opera omnia,* vol. V, pt. 1, as quoted and translated by Dick, *Plurality of Worlds,* 23.

[5] Pierre Duhem, *Medieval Cosmology: Theories of Infinity Place, Time, Void, and the Plurality of Worlds* (Chicago: University of Chicago Press, 1985), 445–46.

[6] Crowe, *Extraterrestrial Life Debate: Antiquity to 1915,* 20.

where the world is named as one, as if only one existed."[7] But this comment seems to have been more of a passing remark than a substantive argument. As with most medieval commentators on this issue, his primary arguments were not from Scripture but from Aristotle: one Craftsman, one ordering, one end—one universe. The unity of the cosmos was essential to its perfection. Division implies imperfection.[8]

Saint Thomas, of course, had to adjust the Aristotelian model of the cosmos in certain ways to make it compatible with Christian faith. Most importantly, he affirmed, contrary to the ancient pagan philosophers, that the matter of the universe had a beginning; the one true God had created it out of nothing (*ex nihilo*). And this one consideration, the creative omnipotence of God—unforeseen by Aristotle or the atomists—eventually presented a serious challenge to Saint Thomas's conclusions about the plurality of worlds.

We should note here that even though Saint Thomas apparently never directly engaged the question of ETI, his carefully-reasoned theology about related matters are of great interest in this matter. His analysis of human nature, original sin, the Incarnation, and the possible scope of God's redemptive activity have all played a significant role in later debates about the potential spiritual and moral status of ETI, their relationship to Christ and the Church, and their ultimate destiny.[9]

---

[7]   Crowe, 23.

[8]   Dick, *Plurality of Worlds*, 26–27.

[9]   For examples of a Thomist approach to ETI in the contemporary conversation, see George, *Christianity*, and Edmund Michael Lazzari, "Would St. Thomas Baptize an Extraterrestrial?" *New Blackfriars*, 99, no. 1082 (January 1, 2018): 440–57.

One such related matter was Saint Thomas's reasoning about a speculation among certain ancient writers (including Saint Augustine and Origen) that the stars themselves are animate—that is, intelligent living creatures. This discussion was perhaps the closest he ever came to writing about a kind of ETI, though of course the notion of animated stars differs considerably from the notion of planetary inhabitants. Saint Thomas concluded that stars might be moved by a kind of soul that was non-human and something like angelic, joined to the celestial bodies as their movers. Such a possibility, he concluded, was not contrary to Catholic faith: Though the Scripture teaches nothing about animated stars, the Bible is written for our salvation, not to instruct us in cosmology.[10]

Another matter related to the modern ETI discussion is Saint Thomas's consideration of whether multiple divine Incarnations could take place. Though he focused only on the possibility of multiple incarnations among humans on Earth, his reasoning could apply as well to the possibility of multiple incarnations among various ETI races on various planets. Saint Thomas concluded that God has chosen to become a Man only once, but He could nevertheless have chosen to do it multiple times if He so willed.

God's power is infinite, he insisted, and His capacity to become incarnate is not exhausted by a single instance or even multiple instances of that action. In addition to His incarnation in Christ, then, God could have chosen to join to His divine nature "another numerically different human nature."[11]

---

[10] See Marie I. George, "Aquinas on Intelligent Extraterrestrial Life," *The Thomist 65,* no. 2 (April 2001): 239–58.

[11] George, citing Thomas Aquinas, *Summa Theologiae,* III 3.7. See also *ST* III 3.7 ad 2.

God's Power Is Not Limited

The Scholastic theology (as it was called) of this great philosopher and his scholarly allies came to dominate the universities of Europe. But three years after he died, in 1277, Étienne Tempier, the bishop of Paris (the city where Thomas had taught), publicly condemned 219 beliefs that were popular at the universities. Étienne considered these beliefs heresies because they seemed to limit the power of God.

Among these condemned notions was the teaching that God "cannot make many worlds." If God is all-powerful, as the Church has always taught, who dares to claim that He finds it impossible to make more than one universe? If He created our universe out of nothing, surely He can create out of nothing just as many other universes as He wishes.

As a result of this public condemnation, many of the theologians of the universities were pressed to reconsider their position on the matter, and the door was open to new speculation about other worlds. Among these, employing significant criticisms of Aristotle's universe, were the Franciscan philosopher William of Ockham (c. 1280–1347); the cleric Jean Buridan (c. 1295–1358), rector of the University of Paris; and Nicole Oresme (1325–82), the bishop of Paris. Though in the end they all concluded that there is no plurality of worlds, their critiques helped to identify the weaknesses in the arguments of Aristotle and Aquinas concerning the matter.[12]

One way to handle Tempier's objection had already been laid out even before the bishop of Paris issued his

---

[12] Michael J. Crowe, "A History of the Extraterrestrial Life Debate," *Zygon* 32, no. 2 (June 1997): 149.

declaration. Michael Scot (1175–1232), a British priest, scholar, and advisor to Frederick II, emperor of the Holy Roman Empire, wrote: "There are those who maintain that God, who is omnipotent, could and still can create, in addition to this world, another world, or several other worlds, or even an infinity of worlds, creating them out of elements similar to those making up this world, or out of different elements. . . . God can do this, but nature cannot withstand it. The impossibility of the plurality of worlds results from the nature of the world itself, from its proximate and essential causes; God, however, can create several worlds, if he so wishes it."[13] Plural universes do not exist, he says, not because of some limitation in God, but because of a limitation in creation itself. The universe, by its nature, is not capable of being multiple; that would create a contradiction.

Yet several prominent thinkers opposed this conclusion that God could not have created multiple worlds without a contradiction in His creation. Richard of Middleton (c. 1249–1308), a Franciscan friar, theologian, and Scholastic philosopher, summed up his position, held by others of the day as well: "I therefore state that God could have and can still now create another universe. There is, in fact, no contradiction in attributing this power to God."[14]

---

[13] *Eximii atque excellentissimi physicorum motuum cursusque siderei indagatoris* Michaelis Scoti *super auctore Sperae, cum quaestionibus diligiter emedatis, expositio confecta Illustrissimi Imperatoris Domini D. Frederici praecibus,* vol. 2, 146, n. [253]; cited in Duhem, *Medieval Cosmology,* 442–43.

[14] *Clarissimi theologi Magistri* Ricardi di Mediavilla *Seraphici ord. min. convent. super quatuor libros Sententiarum Petri Lombardi quaestiones subtilissimae,* lib. 1, dist. XLIII, art. I, quaest. IV, p. 392 [col. B]; cited in Duhem, *Medieval Cosmology,* 452.

Most of those involved in the debate eventually backed away altogether from the claim that multiple worlds are somehow impossible. Instead, they admitted—as the Franciscan theologian Saint Bonaventure (1217–1274) had reasoned even before the condemnation—that God had the power to create many worlds, but had not actually done so. It was more fitting for Him to create one universe rather than many.

Those who still wished to insist that a plurality of worlds is "impossible" found some solace in the conclusions of Albert of Saxony (c. 1320–1390), a German bishop and philosopher. He insisted that the plurality of worlds is impossible according to the principles of physical science. Even so, it is not impossible to God. If He *were* to create multiple worlds, however, it would be a miracle, an ongoing supernatural act, and physics could not explain it.[15]

Inhabited Worlds?

Albert's contemporary, the philosopher Nicole Oresme, bishop of Lisieux (c. 1320–1382), went even further in his critique of Aristotle's model. He challenged the ancient philosopher's arguments for a geocentric universe. Oresme echoed in some ways Origen's position, teaching that God could create and destroy successive worlds in time. Oresme even declared that neither reason nor experience could demonstrate the impossibility of another world on the Moon or a star, or even within the Earth.[16]

---

[15] Duhem, *Medieval Cosmology,* 468.
[16] Dick, *Plurality of Worlds,* 35.

Unlike most of his intellectual predecessors, Oresme went even further to address the more specific question of whether life might exist in these worlds. He affirmed that "God is infinite in his immensity, and, if several worlds existed, no one of them would be outside him or outside his power; *but surely, other intelligences would exist in one world and others in the other worlds* [emphasis added]." Even so, he finally offered a disclaimer that even though the omnipotent Creator could make other worlds, "there has never been nor will there ever be more than one corporeal world."[17]

In the fifteenth century, a yet more radical departure from Aristotle was taken by Cardinal Nicholas of Cusa (1401–1464), a German theologian, philosopher, and astronomer. Cusa turned away decisively from the Scholastic tradition of Saint Thomas and so many others, drawing more from the thought of Plato than from that of Aristotle. In his ideas about the cosmos, he broke fundamentally with the ancient and medieval notions of the world.

Cusa taught that the universe can have no center, so Earth is not the immoveable center, as the Scholastics had taught in following Aristotle. He speculated that there are also other planets like Earth; it is only one among others. The heavenly bodies, even the Sun, the Moon, and the stars, are all composed of the same basic elements as the Earth. For this reason, our position in the universe is neither unique nor even central.[18]

---

[17] Nicole Oresme, *Le livre du ciel et du monde,* eds. Albert Menut and Alexander Denomy, CSB, trans. Albert Menut (Madison: University of Wisconsin Press, 1968), 175; quoted in Crowe, *Extraterrestrial Life Debate: Antiquity to 1915,* 26.

[18] J. Koch, "Nicholas of Cusa," *New Catholic Encyclopedia,* vol. 10, 451.

The cardinal did not shy away from insisting that the celestial bodies could be inhabited or from speculating about their inhabitants: "Life, as it exists here on earth in the form of men, animals, and plants, is to be found, let us suppose, in a higher form in the solar and stellar regions. Rather than think that so many of the stars and parts of the heavens are uninhabited and that this earth of ours alone is peopled—and that with beings, perhaps, of an inferior type—we will suppose that in every region there are inhabitants, differing in nature by rank and all owing their origin to God, who is the center and circumference of all stellar regions." How might these various forms of life differ? "Solar beings," Cusa speculated, might be "bright and enlightened intellectual denizens, and by nature more spiritual than such as may inhabit the moon—who are possibly lunatics—while those on earth may be more gross and material."[19]

In this way, Cusa declared the whole universe to be the stage for an abundance of varied life forms. Nevertheless, he still considered the region of the Earth the most perfect, with a special significance in the universe. Though Earth had no special position as the center of the cosmos, it was special because of God's relationship to the human race.[20]

The cardinal demonstrated in many ways the humility that is so invaluable in considering this matter. "These things,

---

[19] Nicholas of Cusa, *Of Learned Ignorance*, trans. Germain Heron (London: Routledge and Kegan Paul, 1954), 111–18, quoted in Crowe, *Extraterrestrial Life Debate: Antiquity to 1915,* 31. The common root of the English words "lunar" and "lunatic" reflect the ancient notion that intermittent periods of insanity can be triggered by the moon's cycle.

[20] Dick, *Plurality of Worlds,* 42.

however, no man can know unless he be specially instructed by God . . . the manner of his present operation and of his bountifulness to come only God knows. . . . Later I shall add a little more, as far as God gives me to understand, to what it must for the moment suffice to have touched upon in ignorance."[21]

We might have expected Cusa's rather radical break with philosophical tradition to provoke considerable opposition. Yet his appointment as a cardinal, papal legate, and papal advisor, and his participation in the ecumenical Council of Basel (1431), all suggest that at least within the Catholic Church, he was respected and embraced by authorities at the highest levels.

ETI Original Sin, Incarnation, Redemption?

Cusa's contemporary, the French philosopher and theologian William of Vorilong (aka Guillaume de Varouillon, c. 1392–1463), joined the cardinal in pressing the bounds of the ancient conversation. He allowed not just for a plurality of worlds but an infinity of worlds, noting that the pagan philosopher Democritus, as we have seen, had posited an infinity of worlds. Vorilong concluded that if the atheist Democritus had only understood that these worlds "lie hid in the mind of God," rather than thinking them the result of random interaction of atoms, "he would have understood rightly."[22]

---

[21] Quoted in Crowe, *Extraterrestrial Life Debate: Antiquity to 1915,* 33–34.

[22] Grant McColley and H. W. Miller, "Saint Bonaventure, Francis Mayron, William Vorilong, and the Doctrine of a Plurality of Worlds," *Speculum* 12, no. 3 (1937): 386–89, at 388.

More importantly for the ETI conversation, Vorilong suggested that such worlds could be located in our universe, and they could be inhabited. (He seemed to think this situation was probable.) Then he moved to boldly go where no theologian had gone before. Vorilong raised a pointed question concerning these other-worldly inhabitants: Would their existence be compatible with traditional Christian teaching about original sin, the Incarnation, and redemption in Christ?[23]

> If it be inquired whether men exist on that world, and whether they have sinned as Adam sinned, I answer no, for they would not exist in sin and did not spring from Adam. But it is shown that they would exist from the virtue of God, transported into that world, as Enoch and Elias [Elijah] in the earthly paradise. As to the question whether Christ by dying on this earth could redeem the inhabitants of another world, I answer that he is able to do this even if the worlds were infinite, but it would not be fitting for him to go unto another world that he must die again.[24]

Vorilong concludes, then, that since ETI would not be descendants of Adam, they would be without the original sin inherited from him. But even if they somehow had fallen as the human race did, Christ's incarnation and redemptive sacrifice on Earth could provide them redemption. The Son of God would have the ability to be incarnate on other

---

[23] McColley and Miller conclude that although "Vorilong is the earliest of the theologians yet noted" to make this move, "others doubtless preceded him." "Doctrine of a Plurality of Worlds," 387 n. 1.

[24] Quoted in McColley and Miller, 388.

worlds as well, even an infinite number of times. But that scenario of an infinite series of brutal passions and deaths, he insisted, would not be fitting.

We may find ourselves asking, "If these things are indeed true, how could we possibly ever find out about them?" Unlike most modern science fiction writers speculating about ETI, Vorilong does not envision visitors from another inhabited world traveling to ours. But he offers another possibility: "By what means are we able to have knowledge of that world? I answer by angelic revelation or by divine means."[25] In other words, God could tell us through angels or prophets.

Commentators on this text have little to say about Vorilong's reference to the biblical figures Enoch and Elijah. Traditional interpretations of their departure from this life (see Gn 5:24; 2 Kgs 2:11–12) conclude that they were taken up bodily into the sky to reside somewhere beyond the Earth. Vorilong seems to be saying simply that we need not wonder how the inhabitants of other worlds could have been placed there; the fate of Enoch and Elijah shows what divine power can do.

An otherwise unremarkable document from the same period has sometimes been offered as evidence that the Catholic Church condemned the idea of ETI. In a letter written by Pope Pius II and dated November 14, 1459, the Holy Father condemned the following propositions offered by canon Zaninus of Solcia: "God also created another world besides this one, and that in its time many other men

---

[25] McColley and Miller.

and women existed, and that consequently Adam was not the first man."[26]

This document has certain telling parallels to the condemnation by Pope Zachary of Vergilius's teaching that we noted earlier. Pope Pius does not appear to be making a blanket condemnation of the general notion that God has created other inhabited worlds. Rather, he seems to be rejecting the more specific idea that God created a world inhabited by members of the human race before He created our world.

The latter notion would of course imply that Adam and Eve were not the first parents of the entire human race. The more general scenario of God's creating an intelligent race in a prior world, a race not related to ours, would not. As we noted in the case of Pope Zachary, the Catholic Church insists on the unity and solidarity of the human race as descended from Adam. So it is clear why Zaninus's teaching was condemned.

A New Focus

By the end of the fifteenth century, then, we find that the age-old conversation about the plurality of worlds was developing a new focus. Rather than speculating about entire multiple universes, the attention was turning toward multiple worlds within our universe. The notion of these other worlds being inhabited by intelligent creatures now came more to the forefront.

---

[26] *Enchiridion symbolorum: definitionum et declarationum de rebus fidei et morum,* ed. Heinrich Denzinger (Rome: Herder, 1963), #1363 (717c), 344. Translated and quoted in George, *Christianity,* 73.

Finally, Vorilong's novel questions were to be raised by others as well, with a variety of answers proposed. What might be the potential spiritual and moral status of ETI in the light of the Church's Scripture and Tradition: Fallen or unfallen? Redeemed by God's incarnation on Earth, or by some other means?

The conversation was about to become raucous indeed.

3

"A Thousand Labyrinthes"

The Later Renaissance Debates

"Thus Sciences . . . have become Opiones, nay Errores, and lead the Imagination in a thousand Labyrinthes."

—William Drummond

GIVEN THE REMARKABLE intellectual ferment in Western culture of the sixteenth and seventeenth centuries, a number of scientists, philosophers, and theologians entered the ETI arena of debate. Controversy sharpened as clashing scientific models, philosophies, and theologies raised the volume of the conversation, and positions on the central issues multiplied. What led to such developments?

First, the science of astronomy was making great strides. The "heliocentric" ("sun-centered") model of the universe, first proposed by the Greek astronomer Aristarchus of Samos in the third century BC, was given new life by Nicholas Copernicus (1473–1543), a Polish mathematician, astronomer, and Doctor of Canon Law.[1]

---

[1] Copernicus's reputation as an astronomer was such that his advice on reforming the ecclesiastical calendar was requested in 1514 by the

Copernicus's most famous work, *On the Revolution of the Celestial Orbs*, was dedicated to Pope Paul III (1468–1549). In it, the author laid out his arguments with a confidence in "the divine providence of the Creator of all things."[2]

This new model, though forcefully challenged by scientists, philosophers, and theologians alike, came eventually to replace Aristotle's long-established geocentric model. It needed important modifications, but it led in the end to a more accurate understanding of our planet's place in the solar system.[3] It also continued to shift the focus of attention in the "plurality of worlds" debate. Rather than speculations about entire multiple universes, new theories emerged about the "worlds" that could be observed in the sky of *this* universe: the sun, moon, planets, and stars.

Meanwhile, philosophers were challenging more than Aristotle's model of the cosmos, impelled by a revival of ancient ideas both from Plato and from the atomists. The

---

ecumenical Lateran Council. He modestly replied that the length of the year and of the months, and the motions of the sun and moon, were not yet sufficiently known to attempt a reform. Even so, the incident spurred him on to make more accurate observations. Seventy years later, these served as a basis for working out the new Gregorian calendar. John Hagen, "Nicolaus Copernicus," *The Catholic Encyclopedia*, Vol. 4 (New York: Robert Appleton Company, 1908), http://www.newadvent.org/cathen/04352b.htm.

[2] Nicholas Copernicus, *On the Revolutions*, ed. Jerzy Dobrzycki, trans. and commentary Edward Rosen (Baltimore: Macmillan, 1978), Bk. 1, Ch. 9; quoted in Dick, *Plurality of Worlds*, 62.

[3] The geocentric model of the universe came to be called the "Ptolemaic model," after Claudius Ptolemy, a second-century Alexandrian mathematician, astronomer, and geographer. One of his most famous works, the *Almagest*, is the only surviving comprehensive ancient treatise on astronomy and was extremely influential in ancient, Medieval, and Renaissance thought until the Copernican Revolution.

driving notion behind certain arguments, drawn ultimately from Plato's thought, was the principle of *plenitude.* Advocates of this principle, in opposition to Aristotle, asserted that the universe contains all possible forms of existence; whatever can be, including multiple inhabited worlds, will be, and it is good that they are. The newly championed speculations of the atomists tended in this direction as well, and often led to religious skepticism, even atheism, and denial of the human soul's survival after death.[4]

At the same time, advances in technology, most notably the telescope (invented in 1608), allowed researchers to discover more details about the heavenly bodies they studied. These developments gave birth to various astronomical theories based on technical reasoning. Because the new forms of debate focused on the bodies visible in the sky, those who debated now spent considerable time comparing the physical characteristics of such bodies to those of Earth. Conclusions about their comparative composition, physical features, and environmental conditions led inevitably to speculation about their possible inhabitants.[5]

Not surprisingly, theologians found themselves pressed to respond to both scientific and philosophical developments, some of which posed a challenge to traditional Christian beliefs. They were concerned that theology remain faithful to Sacred Scripture and Tradition. But as the Western Christian tradition was itself shattered by various Protestant

---

[4]   This influential philosophical notion is traced historically in Arthur Lovejoy, *The Great Chain of Being* (Cambridge, Mass: Harvard University Press, 1936).

[5]   Dick, *Plurality of Worlds,* 61–62.

movements, theologians of differing convictions debated among themselves about ETI. Catholic and other Christian thinkers proposed a variety of speculations about the subject, but the Catholic Church still took no official position on it.

The Curious (and Unfortunate) Case of Giordano Bruno

The Italian Dominican friar Giordano Bruno (1548–1600) was a philosopher, mathematician, poet, and cosmological theorist.[6] Bruno insisted that the universe is infinite and could have no center. He invoked the principle of plenitude to make such a claim: "Since it is well that this world [Earth] doth exist, no less good is the existence of each one of the infinity of other worlds. . . . Thus is the excellence of God magnified and the greatness of his kingdom made manifest; he is glorified, not in one, but in countless suns; not in a single earth, a single world, but in a thousand thousand, I say in an infinity of worlds."[7]

This statement reflects Bruno's extension of the Copernican model, proposing the idea, novel at the time, that the stars are actually distant "suns" around which revolved their own "earths" (planets). And these heavenly bodies, he claimed, along with meteors, are actually animated with their own souls. In addition, they have animals and intelligent inhabitants.

---

[6] *Cosmology* is the science of the origin and development of the universe.

[7] Giordano Bruno, *On the Infinite Universe and Worlds*, Third Dialogue, trans. Dorothea Waley Singer (New York: Henry Schuman, 1950); quoted in Crowe, *Extraterrestrial Life Debate: Antiquity to 1915*, 40, 44.

His reasoning about ETI went this way: The many worlds are inhabited "if not exactly as our own, and if not more nobly, at least no less inhabited, and no less nobly. For it is impossible that a rational being, fairly vigilant, can imagine that these innumerable worlds, manifest as like to our own or yet more magnificent, should be destitute of similar or even superior inhabitants."[8]

Opposition to the friar's (at the time) controversial claims was heightened by his legendary inflated ego. Though he respected Copernicus, he once boasted, for example, that it was only he himself who "has penetrated into the heavens, past the frontiers of the world, shattered the fantastic walls of the spheres," and located "inhabitants in the sun, moon, and other stars."[9] Such arrogance infuriated his opponents.

Bruno has been called the first martyr for belief in ETI. He was in fact condemned by the Roman Inquisition and burned at the stake by the secular authorities in the year 1600 for his heretical writings and his refusal to recant them. The historical record of the events is incomplete; some important documents of the trial, including the sentence handed down, have been lost. But the surviving evidence does not support the claim that Bruno was executed for his belief in ETI.

In his trials, the multiple charges made against him, based on his writings and witness testimonies, included blasphemy, immoral conduct, and heresy in matters of dogmatic theology. Bruno had propagated overtly heretical theological

---

[8] Bruno, *On the Infinite Universe,* 323; quoted in George, *Christianity,* 74–75.

[9] Translated and quoted in Dick, *Plurality of Worlds,* 64. The original Italian can be found in Giovanni Aquilecchia's edition of Bruno's *La cena de le ceneri* (1955), 2.

positions on the Holy Trinity, the divinity of Christ, the Incarnation, the virginity of Mary, the Mass, and the Eucharist. He insisted that the universe was not created by God out of nothing (as Scripture and Tradition have always taught) but had instead always existed.

Bruno's notions of God tended toward pantheism—the belief that God and the universe are identical, that the universe is a manifestation of God's being. He believed in reincarnation, the "transmigration" of the human soul after death into animals. Perhaps more curiously for a scientist, Bruno was also deeply involved in the practice of magic, divination, and other occult practices. At least one scholar has even concluded that "Bruno pushes Copernicus' scientific work back into a prescientific stage . . . interpreting the Copernican diagram as a hieroglyph of divine mysteries."[10]

Noting these charges is not an attempt to justify Bruno's execution. It simply helps to clarify that his heresy was not his belief in ETI. In 1600, the Catholic Church held no official position on the existence of other populated worlds. It never obligated its members to believe that in all the universe, only our Earth was inhabited by intelligent creatures.

Protestant Views

During this period, the diverse theologies of the new Protestant movements began to manifest their own ideas about ETI. Lambert Daneau (c. 1535–c. 1590), a French jurist and Calvinist theologian, insisted that the notion of life on other planets must be rejected because it is not found in

---

[10] Frances Yates, *Giordano Bruno and the Hermetic Tradition* (London: Routledge and Kegan Paul, 1964), 225.

Scripture. This particular argument against the possibility of ETI can still be heard today.

The German Lutheran theologian Philip Melanchthon (1497–1560), a collaborator of Martin Luther, roundly denounced the notion that God could have created other worlds and given them inhabitants. He agreed with Daneau that Scripture said nothing about God's creation of man anywhere except on earth, and so we must reject the idea. Melanchthon thundered:

> We know that God [in Christ] is a citizen of this world with us, custodian and server of this world, ruling the motion of the heavens, guiding the constellations, making this earth fruitful, and indeed watching over us; we do not contrive to have him in another world, and to watch over other men also. . . . The Son of God is One; our Master Jesus Christ was born, died, and resurrected in this world. Nor does he manifest himself elsewhere, nor elsewhere has he died or resurrected. Therefore it must not be imagined that there are many worlds, because it must not be imagined that Christ died and was resurrected more often, nor must it be thought that in any other world without the knowledge of the Son of God, that men would be restored to eternal life.[11]

Melanchthon wasn't just concerned about the silence in Scripture concerning ETI. His principal objection was that other inhabited planets would suggest that God's special

---

[11] Philip Melanchthon, *Initia doctrinae physicae* (Wittenberg, 1550), fol. 43; translated and quoted in Dick, Plurality of Worlds, 89.

relationship to the human race on earth in Christ is not unique. He also believed that ETI could not be redeemed without a knowledge of Christ. As we will see, these objections recur throughout the continuing debate among Christians to this day.

Johannes Kepler

The celebrated German astronomer and mathematician Johannes Kepler (1571–1630) first wanted to become a Lutheran minister (his university theology professor had studied with Melanchthon), and his Christian faith shaped his scientific endeavor. He believed that God had created the world according to an intelligible plan, which is accessible through the natural light of human reason.[12] For Kepler, mathematics was the key to unlocking nature's secrets. He eventually came to allow that the moon, planets, and even stars might be bodies similar in nature to Earth, each with its own inhabitants.[13]

Kepler spent considerable time studying the moon. Referencing Plutarch's fanciful treatise on that heavenly body, he once wrote "in jest": "As it happens with us, that for utility men and animals follow the natural disposition of the land or of their own province; therefore there are on the moon living creatures, with by far a larger body and hardness of temperament than ours, to be sure, because if there are any there, their day is fifteen of our days long and they endure

---

[12] Peter Barker and Bernard R. Goldstein, "Theological Foundations of Kepler's Astronomy" in *Osiris*, vol. 16, *Science in Theistic Contexts* (Chicago: University of Chicago Press, 2001), 112–13.

[13] Dick, *Plurality of Worlds*, 69–70.

both the indescribable heat and the vertical rays of the sun." Kepler concluded whimsically: "And not absurdly has the moon been believed by superstition to be the place for the purification of souls."[14] As a Lutheran, Kepler probably considered as superstition the notion of a purgatory existing anywhere. His coreligionists would have found this comment especially amusing.

Even so, some of his other works suggests that he is not simply "jesting" here. He would later return to these thoughts about the moon and elaborate on them. In the *Somnium* ("Dream," 1634), describing an imaginary moon voyage, Kepler depicted a variety of lunar inhabitants, attempting to show that if the moon was a body similar to Earth, it was not unreasonable to populate it.[15]

When a brilliant nova appeared in the heavens suddenly in October 1604, Kepler wondered about the composition of the new star and how its matter had been formed. Since he was confident that God had a purpose for all His works, he asked an additional question: *Why* had the new star been ignited? He speculated that it had not been set afire for the purpose of humans on Earth—a planet that was immeasurably small on a cosmic scale. Instead, he proposed that it was done by God for the inhabitants of other planets. Even the stars, he insisted, were inhabited.[16]

The Catholic Italian astronomer Galileo Galilei (1564–1642) published in 1610 his first observations by telescope

[14] Johannes Kepler, *Gesammelte Werke,* II, 218; translated and quoted in Dick, *Plurality of Worlds,* 71–72.
[15] Dick, *Plurality of Worlds,* 84.
[16] Dick, 73.

of the moon, the fixed stars, the Milky Way, and the moons of Jupiter. He sent a copy of his work to Kepler, who immediately began speculations about Galileo's report. Again, the conviction that God does nothing useless spurred him to conjecture: If Jupiter has moons which until that time were hidden from Earth's inhabitants, shouldn't we conclude that those satellites exist, not for our sake, but for the sake of inhabitants living on Jupiter?

Yet he went much further in his speculations about the moon. Galileo had detected a large circular cavity on the lunar surface. Kepler concluded that it was artificially constructed by intelligent inhabitants who "make their homes in numerous caves hewn out of that circular embankment."[17]

Kepler was not unaware of certain theological issues that arise with the proposition that other planets are inhabited. In particular, given traditional Christian teaching about God's special relationship with the descendants of Adam, it seemed to imply a diminished stature for the human race, who no longer occupied a central position in the cosmos. The astronomer posed the dilemma himself: "Well, then, someone may say, if there are globes in the heaven similar to our earth, do we vie with them over who occupies a better portion of the universe? For if their globes are nobler, we are not the noblest of rational creatures. Then how can all things be for man's sake? How can we be the masters of God's handiwork?"[18]

[17] Johannes Kepler, *Kepler's Conversation with Galileo's Sidereal Messenger,* trans. and annotated by Edward Rosen (New York: Johnson Reprint Corporation, 1965), 28; quoted in Dick, *Plurality of Worlds,* 75–76.

[18] Kepler, *Kepler's Conversation,* 43; quoted in Crowe, *Extraterrestrial*

Kepler's solution to the dilemma: "Where we mortals dwell . . . is the primary bosom of the universe. . . . This world of ours does not belong to an undifferentiated swarm of countless others." He believed that our sun was far more brilliant than all the other stars, and that the Earth was the noblest planet within the solar system. It served, then, as the habitation of the noblest of all God's creatures.[19]

Other Voices

Kepler's contemporary, the English natural philosopher Nicholas Hill (1570–c. 1610), was an atomist, a Copernican, and a disciple of Bruno; it is debated whether he was Catholic or Protestant. He added his voice to the conversation in his book *Philosophia epicurea* (1601), in which he asserted that "the superior [heavenly] spheres (as they are commonly spoken of) are made of the same matter as the sphere in which we live, and by analogy contain all things which we have in our world."[20] "All things," he believed, included living creatures who were adapted to the specific environment of their planets.

With Kepler, Hill was aware of the implication in his conclusions that the status of the human race seemed diminished if it was only one of many intelligent races. But he suggested that whatever good was lost in that regard was

---

Life Debate: Antiquity to 1915, 91. As Dick, *Plurality of Worlds*, 87, points out, H. G. Wells used this passage to preface his science fiction work *War of the Worlds* (1897).

[19] Kepler, *Kepler's Conversation*, 34–36; quoted in Crowe, *Extraterrestrial Life Debate: Antiquity to 1915*, 56–57.

[20] Nicholas Hill, *Philosophia epucirea* (Paris, 1601; Geneva, 1619); trans. from the Latin by Dick, *Plurality of Worlds*, 49.

offset by the good of a greater number of souls existing in other worlds.

Not surprisingly, those who still held to Aristotle's cosmic model reacted with abhorrence to the propositions of Copernicus, Kepler, and Galileo. The Anglican clergyman and Oxford scholar Robert Burton (1577–1640), for example, concluded that if Earth is in motion as these astronomers claim, and that "the rest of the planets are inhabited, as well as the moon," then "insolent and bold attempts, prodigious paradoxes, inferences" must surely follow.[21]

Galileo himself was at first skeptical about Kepler's notions of ETI. In 1612, during a controversy with the German Jesuit priest and astronomer Christoph Scheiner (1575–1650) over the discovery of sunspots, Galileo admitted: "I agree with [Scheiner] in regarding as false and damnable the view of those who put inhabitants on Jupiter, Venus, Saturn, and the moon, meaning by inhabitants, animals like ours, and men in particular."[22] But he left open the question of whether ETI that are different in nature from humans on Earth—"extremely diverse, and far beyond all our imaginings"—might exist.[23] The next year, he wrote in a letter to an inquirer that there could be no settled answer to the question of ETI.

---

[21] Robert Burton, *Anatomy of Melancholy* (London: John C. Nimmo, 1893; reprint New York, 1973), 326; quoted in Dick, *Plurality of Worlds*, 85–86.

[22] Galileo Galilei, "Letter on Sunspots," in *Discoveries and Opinions of Galileo,* ed. and trans. Stillman Drake (New York: Doubleday, 1957), 137.

[23] Galileo Galilei, *Dialogue Concerning the Two Chief World Systems: Ptolemaic and Copernican,* trans. Stillman Drake (Berkeley: University of Berkeley Press, 1962), 99.

Meanwhile, literary figures of the period entered the debate. The Anglican clergyman and poet John Donne (1572–1631) concluded, for example, that "God, and Nature and Reason concurre against" the plurality of inhabited worlds.[24] The Scottish poet William Drummond (1585–1649), a member of the Church of England, lamented: "Some afirme there is another World of men and sensitive Creatures, with cities and palaces in the Moone. . . . Thus Sciences . . . have become Opiones, nay Errores, and lead the Imagination in a thousand Labyrinthes."[25]

The Condemnation of Galileo's Teaching

The Catholic Church's oft-cited condemnation of certain aspects of Galileo's teaching in 1616 was not explicitly related to notions of possible ETI.[26] But we find hints of the theological issues in the surrounding Copernican debate in the *Apologia pro Galileo* (Apology for Galileo) of Tomasso Campanella (1568–1639), a Dominican friar, theologian, and philosopher. The work was written in the same year as the condemnation and published six years later.

Campanella's treatise was billed as "an inquiry as to whether that kind of philosophy which Galileo has made

---

[24] John Donne, *Devotions upon Emergent Occasions* (London, 1624), 88; quoted in Dick, *Plurality of Worlds*, 87.

[25] William Drummond, *The Poetical Works of William Drummond of Hawthornden,* ed. L. E. Kastner, vol. 2 (Manchester: At the University Press, 1913), 78; quoted in Dick (1982), 87.

[26] For a detailed account of the circumstances surrounding Galileo's trial, see Dom Paschal Scotti, *Galileo Revisited: The Galileo Affair in Context* (San Francisco: Ignatius, 2017), chapter 5, "Galileo Agonistes: *The Dialogue on the Two Chief World Systems,* The Trial of Galileo and After," 219–65.

famous, is in harmony with or is opposed to the Holy Scripture."[27] In his approach, Scripture must be interpreted taking into account the new discoveries in science.

The author stated nine "charges" that certain unspecified authorities had made against Galileo. The ninth charge was specifically related to the ETI debate: The existence of other inhabited worlds, as Galileo's Catholic and Protestant critics both claimed, was contrary to Scripture: "If the four elements which form our world exist in the stars, it follows from the doctrine of Galileo that, as Mohammed declared, there are many worlds with lands and seas, and with human inhabitants. However, Scripture speaks of only one world and of one created man, so that this belief is opposed to Scripture."[28]

Campanella responded to this charge by pointing out that no decree issued by the Catholic Church prohibited a belief in other worlds. Galileo was not teaching a plurality of worlds in the sense of multiple universes. Instead, he posited numerous small worlds within the one great system of the universe. That notion was contrary not to Scripture but to Aristotle.

Campanella also broached the subject of the relationship of possible ETI to the redemption made possible in Christ. He reasoned:

> If the inhabitants which may be in other stars are men, they did not originate from Adam and are not infected by his sin. Nor do these inhabitants need redemption, unless they have committed some other sin. I am constrained to set forth those passages in Ephesians 1,

---

[27] Quoted in Dick, *Plurality of Worlds*, 91.

[28] Grant McColley, "The Defense of Galileo of Thomas Campanella," *Smith College Studies in History* 22, nos. 3–4 (April–July 1937), 8, 66.

and Colossians 1, "And through him to reconcile all things unto himself, making peace through the blood of his cross, both as to the things that are on earth, and the things that are in heaven." In his *Epistle* on the solar spots Galileo expressly denies that men can exist in other stars . . . but affirms that beings of a higher nature can exist there. Their nature is similar to ours, but is not the same.[29]

Christ did not have to die for the inhabitants of each of the stars, Campanella reasoned. Even if ETI were of the same species as humans on Earth, they would not have been affected by Adam's fall. In other words, they had no need for redemption unless they themselves had sinned. But he did not explore the ramifications of that possibility. As we saw in an earlier chapter, Saint Augustine and other earlier writers would have challenged the notion that human beings could exist somewhere who were not descended from Adam.[30]

In Galileo's controversy, we see manifested a new attitude in scientific discovery. For centuries, under the influence of Aristotle, Plato, and other philosophers, the world was to be understood primarily by philosophical speculation and reasoning, based on philosophical premises about such matters as what would be most "fitting" or "perfect" in a cosmos. The approach now gaining momentum was to understand the world instead through empirical observation.[31]

---

[29] Tommaso Campanella, "The Defense of Galileo," trans. Grant McColley, *Smith College Studies in History* 22, nos. 3 and 4 (1937): 66–67; quoted in Crowe, *Extraterrestrial Life Debate, 1750–1900*.
[30] Dick, *Plurality of Worlds*, 92–93.
[31] Wilkinson, *Search for Extraterrestrial Intelligence*, 22.

The change was ironically displayed in a sermon preached in Florence, Italy, in 1614, by the Dominican friar Tomasso Caccini. In criticizing Galileo, he made a pun on the astronomer's name, which in Italian means "from Galilee." Caccini paraphrased the rebuke of the angels to the Apostles after the Ascension of Christ, reported in Acts 1:11, directing it instead to the astronomer: "Man of Galilee, why do you stand gazing up into heaven?"[32]

Conclusive Arguments from Scripture, Tradition, and Magisterium?

Not long afterward, the French Minim friar Marin Mersenne (1588–1648) entered the ETI debate with his book *Questiones in Genesim* (*Questions on Genesis*), published in 1623. He summarized the common arguments in favor of other worlds: God's omnipotence and virtue required that He create many worlds. Multiple worlds are better than just one, and God always does what is best. There are many species of creatures imaginable that would occupy the distance between God and the angels that do not appear on Earth, but might appear in other worlds.[33]

Despite the arguments in favor of multiple worlds and ETI, Mersenne nevertheless concluded that our world is singular. Yet he admitted that the issue was complicated, and certainty had to be based on many sources of knowledge: experience, reason, and human authority on one hand, and Christian faith as determined by Sacred Scripture, Tradition, and Magisterium.

---

[32] Wilkinson, 22.
[33] Dick, *Plurality of Worlds*, 93.

Unlike some others, Mersenne did not argue against ETI from the silence of Scripture; instead, he concluded that such silence provided no clear resolution of the matter. In considering the Tradition and Magisterium, he pointed out that the issue had not been dealt with in the apostolic Tradition, nor had it been defined by an ecumenical council or papal declaration. The only way to conclude that ETI did not exist based on magisterial teaching, he insisted, was to draw a conclusion from the clear *de fide* ("of faith") premises of the Church's teaching. But he found himself unable to identify any premises that would allow such a deduction.

In the end, Mersenne could not firmly conclude that the Scripture, Tradition, and Magisterium ruled out many inhabited worlds. He explained that several other well-known theologians had come to the same conclusion that the matter could not be determined *de fide*, and that the *possibility* of such multiple worlds was certain because God is all-powerful. Nevertheless, he thought that the most prudent opinion was that our world is singular—though God might produce other worlds in the future.[34]

John Wilkins

Speculations about lunar inhabitants were revived by John Wilkins (1614–1672), a politically influential Anglican priest (later bishop of Chester) and one of the founders of the prestigious Royal Society of London, the oldest national scientific institution in the world. His work *Discovery of a World in the Moone* (1638) found a wide and receptive audience. The

---

[34] Dick, 94–95.

subtitle of his treatise indicated that he proposed "to prove, that 'tis probable there may be another habitable World in that Planet." The work went through multiple printings and editions, some with substantial additions, in the two centuries following. The 1640 edition even explored possible ways for earthlings to make a journey to the moon.

For Wilkins, belief in life on the moon contradicted neither reason nor faith. Aristotle's model of the universe had been flawed, and his arguments, weak. "'Tis not Aristotle," he insisted, "but truth that should be the rule of our opinions." He noted that Campanella, in defending Galileo, had made the same point.[35]

As for Scripture, he held, along with Campanella and Mersenne, that the Bible's silence about a reality did not imply denial of its existence. If the book of Genesis failed to mention God's creation of other worlds, it also said nothing about His creation of the planets, which we know truly exist. "'Tis besides the scope of the Holy Ghost either in the new Testament or in the old, to reveale any thing to us concerning the secrets of Philosophy." He insisted that earlier charges of heresy sometimes made against the idea of a plurality of worlds demonstrated the ignorance of the times in which they were made.[36] In fact, Wilkins declared, far from undermining Christian faith, belief in a lunar world magnified God's wisdom and power.

In defending this idea, Wilkins employed, as others before him had done, the idea of plenitude in God's creation: "There is a great chasm betwixt the nature of men and angels: it may

---

[35] John Wilkins, *Discovery of a World in the Moone,* proposition 2; quoted in Dick, *Plurality of Worlds*, 98–99.
[36] Wilkins, *Discovery of a World*; quoted in Dick, *Plurality of Worlds*, 99.

be the inhabitants of the planets are of a middle nature between both these. It is not impossible that God might create some of all kinds, that so he might more completely glorify himself."[37] When we look at life on earth, he was saying, we see it is God's pattern to create a hierarchy of being, with no rungs on the ascending ladder missing. That fullness in His creation redounds to His glory. Shouldn't we expect Him to fill the gap between human beings and angels with other intelligent beings?

Wilkins even attempted to use the empirical observations of Galileo and others to make his argument for an inhabited moon. Many earlier thinkers had concluded that the moon was simply a reflective disk. God's purpose in creating it was to provide its light to humans on Earth. But the telescope revealed that the moon actually had a landscape, with mountains and what appeared to be seas. So Wilkins suggested that God had created it this way "to make it a fit body for habitation, with the same conveniences of sea and land, as this inferior [lower] world doth partake of."[38]

Wilkins concluded that lunar ETI need not be fallen from grace, as humans are on Earth. But even if they had sinned, he reasoned, Christ could have died for them as well. His thinking reflects how the ETI discussion had come to include not only empirical observations but also scriptural arguments and debates about the scope of redemption in Christ.[39]

We should note in passing that then as now, wits took advantage of such speculations about space travel by Wilkins

---

[37] Wilkins, *Discovery of a World*; quoted in Crowe, *Extraterrestrial Life Debate*.

[38] Wilkins, *Discovery of a World*, proposition 7.

[39] Wilkinson, *Search for Extraterrestrial Intelligence*, 21.

and other writers. (Just as his *Discovery* was being published in 1638, a lunar voyage fantasy appeared by the Anglican bishop Francis Godwin.) The Anglican clergyman Robert South (1634–1716) joked that Wilkins was hoping to obtain a bishopric on the moon. In Samuel Butler's (1612–1680) comic poem "The Elephant in the Moon," astronomers reported sighting such a beast in their telescope, only to discover that a mouse had crawled inside their instrument.[40]

Debates about intelligent lunar life raged for generations. Even lunar cartographers entered the fray: Johannes Helvelius (1611–1687) produced maps showing "seas" on the moon's surface and referred to "selenites," his name for intelligent lunar inhabitants. But the map by Jesuit cartographer Giovanni Battista Riccioli (1598–1671) contained notations that no water exists on the moon and proclaimed in captions above his map that "No Men Dwell on the Moon" and "No Souls Migrate to the Moon."[41]

Shifts in the Conversation

By the time of the later Renaissance debates, then, the conversation about a plurality of worlds had shifted in several important ways.

First, the worlds in debate were now multiple planets in our universe rather than multiple universes. They were thus viewed not so much as an abstract philosophical proposition but as concrete realities existing much closer to our own world and observable by human beings.

---

[40] Crowe, *Extraterrestrial Life Debate*, 1750–1900, 14.

[41] Crowe, 14.

Second, the old philosophical models of the universe were giving way under the weight of empirical observation that revealed their flaws.

Third, the shattering of Western Christian culture by the Protestant movements made room for a greater variety of speculations based on conflicting theological premises and scriptural interpretations.

Fourth, more explicit attention was paid to the question of worlds with intelligent inhabitants.

Finally, with this emerging focus on ETI, questions became more pointed about several issues critical to the Christian understanding of the world: If intelligent species inhabit other planets, what is their relationship to God and to the human race? Can we still hold that humanity has a special status in the cosmos and in its relationship with God? Are these extraterrestrial races fallen or unfallen? And what role does Jesus Christ, the Son of God incarnate as a human being, play in the redemption and ultimate destiny of intelligent extraterrestrials?

In the second half of the seventeenth century, the emergence of the intellectual and cultural movement called the Enlightenment was to complicate the debate even further. As we shall see, while Christians discussed these and related issues in the light of their faith, some of the more skeptical Enlightenment philosophers, scientists, and essayists attempted to use speculations about ETI as a way to challenge and even discredit traditional Christian faith.

4

"Awake Up the Eyes of Your Understanding"

Enlightenment Thinkers Take up the Conversation

"Awake up the eyes of your Understanding and Reason towards the Heavens, contemplating the wonderful things thereof."

—Pierre Borel

WHILE GALILEO IN his later years was struggling with charges of heresy, a young French philosopher was already working on a radically new model of physics and cosmology. René Descartes (1596–1650) published his *Discourse on the Method* in 1637, marking for many historians the beginning of the Age of Enlightenment. But it was Descartes's *Principia philosophiae* (Principles of Philosophy) published seven years later that came to rock the philosophical and scientific worlds, with its proposal of the first complete physical system since the one Aristotle had taught two thousand years earlier.

An overview of the revolutionary Cartesian cosmos, an infinite universe of stars and their planets, is far beyond our scope of inquiry. But his thoughts about the possibility of inhabited worlds, and the influence he exerted on later thinkers, deserve our attention.

Descartes's Ponderings

Descartes was a French Catholic, trained at a Jesuit college, where he met Merin Mersenne, who was to become a lifelong friend and personal adviser.[1] Mersenne's musings about ETI, noted in the previous chapter, would certainly have been known to Descartes. The young scientist was also encouraged in his vocation by the saintly French cardinal Pierre de Bérulle (1575–1629).[2]

Descartes's sense of personal mission as a philosopher and scientist had a mystical dimension. He reports how he once had a dream that he interpreted as a divine revelation. It convinced him that it "was the Spirit of Truth that willed to open for him all the treasures of knowledge." To make advances in knowledge, he insisted, is to progress in the knowledge of God Himself.[3]

Not surprisingly, the third section of the *Principles*, on the visible astronomical world, opened with a declaration of God's greatness and power. But the author also cautioned his

---

[1] Charles Dubray, "Marin Mersenne," *The Catholic Encyclopedia,* Vol. 10 (New York: Robert Appleton Company, 1911), accessed August 8, 2020, http://www.newadvent.org/cathen/10209b.htm.

[2] Bérulle's disciple, St. Vincent de Paul, called him "one of the most saintly priests I have known"; his friend St. Francis de Sales said of him: "He is everything which I should desire to be myself." Clodius Piat, "René Descartes," *The Catholic Encyclopedia,* Vol. 4 (New York: Robert Appleton Company, 1908), http://www.newadvent.org/cathen/04744b.htm.

[3] Piat, "René Descartes," *Catholic Encyclopedia.*

readers that we cannot presume to know the ends for which all things were created by God. In particular, we cannot say that all things in the universe were created exclusively for human beings. "It is . . . not at all probable that all things were created for us in such a manner that God has had no other end in creating them. . . . For we cannot doubt that an infinitude of things exist, or did exist, . . . which have never been beheld or comprehended by man and which have never been of any use to him."[4]

The mature philosopher once declared in his *Rules for the Direction of the Mind* (published posthumously, 1684) that "he who would progress on the road to truth must not delay over any object about which he cannot have a certainty equal to that given by arithmetical and geometrical demonstrations" (Second Rule). This strategy was clearly reflected in his thinking about extraterrestrial intelligence.[5]

Descartes's model of the cosmos implied inhabited planets around the stars, and he apparently wondered about this matter throughout his life. But the trials of Bruno and Galileo made him reluctant to publish such thoughts. Even so, his early private correspondence reveals that he wished to use improved telescopes to discover "whether there are animals on the moon," and late in life he was still pondering whether "perhaps elsewhere there exist innumerable other creatures of higher quality than ourselves."[6]

---

[4]   Descartes, *Works,* 1:271; quoted in Crowe, *Extraterrestrial Life Debate: Antiquity to 1915,* 65.
[5]   Piat, "René Descartes," *Catholic Encyclopedia.*
[6]   Quoted in Dick, *Plurality of Worlds,* 111.

The implications of his cosmology for ETI were evident to at least some of his readers. Three years after the publication of the *Principles*, Descartes received a letter from a troubled correspondent named Pierre Chanut, who commented: "If we conceive the world in the vast extension that you attribute to it, it is impossible that man retains an honorable rank there. [Man] will most probably hold that all these stars have inhabitants or, still better, that they have earths around them, full of creatures more intelligent and better than he."[7]

Descartes replied by saying that indeed, the notion that all things were created for humans can no longer be maintained. Nevertheless: "I do not see at all that the mystery of the Incarnation, and all the other advantages that God has brought forth for man, obstruct him from having brought forth an infinity of other very great advantages for an infinity of other creatures. And although I do not at all infer from this that there would be intelligent creatures in the stars or elsewhere, I also do not see that there would be any reason by which to prove that there were not." In the end, following his declared rule about uncertain matters, he concluded with humility: "I always leave [alone] undecided questions of this kind rather than denying or affirming anything."[8]

Descartes's followers tended to show a similar reluctance in speculating about extraterrestrial intelligence. No doubt the continuing tension between apparent scriptural objections on the one hand, and an affirmation of God's

---

[7]   Quoted in Paolo Rossi, "Nobility of Man and Plurality of Worlds," in Allen Debus, *Science, Medicine and Society in the Renaissance* (New York: Science History Publications, 1972), 2:131–62, at 153.

[8]   As translated in Crowe, *Extraterrestrial Life Debate, 1750–1900*, 16.

omnipotence and creation's plenitude on the other, contributed to their hesitation. They seemed to shy away from theological debates that might complicate the acceptance of their cosmology on purely scientific and philosophical grounds.

Henry More and Pierre Borel

Only two years after Descartes's *Principles* appeared, the English Neo-Platonist Henry More (1614–1687) made a more radical departure from Christian tradition when he published his *Democritus Platonissans, or, An Essay on the Infinity of Worlds out of Platonick Principles* (1646). More was raised in a Calvinist home but rejected the faith of his parents. He secured a fellowship at Cambridge University, remaining within the Church of England but eventually promoting certain ideas that were more at home among Spiritualists and Occultists.[9]

More believed not just that an infinite number of planets revolved around an infinite number of stars but also that the warmth and light of these stars engendered life on those planets "to their great Maker's praise."[10] Yet his claims about other inhabited worlds went much farther. He wrote in impassioned verse:

> long ago there Earths have been
> People with men and beasts before this Earth,

---

[9]   See Richard Ward, *The Life of the Learned and Pious Dr. Henry More: Late Fellow of Christ's College in Cambridge. To Which Are Annexed Divers Philosophical Poems and Hymns* (Wheaton, Ill.: Theosophical Publishing Society, 1911).

[10]   Henry More, *Democritus Platonissans, or, An Essay on the Infinity of Worlds out of Platonick Principles* (Cambridge, 1646), Stanzas 21–22.

And after this shall others be again
And other beasts and other humane birth. . . .
Another Adam once received breath
And still another in endless repedation
And this must perish once in final conflagration.[11]

Such speculation echoed ancient notions of plural worlds in succession, which Saint Augustine and others had opposed as contrary to Sacred Tradition. Even so, More championed a vision of an abundantly creative, omnipotent God whose "endless overflowing goodness" spilled "in every place," creating "infinite several worlds" (Stanza 50).

In his *Divine Dialogues* (1668), More speculated on the status of ETI with regard to redemption in Jesus Christ. He posited that intelligent creatures on other planets were saved by God through revealing to them the mystery of Christ's incarnation and redemption on Earth, which had cosmic consequences. In essence, if the vast distances between their planets and ours prevented interplanetary communication by natural means, God could intervene through supernatural revelation to the extraterrestrials, presumably through angelic visitations or ETI prophets and inspired writers.[12]

Meanwhile, in 1657, the French Protestant physician, chemist, and botanist Pierre Borel (1620–1671) made a rather bold entrance into the ETI conversation, given that he was neither an astronomer nor a theologian. The title of his work served as a summary of its claims: *A New Treatise Proving a Multiplicity of Worlds. That the Planets Are Regions Inhabited,*

---

[11] Henry More, *Divine Dialogues,* vol. 1 (London: 1668), Stanza 76, 523–36.
[12] More, 523–36.

and the Earth a Star, and that It Is out of the Center of the World in the Third Heaven, and Turns Round Before the Sun Which Is Fixed. And Other Most Rare and Curious Things. One Borel scholar has described the book as "a mélange of erudition, of the most recent scientific knowledge, and of naiveté."

Borel believed that the infinite number of inhabited planets in the universe are all enlightened by our central sun, a concession to the traditional conviction that the human race occupies a special place in the cosmos. Even so, the immense stars, infinite in number, could not have been created for humankind alone. Borel insisted that these views were in accord not only with Scripture and with God's nature as Creator but also with empirical observation: "Awake up the eyes of your Understanding and Reason towards the Heavens," he thundered, "contemplating the wonderful things thereof!"[13]

Bernard Fontenelle

In 1686, the French writer and controversialist Bernard le Bovier de Fontenelle (1657–1757) caused a sensation with the publication of his *Entretiens sur la pluralité des mondes* (*Conversations on the plurality of worlds*). A major figure of the French Enlightenment, Fontenelle was known for his antireligious bias and skeptical attitude toward religious claims, despite his training at the Jesuit college in Rouen.

Conversations was directed, not just at scholars, but at the general public, which proved to be enthralled by the work. It was presented as a series of witty and entertaining dialogues between a philosopher and a charming, intelligent

---

[13] Pierre Borel, *A New Treatise,* chapter 5; quoted in Dick, *Plurality of Worlds*, 119.

noblewoman. By 1688, multiple English translations had appeared. By 1800, the book had been translated and published in nine other languages as well.

Part of the appeal of the *Conversations* was its mixture of plausible scientific scenarios with devices developed by the seventeenth-century pioneers of science fiction. Fontenelle was well versed in the emerging scientific observations and theories of his day, having served as the perpetual secretary of the French Academy of Sciences in Paris. But he joined such scientific knowledge to novelistic techniques, fancifully describing the inhabitants of each known planet in our solar system, distinguishing them according to general physical appearance and temperament. He also populated the comets, but not the sun or stars.

Fontenelle insisted that the ideas in his work were contrary to neither reason nor Scripture. In his preface, he anticipated that "scrupulous people . . . will think there is danger in respect to religion in placing inhabitants elsewhere than on earth."

> But what may be surprising to you is that religion simply has nothing to do with the system [of speculations I am proposing], in which I fill an infinity of worlds with inhabitants. It's only necessary to sort out a little error of the imagination. When I say to you that the moon is inhabited, you picture to yourself men like us, and then, if you're a bit of a theologian, you're full of qualms. [But] the descendants of Adam have not spread to the Moon, nor sent colonies there. Therefore the men in the Moon are not sons of Adam.

"Well," he concludes, "it would be embarrassing to Theology [only] if there were men anywhere not descended from him. It's not necessary to say any more about it; all imaginable difficulties boil down to that."[14]

In short, Fontennel insisted, creatures of other worlds would not be true humans descended from Adam. Thus their existence would constitute no threat to the arguments of religious critics who argue that belief in ETI undermines the Christian doctrines of the Incarnation and Christ's redemption. Such creatures would not be subject to the original sin stemming from Adam that requires salvation.

Meanwhile, Fontennel argued, as others had before him, that other worlds with various kinds of intelligent creatures displayed God's omnipotence and creativity, contributing to His glory.[15]

Christiaan Huygens

While Fontenelle was not friendly to religion, his contemporary Christiaan Huygens (1629–1695), a Dutch physicist, mathematician, astronomer, and inventor, was a Protestant who spoke repeatedly in his work of the wisdom of God and His providence. Widely regarded as one of the greatest scientists of all time, Huygens is the only scientist of such stature to have devoted an entire book to the subject of extraterrestrial life.

---

[14] Bernard le Bovier de Fontennel, *Conversations on the Plurality of Worlds,* trans. H. A. Hargreaves (Berkeley: University of California Press, 1990), 5–6.

[15] Dick, *Plurality of Worlds*, 124.

Cosmotheoros (1698) was written late in Huygens's life and published in Latin by his brother after the author's death. It was translated into English the same year under the title *The Celestial Worlds Discover'd: or, Conjectures Concerning the Inhabitants, Plants, and Productions of the Worlds in the Planets.* The book was translated into Dutch, French, German, and Russian within the following two decades.[16]

"It's not improbable," Huygens says as he introduces the work, "that the rest of the Planets have their Dress and Furniture, nay and their Inhabitants too as well as this Earth of ours."[17] The treatise is filled with "probable Conjectures" about the biology, intelligence, morality, science, society, and culture of various kinds of ETI. Where Fontenelle took pleasure in imagining a wide diversity in such aspects, Huygens focused on what he concluded would be their similarities to earthlings.

ETI would probably have senses as we do, he concludes, similar bodily organs, and hands and feet. They would also move in an upright posture as we do. But their bodily shape might otherwise vary considerably from ours.

Since reason is universal, they would be able to distinguish good and evil, true and false, as we do, providing them with a similar sense of justice and morality, and similar scientific endeavors. They would be "adorned with the same Virtues, and infected with the same Vices" as humans are. They would use tools and other instruments to manipulate

---

[16] Crowe, *Extraterrestrial Life Debate: Antiquity to 1915*, 86.

[17] Christiaan Huygens, *The Celestial Worlds Discover'd: or, Conjectures Concerning the Inhabitants, Plants, and Productions of the Worlds in the Planets* (London, 1698), 1; quoted in Crowe, *Extraterrestrial Life Debate: Antiquity to 1915*, 87.

objects in their surroundings; understand and apply some-thing of mathematics; develop forms of transportation, including navigation; communicate through speaking and writing; and have their own forms of music.[18]

Isaac Newton

The Englishman Isaac Newton (1642–1727), like Christiaan Huygens, has been widely regarded as one of the greatest scientists of all time. Unlike Huygens, he never devoted an entire treatise to the discussion of extraterrestrial intelligence. But his published works and unpublished letters and manuscripts reflect his interest in the matter, and his eminence as a physicist, mathematician, astronomer, and philosopher prompted his contemporaries to examine carefully what he wrote.[19]

Newton made impressive calculations about the weights of bodies on other planets as compared to the Earth, given the differences in gravitational pull among planets of various sizes. These calculations raised issues indirectly related to the discussion about ETI. For example, creatures the size of humans might have trouble functioning on larger celestial bodies, where their weight would be considerably heavier: On Jupiter, they would be more than twice as heavy as on earth; on the sun, twenty-three times.

In addition, Newton calculated the density of other planets, a matter that also had implications for life on other planets. Earth is six times denser than Saturn. Could the

---

[18] Huygens, *Celestial Worlds Discover'd*; quoted in Crowe, *Extraterrestrial Life Debate: Antiquity to 1915*, 96–108.
[19] Crowe, 109.

latter planet possibly possess a surface sufficient to support inhabitants?[20]

The most explicit surviving remarks of Newton about the possibility of ETI were discovered by one of his later biographers, David Brewster, and published in 1855. Some details of the manuscript are problematic, but Brewster's version contains these words: "*For in God's house (which is the universe) are many mansions* [see Jn 14:2], *and He governs them by agents which can pass through the heavens from one mansion to another. For if all places to which we have access are filled with living creatures, why should all these immense spaces of the heavens above the clouds be incapable of inhabitants?*"[21] The reference to God and the Gospel allusion reflect Newton's lifelong conviction as an Anglican believer that the order he discovered in the universe could exist only by the intelligent design, activity, and power of its original Creator.

An additional, rather puzzling, comment of Newton was recorded by John Conduitt, the husband of Newton's niece, as part of a conversation the two men had two years before Newton died. Newton allegedly revealed his "Conjecture" that catastrophic "revolutions" occur in the planetary systems around stars that wipe out all life on the planets, implying that intelligent life existed on these bodies. According to Conduitt, Newton "seemed to doubt whether there were not intelligent beings superior to us, who superintended these revolutions of the heavenly bodies, by the direction of

---

[20] Newton, in Crowe, 110–22.

[21] David Brewster, *Memoirs of Life, Writings, and Discoveries of Sir Isaac Newton*, vol. II (Edinburgh, 1855), 172–73; quoted in Crowe, *Extraterrestrial Life Debate, 1750–1900*, 24. Emphasis in the original.

the Supreme Being." But Newton did not elaborate further about the nature of these "intelligent beings superior to us," a description that could refer either to angels or to some form of ETI.[22]

Bentley, Locke, and Berkeley

By this time, the possibility of extraterrestrial intelligence was becoming a popular theme in religious circles, examined in light of its implications for Christian faith. Richard Bentley (1662–1742), a Cambridge-educated Anglican clergyman, took up the subject in a series of Christian apologetic lectures.

With regard to the notion that God has created all things for the sake of the human race on Earth, he insisted that "we need not nor do not confine, define and determine the purposes of God in creating all Mundane [earthlike] Bodies, merely to Human Ends and Uses." Unlike other theologians, however, he added that God *could* have created the universe for humanity because "the Soul of one vertuous and religious Man is of greater worth and excellency than the Sun and His Planets and all the Stars in the World."[23]

Even so, Bentley concluded that the heavenly bodies "were formed for the sake of Intelligent Minds." Just as Earth was created for the sake of humankind, "why may not all other Planets be created . . . for their own Inhabitants which have Life and Understanding?"[24]

---

[22] Quoted in Crowe, *Extraterrestrial Life Debate, 1750–1900*, 25.

[23] Richard Bentley, "A Confutation of Atheism from the Origin and Frame of the World" (London, 1693), in *Isaac Newton's Papers and Letters on Natural Philosophy,* ed. Bernard Cohen (Cambridge, Mass.: Harvard University Press, 1958), 356–58.

[24] Bentley, "Confutation of Atheism," in *Isaac Newton's Papers,* 356–58.

With regard to Scripture, Bentley wrote that "the Holy Scriptures do not forbid him to suppose as great a multitude of [star] Systems and as much inhabited, as he pleases." Even though the Bible spoke only of earthlings, that was no proof that other planets were uninhabited.[25]

Given this position, Bentley had to deal with the dilemma resulting from the affirmation of Scripture and Tradition that all human beings were descended from Adam and thus subject to original sin. In light of possible ETI, that claim would seem to be discredited, since extraterrestrials could hardly be descended from Adam. So Bentley posited, as Fontenelle had done, that this was not a problem because extraterrestrials should not be considered human, but another species. They did not figure into the biblical picture of Adam, the human race, and original sin at all.

Since biblical times, Jews and Christians had spoken of the wonders of nature as evidence of God's glory: "The heavens are telling the glory of God" (Ps 19:1). In Bentley's thought, the notion of multiple inhabited solar systems was added as another kind of evidence for that reality. Such systems demonstrated divine goodness, wisdom, power, and majesty.[26]

When the celebrated English philosopher John Locke (1632–1704) speculated about extraterrestrial intelligence, he also spoke within a religious context. Raised in a Puritan family, his ideas eventually tended in a more Unitarian and ultimately Arian direction. Even so, he maintained the verbal inspiration of the Scriptures and taught that they were fully in keeping with human reason.

---

[25] Bentley, "Confutation of Atheism," in *Isaac Newton's Papers*, 356–58.
[26] Dick, *Plurality of Worlds*, 149.

In his *Essay Concerning Human Understanding* (1689), Locke emphasized that the human capacity for attaining ideas is limited by human senses. Yet intelligent extraterrestrials, he suggested, might have "senses or faculties more or perfecter than we have" and thus develop ideas beyond our own. In fact, sensory limitations were not the only aspect of what he imagined to be a human inferiority to ETI: "He that will consider the infinite power, wisdom, and goodness of the Creator of all things will find reason to think it was not all laid out upon so inconsiderable, mean, and impotent a creature as he will find man to be; who in all probability is one of the lowest of all intellectual beings."[27] Surely, God would have created beings in other worlds more intelligent, powerful, and noble than we are.

The Irish idealist philosopher George Berkeley (1665–1753), a Protestant bishop in the Church of Ireland, was an opponent of Locke's philosophical views. But he seemed to share Locke's pessimism about human nature in the context of comparisons with intelligent extraterrestrial life forms. His *Alciphron, or the Minute Philosopher*, was subtitled *An Apology for the Christian Religion, against Those Who Are Called Freethinkers*. In it, he replied to the objection against Christian belief based on the existence of "so much vice and so little virtue upon earth" with this rejoinder: "And for aught we know, this spot [Earth], with the few sinners on it, bears no greater proportion to the universe of intelligences than a dungeon doth to a kingdom. It seems we are led not only by revelation, but by common sense, observing and inferring from

---

[27] John Locke, *Essay Concerning Human Understanding,* Bk. IV, Ch. III, #23.

the analogy of visible things, to conclude there are innumerable orders of intelligent beings more happy and more perfect than man."[28] Both Locke and Berkeley, then, were confident that ETI exists and is most likely superior to us.

Worst Possible Planet, Best Possible Universe

The German Lutheran polymath Gottfried Wilhelm Leibniz (1646–1716), whose fields of endeavor were legion, is perhaps best known for his optimistic assertion that ours is the best of all worlds. As he insisted early in his work *Theodicy* (1710): "This supreme wisdom [God], united to a goodness that is no less infinite, cannot but have chosen the best" world to create.[29]

In that same treatise, Leibniz laid out an extended treatment of his views on the possibility of other worlds. The French skeptic Voltaire and others had lampooned his optimism about the universe God had created, based on the depth and breadth of evil found among human beings. Leibniz replied: "It is true that one may imagine worlds without sin and without unhappiness . . . but these same worlds would be inferior to ours in goodness. . . . Often an evil brings forth a good whereto one would not have attained without that evil."[30] Leibniz was offering the traditional argument against such an objection, that God allows evil on our planet because He can always bring out of it a greater good.

---

[28] George Berkeley, *Works of Berkeley*, Vol. III (London: Nelson, 1950), 172.

[29] G. W. Leibniz, *Theodicy: Essay upon the Goodness of God, the Freedom of Man, and the Origin of Evil*, trans. E. M. Haggard (New Haven. Conn.: Yale University Press, 1952), 128.

[30] Leibniz, 129.

Yet he took the traditional argument even further by considering the cosmic context beyond Earth. Since at least the fourth century, Catholic theologians had affirmed that Adam's unfortunate fall nevertheless set in motion the events that would lead to the Incarnation of God's Son and our Redemption. As summarized in the *Exultet* of the Catholic Church's Easter liturgy, the Fall was a *felix culpa*, a "happy fault, that earned for us so great, so glorious a Redeemer" in Jesus Christ.[31]

Leibniz affirmed that notion but explored it within the broader background of multiple inhabited worlds. To the whole universe, he declared, Christ bestowed "something more noble than there otherwise would have been amongst created beings."[32]

In the same work, the author took the argument in a different direction in replying to objections that the extensive evil in the world was evidence that this could not be the best possible world. The universe contains, Leibniz wrote, "an infinite number of globes, as great and greater than ours, which have as much right as it to hold rational inhabitants, though it follows not at all that they are human." Beyond Earth, in fact, "it may be that all suns are peopled only by blessed creatures," and that our planet is "almost lost in nothingness. . . . Since all the evils that may be raised in objection before us are in this near nothingness [of our planet], haply it may be that all evils are almost nothingness in comparison

---

[31] Charlton Walker, "Exultet," *The Catholic Encyclopedia,* Vol. 5 (New York: Robert Appleton Company, 1909), http://www.newadvent.org/cathen/05730b.htm.

[32] Leibniz, *Theodicy*, 378.

with the good things which are in the universe."[33] As one commentator has suggested, we could paraphrase Leibniz's position this way: Earth is the worst possible planet in the best possible universe.[34]

This consideration would later be echoed in such diverse settings as the German poetry of Friedrich Gottlieb Klopstock (1724–1803) and the science fiction trilogy of the twentieth-century Anglican scholar C. S. Lewis (1898–1963). Klopstock's *Mesias* (*Messiah*) describes a planet whose inhabitants are unfallen, and whose original ancestor, unlike Adam on Earth, remains immortal. His descendants are

> Persons, as we in form, still fully innocent, not mortal persons,
> And their first father stood fully in masculine youth,
> Although centuries distant from his early years,
> Surrounded by his unaged children. (V, 154–157)

This immortal alien Adam reveals to his descendants the great moral catastrophe that occurred on Earth at the beginning of human history:

> Far from us, on one of the earths, are persons such as we,
> Similar in form; deprived by themselves of innate innocence
> And of godly form—mortal in fact they are!

In Klopstock's cosmic vision, only earthlings have fallen into sin and need redemption through Divine intervention. Even

---

[33] Leibniz, 135.
[34] Crowe, *Extraterrestrial Life Debate*, 1750–1900, 29.

so, "the triumph of Christ extended to the stars of innocent persons / And of immortals."[35]

Would We Baptize Aliens?

As a devout German Lutheran, Leibniz was deeply concerned about theological issues related to the possibility of other inhabited worlds. Unlike most others writing about the subject, he considered the possibility that travel between the planets might be possible, leading to pressing religious issues.

> If someone . . . came from the moon, we would take him to be a lunarian, and yet we might grant him . . . the title *man*. . . . But if he asked to be baptized, and to be regarded as a convert to our faith, I believe that we would see great disputes arising among the theologians. And if relations were opened up between ourselves and these planets—whom M. Huygens says are not much different from men here—the problem would warrant calling an Ecumenical Council to determine whether we should undertake the propagation of the faith in regions beyond our globe.

In this passage, he may have simply been poking fun at the Catholic Church. But these dilemmas that would arise from interplanetary contact would nevertheless be real.

The speculative scenario continues:

---

[35] Friedrich Klopstock, *Der Messias*, in Klopstock's *Ausgewählte Werke*, ed. K. A. Schleiden (Munich, 1962); quoted in Crowe, *Extraterrestrial Life Debate, 1750–1900*, 145.

No doubt some would maintain that rational animals from those lands, not being descended from Adam, do not partake of redemption by Jesus Christ. . . . Perhaps there would be a majority decision in favor of the safest course, which would be to baptize these suspect humans conditionally. . . . But I doubt they would ever be found acceptable as priests of the Roman Church, because until there was some revelation their consecrations would always be suspect.

Leibniz concludes that "fortunately we are spared these perplexities by the nature of things"—that is, by the great distances involved in interplanetary travel. "Nature has seen fit to keep these [beings from other worlds] at a distance from us so that there will be no challenge to our superiority on our own globe." But he seems to be the first on record to raise particular questions that certain Catholic writers have raised in our day, when so many are convinced that ETI contact is likely or has already been made.[36]

Astronomers and Poets

Seventeenth-century philosophers and theologians were not alone in their enthusiastic affirmation of ETI. A number of astronomers and other scientists promoted the idea as well. But their writings often included religious aspects, and their speculations sometimes launched out in novel directions.

Edmond Halley (1656–1741), the English astronomer, mathematician, meteorologist, and geophysicist for whom the famous comet is named, not only insisted that other planets

---

[36] Klopstock, in Crowe, 314, 472–73.

were inhabited but also proposed that habitable globes exist beneath the Earth's surface as well. Though he first posited the notion to explain apparent shifts in the world's magnetic poles, he boasted: "I have shew'd a possibility of a much more ample Creation, than has hitherto been imagin'd."[37]

The Cambridge professor William Whiston (1667–1752) was a theologian as well as a mathematician, though he made serious departures from Christian tradition in denying the Blessed Trinity and the existence of hell. A disciple of Newton and friend of Halley, Whiston extended the realm of possible ETI dramatically in his thinking. He suggested that inhabitants dwell within the interior of the Earth, sun, planets, and comets. Even in the atmospheres of planets, he speculated, "not wholly Incorporeal, but Invisible Beings" dwell.[38]

Whiston's lectures at a London coffeehouse apparently introduced the great English Catholic poet Alexander Pope (1688–1744) to the notion of multiple inhabited worlds. In his philosophical poem *An Essay on Man* (written 1732–34), Pope taught that "the proper study of mankind" must include consideration of the extraterrestrials God has created:

> He, who thro' vast immensity can pierce,
> See worlds on worlds compose one universe,
> Observe how system into system runs,
> What other planets circle other suns,

---

[37] Edmond Halley, *Miscellanea curiosa*, 3rd ed., Vol. I (London, 1726), 55–59; quoted in Crowe, *Extraterrestrial Life Debate, 1750–1900* (1986), 31.

[38] Crowe, *Extraterrestrial Life Debate, 1750–1900* (1999), 31.

> What vary'd Being peoples ev'ry star,
> May tell why Heaven has made us as we are.[39]

These lines made such an impression on the German philosopher Immanuel Kant (1724–1802) that he quoted them in his published theories of the universe, which included speculations about the various inhabitants of the planets in our solar system.[40]

Pope's poem was rivaled in popularity by *Night Thoughts*, published between 1742 and 1745 by his contemporary the Anglican clergyman Edward Young (1683–1765). Translated into French, German, Italian, Magyar, Portuguese, Spanish, and Swedish, this work was divided into nine "Nights," the final "Night" being focused on extraterrestrial themes.

Referring to Earth, the poet asks:

> Canst thou not figure it an isle, almost,
> Too small for notice in the vast of being?
> Sever'd by mighty seas of unbuilt space
> From other realms; from ample continents
> Of higher life, where nobler natives dwell.

Those "nobler natives" know their Creator and worship him:

> Each of these stars is a religious house;
> I saw their altars smoke, their incense rise;
> And heard hosannas ring through every sphere.

"Ten thousand worlds, ten thousand ways devout," he concluded, "all nature sending incense to the Throne."

---

[39] Alexander Pope, *An Essay on Man*, Epistle 1, lines 23–8.
[40] Crowe, *Extraterrestrial Life Debate, 1750–1900* (1999), 31.

Young was aware that the existence of ETI would raise a number of theological questions regarding their nature, their moral status, their history, and their destiny. He queries the extraterrestrials themselves about such matters:

> Whate'er your nature, this is past dispute,
> Far other life you live, far other tongue
> You talk, far other thought, perhaps, you think,
> Than man. How various are the works of God!
> But say, what thought? Is Reason here enthroned?
> And absolute? Or sense in arms against her?
> Have you two lights? or need you no reveal'd? . . .
>
> And had your Eden an abstemious Eve? . . .
> Or, if your mother fell, are you redeemed? . . .
> Is this your final residence? If not,
> Change you your scene, translated? Or by death?
> And if by death, what death?—Know you disease?[41]

Young's poem compactly raised several critical questions.

Are the extraterrestrials ruled by reason, or do they find their passions in rebellion against their reason, as we do? Is their knowledge of God gained through both natural reason and revelation, as we do, or is their reason so perfect that they need no revelation? Are they unfallen? If fallen, are they redeemed? Do they suffer? Are they immortal, living forever on their planet? If not, are they translated into the next life as Enoch and Elijah were? Or if they die, what kind of death do they die?

---

[41] George Gilfillan, *Young's Night Thoughts* (London, 1833; Project Gutenburg, 2010), IX, 1603–7, 1881–3, 1898–1900, 1766–81, https://www.gutenburg.org/files/33156/33156-h/33156-h.htm.

Young's stirring sentiments found deep resonance in a wide and diverse audience. The French emperor Napoleon, the English Romantic poet William Blake, and John Wesley, the founder of the Methodist tradition (who actually edited an edition of the poem), all treasured the work.[42]

The English Congregational clergyman Isaac Watts (1674–1738) is known most widely for composing some 750 hymns, many still popular today. In his 1709 poem "The Creator and Creatures," he addresses the Creator:

> Thy voice produced the seas and spheres,
> Bid the waves roar, and planets shine;
> But nothing like thy Self appears.
> Through all these spacious works of thine.[43]

Some scholars have interpreted these lines to mean that Watts rejected the notion of other inhabited worlds. But they can also be read to mean that nothing in the universe is as magnificent as God, or that the Son of God was incarnated only on Earth. These latter interpretations are more compatible with the hymnist's observation in his *Knowledge of the Heavens and the Earth Made Easy* (1728) that "'tis probable that [the planets] are all Habitable Worlds furnished with rich Variety of Inhabitants to the Praise of their great Creator."[44]

---

[42] As we will see, in these few compact lines, Young raises several of the essential theological and moral questions that the Church would need to ask of ETI if we were to encounter such beings.

[43] *Minor English Poets 1660–1780*, ed. David P. French, vol. III (New York, 1967), 635.

[44] Isaac Watts, *Knowledge of the Heavens and the Earth Made Easy; or, The First Principles of Astronomy and Geography*, 2nd ed. (London, 1728), 103.

Multiple Incarnations

Among those who affirmed the existence of intelligent extraterrestrials, the relationship of Christ to ETI remained a matter of considerable debate. Henry More, as we noted, concluded that intelligent creatures on other planets were saved by God through revealing to them the mystery of Christ's incarnation and redemption on Earth. But other authors came to quite different conclusions on the matter.

In his arguments, Richard Bentley simply dismissed any "frivolous Disputes" involving the relationship of ETI to the fall of Adam and the incarnation of Christ. They need not be human just because they are rational, he suggested; God "may have made innumerable Orders and Classes of Rational Minds; some higher in natural perfections, others inferior to Human Souls. But a Mind of superior or meaner capacities than Human would constitute a different Species."[45]

William Haye (1695–1755), a Whig member of Parliament, presented his views in *Religio Philosophi: or, The Principles of Morality and Christianity Illustrated from a View of the Universe, and Man's Situation in It* (London, 1751). In some ways he echoed Young's thoughts, affirming that all the planets are "inhabited as well as the Earth. . . . Praise and thanksgiving are continually ascending to [God's] throne . . . from every quarter of the Universe."[46]

But Hay went further in declaring that all species form together "a general religion, a joint Communion, a Universal Church." This truth "bids us love them, not as our own

---

[45] Watts, *Knowledge of the Heavens*, 358–59, quoted in Crowe, *Extraterrestrial Life Debate: Antiquity to 1915*, 116–19.
[46] Quoted in Crowe, *Extraterrestrial Life Debate, 1750–1900*, 86.

Species, but as our Fellow-Creatures, and as Members of the same Church and Communion."[47]

Even so, Hay insists, it is "most probable" that they are fallen as we are, so that God must call them back "to a Sense of their Duty [by means] which may be as various as the Globes themselves." In what ways might God deal with the extraterrestrial sinners? On some planets "as a tremendous Judge, . . . in others as an indulgent Parent. In some only alarming, in others correcting; in some destroying, in others rebuilding; in some changing only individuals, in others entire Species; and exalting the Rational Creatures of each Globe from a Material to a Spiritual, from a Mortal to an Immortal State; transforming them into Angels; and from those Seminaries perpetually increasing the Hosts of Heaven."[48] In redeeming at least some of these creatures, Hay concluded, God may have accomplished multiple ETI incarnations.

The Second Person of the Trinity, Hay added, intending "to instruct, redeem, judge, and govern the race of Adam . . . united to himself Jesus: and for the same or similar ends he may have, and probably hath, united to himself other rational Creatures in other Planets. Jesus is not their Saviour, nor they the Saviours of Mankind."[49] Understandably, such statements, with echoes of the ancient Nestorian heresy, would not have been well received in many quarters.[50]

---

[47] Crowe, *Extraterrestrial Life Debate, 1750–1900*.

[48] Crowe, *Extraterrestrial Life Debate, 1750–1900* (1999), 86–87.

[49] Crowe, 86–87.

[50] The fifth-century Nestorian heresy declared that the divine Son of God was joined to a man (Jesus) so that the resulting union between God and humankind was simply a union of wills between two persons, one divine and one human. The Council of Ephesus (AD 431) rejected that notion and established that in Christ, there is only one

The "Men-God"

A similar position was taken by the *Traité de l'infini créé* (*Treatise on created infinity,* 1769), whose author's identity is debated.[51] Following Descartes, the writer declared the absolute infinity of the universe in both space and duration. He concluded that there exists "an infinity of earths sprinkled in the universe, and in each one some men who profit from the space wherein they are enclosed." He claimed to base his position on both physics and metaphysics: "We raise our proofs from the side of God, and we join theology to philosophy, the only good way to establish and prove a system."[52]

His soteriology, however, fundamentally recast Christian teaching about the Incarnation and Redemption as Hay's had done. At the heart of his position, too, was the notion of multiple divine incarnations across multiple planets.

Just as God the Son, the Second Person of the Blessed Trinity, had joined to His divine nature a human nature in Jesus Christ, He had also taken to Himself ETI natures (to all of which creatures he gave the general term "men"). The "God-Man" of traditional Christian theology thus is shown throughout the cosmos to be many *hommes-Dieu,* "Men-God": "man in the plural, God in the singular, because the *hommes-Dieu* would be several in number as to human

---

divine Person who has taken on a complete human nature. Correctly understood, the distinction is essential and, as we shall see in chapter 13, has important implications for Christian debates about the possible relationship of ETI to Christ's incarnation and redemption.

[51] The treatise was long thought to be written by the French priest-philosopher Nicolas Malebranche (1638–1715), but more recent scholarship suggests that the author was the French priest Jean Terrasson (1670–1750).

[52] Translated and quoted in Dick, *Plurality of Worlds,* 139.

[creaturely] nature, but only one as to Divine nature."[53] But he did not go so far as to say, as Hay seemed to insist, that the multiple incarnations had no saving relationship to one another, nor did he teach that redeemed ETI eventually became angels, "increasing the Hosts of Heaven."

By the mid-eighteenth century, then, the notion of ETI had been promoted by a number of thinkers, including some of the most prominent intellectuals of the day. Proposed by scientists, philosophers, theologians, poets, and others, as one historian of the development has termed it, "the era of the extraterrestrial had begun."[54] Much of public opinion seemed to follow their lead. But as we shall see, firm opponents of the idea did not remain silent.

---

[53] Dick, 139.
[54] Crowe, *Extraterrestrial Life Debate, 1750–1900* (1999), 37.

5

Against the "World-Mongers"

ETI Skeptics Strike Back

"There are indeed many and weighty authors who stand in the battle line for the lunar inhabitants. Nevertheless, victory is certainly ours, for they are not easily armed by faith or reason."

—Gerhard DeVries

THE NEW WAVE of thinkers championing the new cosmic models—and with those models, the notion of inhabited worlds—was not without its adversaries. These opponents typically represented the more traditional leaders and spokesmen for the academic, scientific, philosophical, and theological communities of Europe. The sensitive nature of the situation was reflected in a letter (1642) sent by Pierre de Cazre, rector of the College of Dijon, to the French priest and astronomer Pierre Gassendi. He warned the scientist that

> if the earth is doubtless one of the planets and also has inhabitants, then it is well to believe that inhabitants exist on the other planets and are not lacking in the fixed stars, [and] that they are even of a superior nature and in proportion as the other stars surpass

the earth in size and perfection. This will raise doubts about [the book of] Genesis which says that the earth was made before the stars and that they were created on the fourth day to illuminate the earth and measure the seasons and years. Then in turn *the entire economy of the Word Incarnate and of scriptural truth will be rendered suspect.*[1]

Few were apparently aware at that time of the ancient admonition issued many centuries before by Saint Augustine, who cautioned that, when interpreting the first chapters of Genesis, "No Christian will dare say that the narrative must not be taken in a figurative sense."[2]

"Absurd and False Opinions"

The Dutch philosopher Gerhard DeVries (1648–1705), chair of philosophy at the University of Utrecht, published in 1678 his *Dissertatio academica de lunicolis* (*Academic dissertation on the lunar inhabitants*). He represented the older, established tradition of medieval thought, which at that time was still strongly entrenched in Holland. DeVries focused on the issue of inhabitants of the moon, which for many represented the test case for the existence of ETI.

"There are indeed many and weighty authors," he admitted, "who stand in the battle line for the lunar inhabitants. Nevertheless, victory is certainly ours, for they are not easily

---

[1]   Quoted in Crowe, *Extraterrestrial Life Debate, 1750–1900,* 17–18; emphasis in the original.

[2]   St. Augustine, *De Genesi ad Litteram,* vol. 41 in *Ancient Christian Writers: The Works of the Fathers in Translation*, ed. J. Quasten, W. Burghardt, T. Lawler (Mahwah, N.J.: Paulist Press, 1982), 19.

armed by faith or reason. And both [faith and reason] are fighting for me."[3]

In addition to the typical scientific and philosophical arguments, DeVries offered arguments from Scripture and faith. Genesis 1:16, he recalled, compared the moon to the sun as the lesser light, not to the earth. So the moon belonged to the heavens; it was a celestial body, not a terrestrial body, composed of the same elements as Earth. As additional scriptural support, DeVries presented the traditional argument from silence, noting that the Bible describes Earth in detail, but said nothing about forests, seas, and inhabitants on the moon.

Finally, DeVries argued that if there were intelligent lunar inhabitants, and if they were saved by God, it would reduce the number of souls saved on earth. He apparently subscribed to the notion that a divinely pre-ordained number of places in heaven have been reserved for the blessed. After the fall of the bad angels, redeemed humans were destined to take the places that would have been occupied by the angels who fell. If the number of places was limited and fixed, then more redeemed extraterrestrial souls would mean fewer places in heaven for human souls.[4]

---

[3] Gerhard DeVries, *"Dissertatio academica de lunicolis,"* in Daniel Voet, *Physiologia, sive, de natura rerum libri sex, recogniti, ac notis illustrati a Gerardo De Vries ... accedit hujus Dissertatio germina, altera de lumine, altera de lunicolis,* 3rd ed. (Utrecht: Trajecti ad Rhenum, 1694), 254; quoted in Dick, *Plurality of Worlds,* 121.

[4] A version of this idea can be found at least as early as St. Augustine's *Enchiridion* (c. 420), 9:28–29. He taught that redeemed humans would "fill up the loss which that diabolical disaster had caused in angelic society." But he did not seem to think the number of places available to redeemed humans was limited to the number of the fallen angels: "The

In short, from DeVries's perspective, not only science and philosophy, but also Scripture and faith made it clear that God had not populated the moon or any other celestial body. The notion of lunar inhabitants (and its implications for other inhabited worlds) was thus for DeVries not a conclusion based on God's omnipotence and the plenitude of His creation. Instead, it was "a common refuge of those who presume to defend absurd and false opinions of every kind as truth."[5]

All Things Created for Humankind

The promoters of ETI often based their arguments theologically on the notion that all things we intelligent creatures can perceive in the universe are created for our appreciation, use, and enjoyment, so that we will give glory to our Creator: "And God said, 'Let there be lights in the firmament of the heavens to separate the day from the night; and let them be for signs and for seasons and for days and years . . . and to give light upon the earth" (Gn 1:14–15). "The heavens are telling the glory of God, and the firmament proclaims his handiwork" (Ps 19:1).

If there are countless heavenly bodies in the cosmos that no human being will ever see, then how could all those bodies hidden from our view be created for earthlings? Instead, they argued, God must have created those bodies for the sake of other intelligent creatures inhabiting distant worlds.

---

heavenly Jerusalem, our mother and the commonwealth of God, shall not be defrauded of her full quota of citizens, but perhaps will rule over an even larger number" (29).

[5]   DeVries, *"Dissertatio academica de lunicolis,"* 259, quoted in Dick, *Plurality of Worlds,* 122.

A second line of theological argument for extraterrestrial intelligence relied on the idea of divine plenitude that we noted in chapter 3. It reasoned that God fills every corner of His universe with creatures, and He would be "wasting" the greatest portion of His creation if He left it uninhabited, lavishing His favor only on lowly earthlings.

The Englishman Thomas Baker (1656–1740), a fellow of St. John's College in Cambridge, was an opponent of such arguments and went to battle against the "World-Mongers," as he called them. He concluded a chapter in his *Reflections upon Learning* (1699) with a challenge to those who judged things only by their size and who consequently asserted that the Creator would waste the vast heavenly bodies if He left them without inhabitants. Baker responded to that assumption: "There is more Beauty and contrivance [creative skill] in the Structure of the Human Body, than there is in the Glorious Body of the Sun, and more perfection in one Rational immaterial Soul, than in the whole Mass of Matter. . . . There cannot then be any absurdity in saying, that all things were created for the sake of this inferior World, and the Inhabitants thereof, and they that have such thoughts of it, seem not to have consider'd, who it was that died to redeem it."[6]

For Baker, the Son of God walked on this tiny planet and gave His life for its inhabitants. Given such a demonstration of divine favor, we should not be surprised if no other planets are like it; even if they are much larger, their massive size is no indication of greater importance.

---

[6] Thomas Baker, *Reflections upon Learning* (London, 1699), 97–98.

The Anglican clergyman Robert Jenkin (1656–1727) took to a whole new level the old argument against ETI that all things, even other worlds, have been created for the sake of the human race, not for inhabitants of other worlds. He included a chapter devoted to making that claim in his *Reasonableness and Certainty of the Christian Religion* (1711), which had to do with the eternal destiny of human beings.

In an unusual twist of speculation, Jenkin asserted that although the planets could have been created for alien habitation, he thought it more probable that they were designed to serve "either for Mansions of the Righteous, or Places of Punishment for the wicked, after the Resurrection."[7] Other inhabitable planets, he suggested, were created not for ETI but to be the places of everlasting reward or punishment for earthlings.

The Hutchinsonians

Among the most influential of the ETI opponents of this period were the followers of John Hutchinson (1674–1737), an English theologian, natural philosopher, and author of *Moses's Principia* (1724–27). He challenged Isaac Newton's science, proposing instead a system of his own, based in part on his conviction that Old Testament Hebrew, if read properly, reveals God's designs for the universe.

The Hutchinsonians, as they were called, attracted several prominent Anglican figures who tended to be Augustinian, High Church, and scriptural literalists. Among these was Alexander Catcott (1725–79), who sought to debunk the

---

[7] Robert Jenkin, *The Reasonableness and Certainty of the Christian Religion*, Bk. II (London, 1700), 218–23:222.

notion of ETI because it had been used by the Deists to attack the Christian faith.[8]

An Anglican bishop had declared that the belief in plural worlds "may be of great use, in *abating our pride*, and *exalting our notions* of the *great Creator.*" On the contrary, Catcott argued, such pluralism actually leads to pride "by giving room to the wildest genius to indulge his extravagant fancy in acting the god and making (out of his own little head) an *infinity of worlds.*" He further countered that pluralism does not exalt our notion of God; instead, it will "tend in weak minds to lessen the idea of his *goodness* and *concern* for *man;* and so introduce infidelity and atheism in the world."[9]

Cosmic Life after Death

As an interesting aside, we should note that Jenkin was not the only one to ponder the cosmic location of postmortem human existence. In fact, several eighteenth-century books were written to designate where hell in particular might be located in the physical universe. The Anglican clergyman Tobias Swinden (1659–1719) attracted considerable attention with the publication of his *Enquiry into the Nature and Place of Hell* (1714), which was translated into French and German as well. Swinden declared that the sun, because of its fiery nature and vast size, was the most probable location of hell. Other stars could possibly have inhabited planets surrounding them, but he thought them unlikely locations

---

[8] Crowe, *Extraterrestrial Life Debate, 1750–1900*, 90.
[9] Quoted in Crowe, 92; 574, n. 28; emphasis in the original.

for hell, because such inhabitants were probably not fallen as humans are, and the Bible speaks of only one hell.[10]

Noting the Gospel's reference to "many rooms" in God's house (see Jn 14:2), the London printer Jacob Ilive (1705–83) offered a much more startling proposition. Rather than seeking to locate hell in the depths of the Earth (as was traditionally thought) or even in the Sun (as Swinden had proposed), he declared that "*this Earth Is Hell . . . [and] the Souls of Men are the Apostate Angels.*"[11] The harsh estimate of humanity's status held by Locke and Bentley was thus mild by comparison to Ilive's rather novel claims.

"A Golden Celestial Ladder"

A perhaps even more radical departure from Christian tradition in this regard was posited by Johann Gottfried Herder (1744–1803), the great German scholar whose vast erudition was displayed in several academic disciplines, including astronomy. Herder took up the theme of how human beings might be related to other inhabited worlds as an aspect of their life after death.

In his Über die Seelenwanderung (*On the Transmigration of Souls,* 1785), he wrote: "Perhaps also resting places, regions of preparation, other worlds are ordained for us, on which we, as on a golden celestial ladder, ever more easily, more actively, more happily climb to the source of all life,

---

[10] Crowe, 37.

[11] Jacob Ilive, *Oration … Proving I. The Plurality of Worlds. II. That this Earth is Hell. III. That the Souls of Men are the Apostate Angels. IV. That the Fire which shall punish those who shall be confined to this Globe after the Day of Judgement will be Immaterial …* (London, 1733).

and always seek but never reach the center point of the pil-grimage, the lap of the Deity. . . . Where I meanwhile may be, and through whatever worlds I am led, I am and remain always in the hand of the Father, who brought me here and calls me further: always consequently in God's infinite lap."[12]

In this way, Herder adapted the ancient Eastern religious notion of reincarnation. He rejected the idea that humans could be reincarnated on earth as animals or other human beings. But he believed that after our earthly death, we could live multiple lives on other planets, moving up "a golden celestial ladder" in preparation for our final union with God.

"The Coils of the Great Serpent of Eternity"

In a more literary vein, we find the notion of postmortem spirits, both human and ETI, coming together in a chilling scene in the German Romantic novel *Siebenkäs* (1796–97), by Johann Paul Friedrich Richter (1763–1825). Under the pen name Jean Paul, the author expressed his utter horror and despair at the thought of a universe without God. The chapter entitled "*Rede des todten Christus*," "Speech of the Dead Christ," is the most widely known and translated of all his works.

The narrator recalls a dream in which he finds himself in a cosmic graveyard, where spirits of the dead wander among open caskets. They gather in a church, where the last to emerge from his coffin, with a wound in his breast,

---

[12] Johann Gottfried Herder, Über die Seelenwanderung: Drei Gespräche, in Herder, *Sämtliche Werke*, ed. Bernard Suphan, Vol. XV (Hildesheim, 1967 reprint of the Berlin 1888 original), 272; quoted in Crowe, *Extraterrestrial Life Debate, 1750–1900*, 150.

is queried by the others: "Christ! Is there no God?" Christ replies, "There is none," and goes on:

> I have traversed the worlds, I have risen to suns, with the milky ways, I have passed athwart the great waste spaces of the sky; there is no God. And I descended to where the very shadow cast by Being dies out and ends, and I gazed into the gulf beyond, and cried, "Father, where art Thou?" But answer came there none. . . . And when I looked up the boundless universe for the Divine eye, behold, it glared at me from a socket empty and bottomless. . . . Shriek on, then, discords, shatter the shadows with your shrieking din, for HE IS NOT!

Each of the inhabited worlds, Jean Paul declared, shakes forth "its glimmering souls on to the Ocean of death," where "every soul in this vast corpse-trench . . . is utterly alone." And though there is no God, "the coils of the great serpent of eternity [are] all twined about those worlds."[13]

"In all this wide universe," Jean Paul concludes, "there is none so utterly solitary and alone as the denier of God."[14] What modern work of space science fiction or horror comes even close to the absolute terror of this scene? What atheist could read it thoughtfully without a least a moment of pause?

---

[13] Jean Paul, *Flower, Fruit, and Thorn Pieces; or, the Wedded Life, Death, and Marriage of Firmian Stanislaus Siebenkäs*, trans. Alexander Ewing (London, 1895), 260–65; quoted in Crowe, *Extraterrestrial Life Debate, 1750–1900*, 154–55.
[14] Paul, in Crowe, 260.

The Debate in Italy

Meanwhile, the ETI debate was heating up farther south and east. In Italy, the battle was taken up by Giovanni Cadonicci (1705–86), theologian, Church historian, and canon of the Cathedral of Cremona. Some works of French and English pluralist authors had been translated into Italian, offering Cadonicci a chance to respond with a rebuttal to pluralism on the basis of both theology and physics (*Confutazione teologica-fisica*, 1760).[15]

For Cadonicci, earthlings were the only rational physical beings in the universe. (Angels are rational but not physical because they are pure spirit.) His work criticized some aspects of the science behind the pluralist writers, such as their failure to provide evidence from astronomical observation that the stars are circled by planets. But his critique was largely theological and philosophical.[16]

Cadonicci cited, for example, the medieval arguments for a single cosmos offered by Saint Thomas Aquinas, which (as we saw in an earlier chapter) were themselves based in part on the ancient philosophical assumptions of Aristotle. He discussed whether human beings could be transported to other planets by demons. And he insisted that the Christian understanding of redemption ruled out the possibility of intelligent extraterrestrial life.[17] "What better reason do we have [for rejecting ETI] . . . than that of [God's] ordaining

---

[15] Giovanni Cadonicci, *Confutazione teologica-fisica del sistema di Gulgielmo Derham inglese, che vuole tutti i planeti de creature ragionevoli, come la terra, abitati* (Brescia, 1760); cited in Crowe, *Extraterrestrial Life Debate, 1750–1900*, 155–56.

[16] Cadonicci, in Crowe, 5.

[17] Cadonicci, in Crowe, 21, 131, 177–78.

the redemption of the human species . . . into which he descended, became incarnate, took flesh, lived, preached, died, and where he wanted his cross to replace the triumph of the Devil and death?"[18]

Cadonicci had concluded that if other planets were inhabited, then God the Son would "have become incarnate, lived, died, and resurrected in all the planets."[19] He found that possibility unacceptable.

But in Italy as elsewhere, the ETI debate remained lively. One important contribution came from the internationally known Jesuit priest, scientist, philosopher, and poet Roger Joseph Boscovich (1711–87), who taught at the Collegium Romanum and the University of Padua. Boscovich also played a major role in founding the Brera Observatory near Milan.[20]

In his *Philosophiae naturalis theoria* (1758), he advanced the startling notion (based on a chemical theory about the nature of fire) that "in the sun itself, & in the stars, . . . there may exist bodies . . . [that] may grow & live without the slightest injury of any kind to their organic structure."[21] More remarkable still was his speculation that matter ultimately consists not of hard atoms with mass, but rather as centers of force with attractive and repulsive forces. Perhaps such bodies of matter, he proposes, can interpenetrate one another: "There might be a large number of material & [perceptible] universes existing in the same space, separated one from the other in such a way that one was perfectly

---

[18] Cadonicci, in Crowe, 202.

[19] Cadonicci, in Crowe, 340.

[20] Crowe, *Extraterrestrial Life Debate, 1750–1900*, 156–58.

[21] Roger Joseph Boscovich, *A Theory of Natural Philosophy*, trans. J. M. Child (Cambridge, Mass.: Harvard University Press, 1966), 166.

independent of the other, & the one could never acquire any indication of the existence of the other."[22]

He elaborated: "What if there are other kinds of things that are different from those about us, or even exactly similar to ours, which have, so to speak, another infinite space, which is distant from this our infinite space by no interval either finite or infinite, but is so foreign to it, situated, so to speak, elsewhere in such a way that it has no communication with this space of ours; & thus will induce no relation of distance." These multiple universes could in fact, he goes on to suggest, exist "in a time situated outside the whole of our eternity."[23]

The breadth of Boscovich's theory is stunning: God could have created, not just intelligent life on other planets, but entire parallel inhabited universes in parallel eternities. And in a work published after his death, the theorist even considered the possibility of "a sequence of similar universes," some of which were in size like tiny grains of sand compared to others.[24] His vision in many ways foreshadowed much later speculations in cosmology and physics, such as the multiverse theory and the many dimensions posited in string theory.

---

[22] Boscovich, 184.

[23] Boscovich, 199.

[24] Quoted in Zeljko Marković, "Boscovich's *Theoria*," in Lancelot Law Whyte, ed., *Roger Joseph Boscovich* (London: Allen & Urwin, 1961), 125–52:150.

An ETI Rumpus in Russia

When theories of extraterrestrial intelligence reached Russia in the early eighteenth century, they caused a commotion at the highest levels of government. Tsar Peter the Great (1672–1725), seeking to Westernize and modernize his nation's culture, encouraged the translation of erudite European books into Russian. Huygen's *Cosmotheoros* was translated by a friend and personal advisor of the tsar, who commanded that it be published by Mikhail Petrovich Avramov.

When Avramov read the book, he was scandalized. It was a work of "Satanic perfidy," he insisted, whose author was "delirious," and whose translator had "with godless flattery deceived" the tsar.[25] He later told the Empress Elizabeth: "I examined this book which was contrary to God in all ways, and with my heart quaking and my soul overawed, I fell before the Mother of God with sobbing and bitter tears, frightened to publish and frightened not to publish."[26] In desperation, Avramov obeyed the tsar. But he published only thirty copies of it and did his best to conceal these.

Nevertheless, in 1724 another publisher printed the book, and in 1730 another translator completed his edition. The Holy Synod of the Russian Orthodox Church attempted to suppress the publication of the second translation, but succeeded only in delaying the process.

The controversial Mikhail Vasilyevich Lomonosov (1711–65), once praised by novelist Alexander Pushkin as "Russia's first university," came to the defense of claims for a plurality

---

[25] Valentin Boss, *Newton and Russia: The Early Influences 1698–1796* (Cambridge, Mass: Harvard University Press, 1972), 61.

[26] Quoted in Boss, 64.

of inhabited worlds. In his poem "Evening Reflections on Seeing the Aurora Borealis" (1743), he taught:

> And Science tells us that each twinkling star
> That smiles above us is a peopled sphere,
> Or central sun, diffusing light afar;
> A link in nature's chain:—and there, even there
> The Godhead shines displayed—in love and light,
> Creating wisdom—all-directing might.[27]

The sentiments expressed here are sweet, but Lomonosov also had an acid wit. He was a deist and a sharp critic of the Orthodox Church, so he could treat the same topic in biting satire.

In his poem "Hymn to a Beard" (1757), Lomonosov satirized Russian priests, who were at that time the only Russian men permitted to wear beards:

> True it be that all the planets
> Resemble ours as earthlike objects.
> Be on one of them a long-hair
> Priest, or self-appointed prophet:
> "By my beard, I swear to you,"
> He said, "The earth is through and through
> A lifeless planet; all is bare."
> One who remonstrated: "Man lives there."
> At the stake they burned him
> To punish this free-thinker's sin."[28]

---

[27] Leo Wiener, *Anthology of Russian Literature* (New York: G. P. Putnam, 1902), 253.

[28] Quoted in Otto Struve, "Lomonosov," *Sky and Telescope*, 13 (1954), 118–20.

An enraged Holy Synod reacted by asking the empress to issue a legal declaration that "none henceforth shall dare to write or print anything either of the multitude of worlds, or of anything else in opposition to the sacred faith, or in disagreement with honorable morals, under penalty of most severe punishment."[29] Lomonosov replied in a later scientific paper that ancient texts by the Church Fathers Saint Basil the Great and Saint John of Damascus show that Scripture does not rule out a plurality of inhabited worlds.[30]

Objections Anticipated

Christiaan Huygens's book provoked the storm of religious opposition to the notion of ETI developing in Russia. Yet the same book had actually noted and anticipated such opposition in the previous century. He had written: "When they hear us talk of new Lands, and Animals endued with as much reason as themselves, [they] will be ready to fly out into religious Exclamations, that we set up our Conjectures against the Word of God. For we do not read there one word of the Production of such Creatures, no not so much as of their existence, nay rather we read the quite contrary."

His reply to such critics was blunt: "Either these Men resolve not to understand, or they are very ignorant: For they have been answer'd so often, that I am almost asham'd to repeat it: That it's evident God had no design to make

---

[29] Quoted in Boris Menshutkin, *Russia's Lomonosov: Chemist — Courtier — Physicist — Poet*, trans. J. E. Thal, E. J. Webster, and W. C. Huntington (Princeton, N.J.: Princeton University Press, 1962), 149; cited in Crowe, *Extraterrestrial Life Debate, 1750–1900*, 160, 584.

[30] I have been unable to access the original references to discover which specific texts, if any, Lomonosov identified.

a particular enumeration in the Holy Scriptures, of all the Works of his Creation."

Huygens and others had grown weary of the argument from scriptural silence. "It is plain," he insisted, "that under the general name of Stars or Earth are comprehended all the Heavenly Bodies," even the moons of Jupiter and Saturn, which had been only recently discovered. (He himself had discovered Titan, the first of Saturn's moons.)[31]

Huygens responded as well to the objection that God had created all things for the use of Man, not for other intelligent creatures: "Since then the greatest part of God's Creation, that innumerable multitude of Stars, is plac'd out of the reach of any man's Eye . . . so that they don't seem to belong to us; is it such an unreasonable Opinion, that there are some reasonable [i.e., reasoning] creatures who see and admire those glorious Bodies at a nearer distance?"[32]

The author finally concluded his reply to religious objections with a response to one more criticism: the insistence that "it does not become us to be so curious and inquisitive in these things which the Supreme Creator seems to have kept for his own knowledge."

> But these Gentlemen must be told, that they take too much upon themselves when they pretend to appoint how far and no farther Men shall go in their Searches, and to set bounds to other Men's Industry; just as if they had been of the Privy Council of Heaven: as if they knew the Marks that God has plac'd to knowledge: or

---

[31] Huygens, *Celestial Worlds Discover'd*, 1–11; quoted in Crowe, *Extraterrestrial Life Debate: Antiquity to 1915*, 86.

[32] Huygens, in Crowe, 89.

> as if Men were able to pass those Marks. . . . That vig-
> orous Industry, and that piercing Wit, were given Men
> to make advances in the search of Nature, and there's
> no reason to put any stop to such Inquiries.

If our forefathers had demonstrated such a negative attitude toward scientific inquiry, Huygens noted, we might never have discovered the New World.[33]

Emanuel Swedenborg

In fairness to the religious writers who sometimes vehemently opposed the notion of extraterrestrial intelligence, we must note two matters of context. First, the more spiritually minded proponents of ETI were often known to combine their scientific ideas with religious notions that were antithetical to Christian thought. As we have seen, Bruno propagated heretical theological positions on the Holy Trinity, the divinity of Christ, the Incarnation, the virginity of Mary, the Mass, and the Eucharist. Whiston denied the Blessed Trinity and the existence of hell. Herder combined notions of extraterrestrial life with reincarnation, a position that was eventually to find several influential adherents in France.

Another case in point would be Emanuel Swedenborg (1688–1772), son of a Swedish Lutheran bishop, a scientist and engineer who turned religious prophet. His teachings were largely based on numerous alleged visions which led him to write books that were received by his followers as a kind of divinely inspired scripture. The Swedenborgians, or the Church of the New Jerusalem, as they are formally called,

---

[33] Huygens, in Crowe, 90.

could read his claims about extraterrestrial intelligence in his book *Earths in Our Solar Systems Which Are Called Planets and Earths in the Starry Heavens; Their Inhabitants, and the Spirits and Angels There, From Things Heard and Seen.*

Swedenborg believed that God appeared to him and appointed him to teach the true Christian religion, which had been obscured through the centuries. He rejected belief in the Blessed Trinity. In one of his lesser works, he insisted that the Last Judgment had already taken place, and that he himself had witnessed it. He also taught that Christ's second coming had already taken place, but not through Christ's appearance in person. Rather, it was a revelation of Christ through the teachings of Swedenborg.

The alleged mystic claimed to converse frequently with angels and the spirits of deceased human beings on earth. But other intelligences came to speak to him as well, he insisted:

> It has been granted me of the Lord to discourse and converse with spirits and angels who are from other earths [that is, planets], with some for a day, with some for a week, and with some for months; and to be instructed by them concerning the earths, from which and near which they were; and concerning the lives, customs, and worship of the inhabitants thereof, with various other things worthy to be noted: and whereas in this manner it has been granted me to become acquainted with such things, it is permitted to describe them according to what has been heard and seen.

Swedenborg believed that "all spirits and angels are from the human race," even those associated with other planets. He claimed to communicate with spirits from the moon, Mercury, Venus, Mars, Jupiter, Saturn, and planets beyond our solar system.[34]

With regard to Christ's role for intelligent extraterrestrials, Swedenborg taught that the Divine Word became incarnate only on our earth. But Christ's primary purpose in coming to our planet appears to have been for him more a matter of revealing truth than offering a redemptive sacrifice. The truth that Christ came to reveal now spreads from our earth to ETI throughout the universe.[35]

In the following century, several other religious leaders who claimed mystical or prophetic experiences would also incorporate intelligent extraterrestrials into their claims of revelations from God about the cosmos. Joseph Smith (1805–44), founder of the Church of Jesus Christ of Latter-Day Saints (the Mormons), taught that the universe contains a vast number of inhabited planets, while Ellen G. White (1827–1915), who became the prophetess of the Seventh-Day Adventist movement, reported visions of ETI.[36]

---

[34] Emanuel Swedenborg, *Earths in the Universe* (London: Swedenborg Society, 1970), 1; quoted in Crowe, *Extraterrestrial Life Debate: Antiquity to 1915*, 216.

[35] Swedenborg, 113, in Crowe, 221.

[36] Wilkinson, *Search for Extraterrestrial Intelligence*, 26.

Benjamin Franklin, John Adams, and Thomas Paine Embrace ETI

Another useful case in point can be found in the thought of several influential Deists who were prominent in the early history of the American republic: Benjamin Franklin, John Adams, and Thomas Paine. Unlike the exotic mystical claims of Swedenborg, Deism was a highly rationalized religious system spawned by the Enlightenment. Deists rejected the mysteries and miracles of traditional Christian thought, denying the Blessed Trinity, the Incarnation, Divine Revelation, and many more essentials of Christian belief.

The American polymath Benjamin Franklin (1706–90) is widely known as one of the Founding Fathers of the United States. Less well known are his pronouncements about extraterrestrial intelligence and the religious implications of their existence.

In 1728, Franklin drafted his "Articles of Belief" soon after returning from a visit to England. They expressed not only his religious convictions but also his views about ETI, views which may have been indirectly influenced by Isaac Newton through a common acquaintance. Franklin declared:

> I believe there is one Supreme most perfect Being, author and father of the gods themselves. . . . I conceive, then, that the INFINITE has created many beings or gods, vastly superior to man, who can better perceive his perfections than we, and return him a more rational and glorious praise. . . . It may be that these created gods are immortal, or it may be that, after many ages, they are changed, and others supply

their places. Howbeit, I conceive that each of these is exceeding wise and good, and very powerful; and that Each has made for himself, one glorious sun, attended with a beautiful and admirable system of planets. It is that particular wise and good God, who is the author and owner of our system, that I propose for the object of my praise and adoration.[37]

In short, though a Deist, toward the end of his life Franklin professed a kind of ETI polytheism.

John Adams (1735–1826), another American Founding Father and the second president of the new nation, wrote in his diary the year after he graduated from Harvard (1756): "Astronomers tell us, with good Reason, that not only all the Planets and Satellites in our Solar System, but all the unnumbered worlds that revolve around the fixt Starrs are inhabited, as well as this Globe of Earth. Mankind are no more in comparison of the whole rational Creation of God, than a point to the orbit of Saturn. Perhaps all these different Ranks of Rational Beings have in a greater or less Degree, committed moral Wickedness."

If the latter is the case, Adams reasoned, a Calvinist should be pressed to accept one or the other of two alternatives: "Either God Almighty must assume the respective shapes of all these different Species, and suffer the Penalties of their

---

[37] Benjamin Franklin, "Articles of Belief and Acts of Religion," in *Works of Benjamin Franklin, with notes and a life of the author by Jared Sparks* (Boston: Hilliard, Gray, and Company, 1840), 2:1–3; quoted in Crowe, *Extraterrestrial Life Debate: Antiquity to 1915*, 205–6.

Crimes, in their Stead, or else all these Being[s] must be consigned to everlasting Perdition."[38]

Adams apparently maintained his interest in such matters throughout life. Eighteen months before he died in 1826, in a private correspondence, he spoke bitterly of Christian faith in light of his understanding of the vast cosmos and its presumed inhabitants. Adams scoffed at those who "believe that great Principle which has produced this boundless universe . . . came down to this little ball, to be spit upon by the Jews. And until this awful blasphemy is got rid of, there never will be any liberal science in the world."[39]

Thomas Paine (1737–1809) was an English-born political activist perhaps best known for his pamphlet *Common Sense* (1776), which gave considerable support to the American revolutionary cause. In his work *The Age of Reason* (1793–94), Paine championed Deism and vehemently attacked institutional religion. The book included an extended argument that accepting the existence of extraterrestrial intelligence required rejection of the Christian faith. He wrote:

> Though it is not a direct article of the Christian system, that this world that we inhabit is the whole of the habitable creation, yet it is so worked up therewith, from what is called the Mosaic account of the Creation, the story of Eve and the apple, and the counterpart of that story, the death of the Son of God, that to believe otherwise, that is to believe that God created

---

[38] John Adams, *Diary and Autobiography of John Adams*, L. H. Butterfield, ed. (New York: Atheneum, 1964), 1:22; quoted in Crowe, *Extraterrestrial Life Debate: Antiquity to 1915*, 207–8.

[39] Adams, in Crowe, 208.

a plurality of worlds, at least as numerous as what we called stars, renders the Christian system of faith at once little and ridiculous, and scatters it in the mind like feathers in the air. The two beliefs cannot be held together in the same mind; and he who thinks that he believes both, has thought but little of either.[40]

Paine's dismissive attitude seems to reveal his own ignorance of the age-old ETI conversation among intelligent and devout Christians.

This influential skeptic used another argument we have seen to discredit the Christian faith in light of a plurality of worlds: the prospect of endless divine Incarnations for the purpose of endless redemptive deaths:

From whence then could arise the solitary and strange conceit, that the Almighty, who had millions of worlds equally dependent on his protection, should quit the care of all the rest, and come to die in our world, because they say one man and one woman had eaten an apple! And on the other hand, are we to suppose that every world in the boundless creation, had an Eve, an apple, a serpent, and a redeemer? In this case, the person who is irreverently called the Son of God, and sometimes God himself, would have nothing else to do than to travel from world to world, in an endless succession of death, with scarcely a momentary interval of life.[41]

---

[40] Thomas Paine, *The Age of Reason, in Representative Selections*, ed. Harry Hayden Clark (New York: Hill and Wang, 1961), 273–284; quoted in Crowe, *Extraterrestrial Life Debate: Antiquity to 1915*, 224.
[41] Paine, in Crowe, 229.

Christians who read such inflammatory claims might well have found themselves, not becoming skeptics about their religion, but rather skeptics about extraterrestrial intelligence. Some of the fifty responses published to *The Age of Reason* not surprisingly focused on Paine's arguments against Christian faith based on ETI.

Prominent Early American ETI Advocates

Despite Paine's insistence that traditional Christians could not believe in a plurality of worlds without affirming a contradiction to their faith, in early America several prominent religious figures publicly embraced both Christian faith and ETI. One of them was Cotton Mather (1663–1728), the influential Puritan divine and prolific writer of Massachusetts whose father was president of Harvard College and whose scientific endeavors led to his election to the Royal Society in England.

In his work *The Christian Philosopher* (1721), for example, Mather concluded a passage on the stars with this prayer: "*Great* God, what a Variety of *Worlds* hast thou created! . . . How stupendous are the Displays of thy *Greatness*, and thy Glory, in the Creatures, with which thou hast replenished those worlds! Who can tell what Angelical Inhabitants may there see and sing the *Praises* of the Lord!"[42] Perhaps through Mather's influence, by the 1740s, the plurality of worlds was taught at Harvard.

---

[42] Cotton Mather, *The Christian Philosopher* (Gainesville, Fla.: Scholars Facsimiles and Reprints, 1968, facsimile reproduction of the London 1721 original), 2; quoted in Crowe, *Extraterrestrial Life Debate, 1750–1900* (1986), 107.

A second example of the evangelical embrace of ETI was Timothy Dwight (1752–1817), a president of Yale College. A disputation on the plurality of worlds had been held at Yale the year Dwight was born; by the time he became president, belief in ETI was well within the mainstream at the college. Dwight was a vocal critic of Deism, and in the 173 apologetics-oriented sermons he repeated to his students every four years, he often entertained the possibility of extraterrestrial intelligence.

The beauty and diversity of inhabited worlds reflect the greatness of their Creator, Dwight insisted. In response to Paine's mockery of the necessity of endless divine incarnations and bloody deaths, he concluded that among the numerous forms of intelligent life existing on the moon or other planets, only earthlings fell into sin and needed redemption. So the incarnation of God's Son had taken place only once, on Earth.[43]

Dwight's evangelical contemporary, the Anglican pastor John Wesley (1704–91), who founded the Methodist movement, apparently experienced a change of heart on the matter of ETI. An entry in his *Journal* suggests that he had been convinced of the pluralist position, but changed his mind after reading Huygen's work and that of the Hutchinsonians. He modestly suggested to ETI advocates: "Be not so positive."[44] Yet his cautious words were not at all heeded on either side of the strenuous debates in the centuries to come.

---

[43] Crowe, *Extraterrestrial Life Debate, 1750–1900* (1986), 107; Dick, *Plurality of Worlds*, 25–26.
[44] John Wesley, *The Works of Rev. John Wesley* (Grand Rapids, Mich: Baker Book House, 1978, reprint of the London 1878 edition), 13:396; 399; 2:515.

6

"A Blasphemy to Doubt It"

ETI Debates of the Nineteenth Century

"In the controversy about the Plurality of worlds, it has been considered . . . to be so necessary that the Creator should have filled with living beings the luminaries which we see in the sky, and the other cosmical bodies which we imagine there, that it almost amounts to a blasphemy to doubt it."

—Saint John Henry Newman

BY THE NINETEENTH century, the notion of extraterrestrial intelligence was no longer widely viewed among the well-read in Europe and the United States as an eccentric and impious speculation. In many ways, it had become instead a near-dogma among astronomers, and a common assumption among many theologians as well. Saint John Henry Newman (1801–90), the English Catholic convert, theologian, cardinal, and man of letters, complained in his celebrated *Essay in Aid of a Grammar of Assent* (1870) that any doubts about the matter in the religious circles of his day were seen as "blasphemy."

We should note, however, that the popular reconciliation of science and faith with regard to ETI had taken place largely at the level of a general belief in "Nature's God." The notion that God had created many inhabited planets readily supported the claim that such creative plenitude displayed His power, wisdom, and goodness. Even Deists who harshly criticized the Christian faith, such as the American founding fathers we have noted, could embrace pluralism without compromising their rather unadorned beliefs about the Creator.

On the other hand, the more distinctive tenets of a specifically Christian faith—doctrines of original sin, the Incarnation, redemption, and human destiny—were not so easily reconciled with the affirmation that extraterrestrial intelligence exists. As we have seen, at the very least, claims about ETI raised serious questions about the relationship of Jesus Christ to the inhabitants of other planets. These issues had been raised in earlier centuries, to be sure. But in the nineteenth century, ETI's champions had to focus more of their attention on demonstrating how such creatures would fit into the traditional Christian panorama of salvation.

ETI and Jesus Christ: Timothy Dwight

We noted in an earlier chapter the efforts of Timothy Dwight (1752–1817), an American Protestant minister and president of Yale University, to persuade his students that the Deists' use of pluralism to challenge Christian faith was insupportable. Drawing from the traditional notion of plenitude (the existence of multitudes of ETI affirms God's greatness and wisdom), Dwight preached that throughout God's "vast empire, he surrounded his throne with intelligent creatures, to fill the immense and perfect scheme of being." Astronomy, he suggested, had revealed that the cosmos is even more magnificent than the universe revealed by the prophets.[1]

This much, even the Deists could affirm. But Dwight emphasized that God's greatest benefit to those on Earth was Jesus Christ, the divine Son of God incarnate, and the redemption He accomplished on our behalf. So he had to address specifically the relationship of Christ to ETI. In one of his many sermons, collected in the five-volume *Theology Explained and Defended*, he declared: "Throughout immensity, [Christ] quickens into life, action, and enjoyment, the innumerable multitudes of Intelligent beings. The universe, which he made, he also governs. The worlds, of which it is composed, he rolls through the infinite expanse with an Almighty and unwearied hand. . . . From the vast storehouse of his bounty he feeds, and clothes, the endless millions . . . and from the riches of his own unchangeable Mind informs the innumerable host of Intelligent creatures with ever-improving virtue, dignity and glory."[2]

Dwight was of course echoing various scriptural passages in speaking of Christ's universal role as Creator and Governor: "All things were made through him, and without him was not anything made that was made" (Jn 1:3). He is "upholding the universe by his word of power" (Heb 1:3).

In the last volume of the same work, Dwight's analysis of a different biblical text foreshadows later interpretations

---

[1] Timothy Dwight, *Theology Explained and Defended in a Series of Sermons*, 5 vols. (Middletown, Conn.: 1818), vol. I, 78–79; quoted in Crowe, *Extraterrestrial Life Debate, 1750–1900*, 175–76.
[2] Dwight, *Theology Explained*, vol. I, in Crowe, 203.

suggesting that divine revelation in Scripture is given to humanity and thus focused on the human situation, so its scope may not include specifics about God's plans for ETI. In 2 Peter 3:10, for example, which declares that at Christ's second coming, "the heavens will pass away," the word "heavens" means only a portion of the universe, according to Dwight: "Other Intelligent beings, therefore, and the worlds which they inhabit, may be concerned in this wonderful production, only in a mediate and remoter sense."[3]

Much that appeared in Dwight's sermons were a rebuttal to the claims of Thomas Paine's infamous attack on the Christian faith. As we saw in a previous chapter, Paine mocked the notion of the Incarnation in light of an infinity of inhabited worlds. He declared that if salvation required such an act, God would have to spend most of His time dying for extraterrestrial intelligences throughout the cosmos, with endless divine incarnations to achieve endless redemptive deaths.

Dwight responded: "This world was created, to become the scene of one great system of Dispensations toward the race of *Adam*. . . . It was intended, also, to be a theatre of a mysterious and wonderful scheme of providence. The first rebellion in the Divine Kingdom commenced in heaven [among the angels, led by Lucifer]: the second existed here. The first was perpetuated by the highest, the second by the lowest, order of the intelligent creatures. These two are with high probability the only instances, in which the Ruler of all things has been disobeyed by his rational subjects."[4]

---

[3]   Dwight, *Theology Explained*, vol. V, in Crowe, 508.
[4]   Dwight, in Crowe, 508.

In short, Dwight proposed that Christ's incarnation and atonement have most likely taken place only on Earth, because the inhabitants of this planet alone have fallen and stand in need of redemption. "In this world there exists a singular [that is, unique] and astonishing system of Providence; a system of mediation between God and his revolted creatures. . . . This system, never found elsewhere, is accomplished here."[5]

If we need evidence that in the years following Dwight's pluralist sermons, belief in the existence of ETI was growing among American evangelical Christians, we need only consider the consequences of what has been called "the great moon hoax" of 1835. The New York *Sun,* a penny daily, published a series of reports claiming that the famous astronomer John Herschel had discovered lunar inhabitants by the use of a telescope. The hoax was actually an attempt at satire, but tens of thousands of gullible readers embraced the revelations as true; as the poet Edgar Allen Poe later recalled, "not one person in ten discredited" the account.[6]

According to contemporary reports, "some of the grave religious journals made the great discovery a subject of pointed homilies." An American pastor told his congregation that he might have to solicit funds to purchase Bibles for the lunar inhabitants, and certain philanthropists appointed committees to inquire about whether those on the moon might need material aid, or help in abolishing slavery if it existed among them.[7]

---

[5] Dwight, in Crowe, 509.
[6] Quoted in Crowe, *Extraterrestrial Life Debate, 1750–1900*, 213.
[7] Crowe, 212–13.

"The Fall of a Single Leaf"

Across the Atlantic, another evangelical Protestant pastor was challenging Thomas Paine's infidelity through reference to the ETI debate. Thomas Chalmers (1780–1847), a Scottish pastor who achieved considerable fame and influence through his thoughtful and eloquent sermons preached in Glasgow, delivered seven weekday sermons in November 1815 that created an international sensation. The book in which they were published two years later became a bestseller, entitled *A Series of Discourses on the Christian Revelation Viewed in Connection with the Modern Astronomy* (1817).[8]

Chalmers employed much the same strategy in his arguments as Dwight, with perhaps even more detailed facts and speculations from the astronomical science of his time. (He had at one time seriously considered a scientific career.) He sought "to extract a sentiment of piety from the works and the appearances of nature," and he invoked the plenitude argument for a Creator who filled the universe with life, including intelligent life.[9]

For Chalmers, the great virtue of humility was a natural consequence of studying astronomy. "We should learn not to look on our earth as the universe of God, but as one paltry and insignificant portion of it; that it is only one of the many mansions that the Supreme Being has created for the accommodation of his worshippers." Consequently, the

---

[8] Thomas Chalmers, *A Series of Discourses on the Christian Revelation Viewed in Connection with the Modern Astronomy* (New York: American Tract Society, 1850); excerpted in Crowe, *Extraterrestrial Life Debate: Antiquity to 1915*, 240–61.

[9] Chalmers, in Crowe, 246.

earth and that portion of the cosmos surrounding it could vanish without making much difference to the rest of God's vast creation.[10]

Dwight had argued that the scriptural prophecy of the heavens passing away might be interpreted as involving only a portion of the heavens, with other intelligent races across the universe being affected only indirectly, if at all. Chalmers took that speculation to a new level with haunting, humbling apocalyptic scenes about the final demise of the world in which earthlings live, echoing the language of Scripture:

> Though this earth were to be burned up, though the trumpet of its dissolution were sounded, though yon sky were to pass away as a scroll, and every visible glory, which the finger of the Divinity has inscribed on it, were to be put out forever—an event, so awful to us, and to every world in our vicinity, by which so many suns would be extinguished, and so many varied scenes of life and of population would rush into forgetfulness—what is it in the high scale of the Almighty's workmanship? a mere shred which, though scattered into nothing, would leave the universe of God [as] one entire scene of greatness and of majesty.

"The universe at large," Chalmers concluded, "would suffer as little by the destruction of our planet as the verdure and sublime magnitude of a forest would suffer by the fall of a single leaf."[11]

---

[10] Chalmers, in Crowe, 254.
[11] Chalmers, in Crowe, 254.

Yet Chalmers used this terrifying observation to press
home the startling biblical conviction that in our insignificance, God still cherishes us (see Ps 8:3–8). "Now, it is this
littleness, and this insecurity, which make the protection of
the Almighty so dear to us, and bring, with such emphasis, to every pious bosom, the holy lessons of humility and
gratitude. The God who sitteth above, and presides in high
authority over all worlds, is mindful of man." No wonder,
then, that "we may feel the same security in his providence,
as if we were the objects of his undivided care."[12]

Christ's Relationship to ETI: Two Alternatives

In his lyrical descriptions of God's mercy extended to the
human race in the Incarnation, Chalmers touched on the
issue of Christ's relationship to ETI. He seemed to offer two
alternatives. On the one hand, he called his listeners to ponder how "rather than lose the single world which had turned
to its own way," God would "lay upon his own Son the bur-
den of its atonement." Here, he suggested that on our planet
alone has intelligent life rebelled against God.[13]

On the other hand, Chalmers also pondered whether the
merits of Christ's work on Earth extend to extraterrestrials
as well: "The plan of redemption may have its influences
and its bearings on those creatures of God who people other
regions."[14] Do these words mean that at least some ETI
may be fallen and can be saved by what has occurred on
our planet? Or do they merely suggest that Christ's work on

---

[12] Chalmers, in Crowe, 255.

[13] Chalmers, in Crowe, 257.

[14] Chalmers, in Crowe, 258.

Earth could have beneficial consequences even for unfallen races across the cosmos—such as demonstrating to them more fully the depths of God's kindness?

Quoting Jesus's pronouncement that "there will be more joy in heaven over the one sinner who repents" (Lk 15:7), Chalmers depicts a cosmic version of that Gospel principle: The entire universe may be rejoicing over the repentance of one earthling. Perhaps the universe is actually "one secure and rejoicing family [in which our] alienated world is the only strayed, or only captive member."[15]

One of Chalmers's contemporaries, the prominent English Baptist minister John Foster (1770–1843), accepted the existence of intelligent extraterrestrials but challenged some of Chalmers's speculations about the relationship of Christ to ETI. In an article published in the British journal *Eclectic Review*, he doubted that ETI knows anything about what has happened on our planet. He also posited that extraterrestrials have experienced religious events on their own orbs just as significant as any on ours. As a result, the events on Earth would not be noteworthy on other planets.[16]

In addition, Foster concluded that unfallen races on other worlds could help explain the problem of evil on Earth. The great evil, sin, and misery on our planet, he speculated, does not characterize the condition of intelligent life elsewhere.[17]

---

[15] Chalmers, in Crowe, 259.

[16] John Foster], *Eclectic Review*, 8 (1817), 212.

[17] [Foster], 212.

"The Blood of the Victim Bathed the Universe"

While evangelicals on both sides of the Atlantic were speculating about ETI, the French Catholic philosopher Comte Joseph de Maistre (1754–1821) was also addressing directly and confidently the issue of Christ's relationship to extraterrestrials. In his *Soirées de Saint-Pétersbourg* (1821), he criticized certain theologians who reject the notion of ETI "for fear that it disturbs the doctrine of redemption," instead insisting that "the other planets are mere globes, *destitute of life and beauty*, which the Almighty has launched into space, apparently like a tennis-player, for his amusement solely."[18]

His position on the possible need for multiple divine incarnations was straightforward: "If the inhabitants of other planets are not like us guilty, they have no need of the same remedy, and if, on the contrary, the same remedy is necessary for them, are the theologians of whom I speak then to fear that the power of the sacrifice which has saved us is unable to extend to the moon?"[19]

If intelligent extraterrestrials are morally unfallen, he insisted, they have no need of redemption. If they are fallen, then the merits of Christ's sacrifice can reach them as well. There is no need for the Son of God to die again and again on various worlds, as Paine had argued.

Maistre cites the influential third-century Christian theologian Origen (c. 184–c. 253) in support of his position. It was Origen's "well known opinion," Maistre insisted,

---

[18] Comte Joseph de Maistre, *Soirées de Saint-Pétersbourg*, vol. II (Paris, n.d.), 318–19; trans. Eugene Lynch, "On Sacrifices," in *The United States Catholic Magazine and Monthly Review* (1845, vol. 4), 300–305.

[19] De Maistre, 304.

that the blood shed on Calvary had been useful not
only to men, but to the angels, the stars, and all created beings; an opinion which will not seem surprising if we call to mind what St. Paul says: "Because it
hath pleased God to reconcile all things unto himself,
through him who is the beginning, the first born from
the dead, making peace through the blood of his cross,
both as to things that are in heaven, and the things
that are on earth" [Col 1:20; Eph 1:10]. And if every
creature groaneth [in misery, because of the effects of
Adam's fall], according to the profound doctrine of
the same apostle [see Rom 8:23], why should not also
every creature be consoled?

Origen's memorable words in this regard were interpreted by
the Frenchman to refer (at least in principle) to ETI: "The
altar was at Jerusalem, but the blood of the victim bathed
the universe."[20]

Maistre went on to note how the Church Fathers Saint
Jerome and Saint John Chrysostom spoke of the merits of
Christ's sacrifice extending to the entire cosmos. "The great
and holy adversary of Origen [that is, Jerome] assures us
that, at the beginning of the fifth century, it was a received
opinion that 'the fruits of the redemption belonged to the
heavens as well as to the earth'; and St. Chrysostom did not
hesitate to avow that the same sacrifice . . . would operate
to benefit the whole universe." Finally, he cited the words
of a hymn sung for the Lauds of Passion Sunday: "Earth,

---

[20] De Maistre, 304–5.

sea, and stars, the universe itself, are in this blood washed clean!"[21]

Joseph Smith and Ellen G. White

We noted in an earlier chapter that two nineteenth-century religious movements, both born in America, incorporated notions of ETI into their teaching. Together, these two movements have come to shape the religious beliefs of millions around the world.

Joseph Smith (1805–44), founder of the Church of Jesus Christ of Latter-day Saints (the Mormons), passed on to his followers a number of writings that affirmed the existence of multiple inhabited worlds. As a result of many divine revelations Smith claimed to have received, he embraced several notions related to ETI that were widely accepted in Europe and America at that time: other planets of our solar system are inhabited by intelligent beings; the universe is infinite; fixed stars are like our sun and orbited by planets; these planets, too, are inhabited by intelligent beings; these solar systems are infinite in number.

In addition, Smith taught several ideas related to ETI that were distinctive (though not unique) to his movement: Various kinds of beings inhabit various worlds; Earth is the most wicked of all worlds; resurrected beings also inhabit worlds; and Christ's redemption is universal across worlds.[22]

---

[21] De Maistre, 304.

[22] Crowe, *Extraterrestrial Life Debate: Antiquity to 1915*, 324–25. Crowe's analysis is based on that of Erich Robert Paul in *Science, Religion, and Mormon Cosmology* (Urbana: University of Illinois Press, 1992), 85.

Ellen G. White (1827–1915), the primary "prophetess" of the Seventh-Day Adventist movement, claimed to have received hundreds of divine revelations, some of them involving ETI. Her "first view of the planetary world" involved visions of Jupiter, Saturn, and their moons. "The inhabitants are a tall, majestic people," she reported, "so unlike the inhabitants of earth. Sin has never entered here."[23]

Satan and the other fallen angels, White taught, had attempted to spread rebellion against God throughout the universe. But they had been successful in that attempt only on Earth. Christ's redemptive work was made necessary by Adam's fall.

> But the plan of redemption had a yet broader and deeper purpose than the salvation of man. It was not for this alone that Christ came to earth; it was not merely that the inhabitants of this little world might regard the law of God as it should be regarded; but it was to vindicate the character of God before the universe. . . . The act of Christ in dying for the salvation of man would not only make heaven accessible to men, but before all the universe it would justify God and his Son in their dealing with the rebellion of Satan.[24]

Though the Incarnation was unique to Earth, and no extraterrestrial inhabitants needed redemption, ETI benefited from what had happened on our planet because it revealed God and His providence more completely throughout the cosmos.

---

[23] Quoted in Crowe, *Extraterrestrial Life Debate: Antiquity to 1915*, 329.
[24] Crowe, 330–31.

"My Life Is Ever Suffering for Love"

Dwight, Chalmers, and Maistre all sought to respond to Paine's mockery of endless divine incarnations for the purpose of endless redemptive deaths. Smith's and White's alleged visions also implied a response to such skepticism. The Incarnation on Earth was unique, they all affirmed. Either inhabitants of other planets were unfallen and needed no redemption or they were fallen and could be redeemed by the work of the God-man who had suffered, died, and risen again on our planet.

The English poet Philip James Bailey (1816–1902) also responded to the skeptic's critique, but not by proposing that multiple incarnations were unnecessary. Instead, in his book-length poem *Festus* (1839), one passage boldly proposes these words of Christ to an angel who cares deeply for the earthlings who have been placed in his care:

> Think not I lived and died for thine alone,
> And that no other sphere hath hailed me Christ.
> My life is ever suffering for love.
> In judging and redeeming worlds is spent
> Mine everlasting being.[25]

Bailey thus embraced the possibility Paine had scorned, seeing it as a potential demonstration of the depth and intensity of divine love.

---

[25] Philip James Bailey, *Festus: A Poem*, 1st American ed. (Boston: B.B. Mussey, 1845), 25.

Other Protestant Pastors

In the second half of the century, several other American and Canadian Protestant figures entered the ETI debate. Most attempted simply to respond to other writers, developing or challenging the common positions on the matter that we have noted.

In 1871, the Baptist pastor Edwin T. Winkler (1823–83) published in the *Baptist Quarterly* an essay echoing earlier notions that the incarnation of Christ is unique to Earth, but its influences reach throughout the cosmos. Recalling how a little band of Spartan soldiers once won a victory that changed the course of Western history, Winkler drew an analogy to possible cosmic scenarios: "As a battle may be fought at some grey pass of Marathon . . . that shall change the fortunes of a world for a thousand years, so here, on this small world, a triumph may have been achieved by the Son of God, that distributes its spoils to all systems, through all times; and for the temptation and anguish of Jesus of Nazareth, the sweet influences of the Pleaides may be fuller of vernal promise . . . and seasons of salvation may have befallen all the signs [that is, constellations] of the zodiac."[26]

Winkler also echoed David Brewster's notion of Adam's redeemed descendants living on other celestial orbs in eternity. He speculated that on some heavenly body, "my loved and lost are gathered. There the wasted cheeks are flushed with immortal beauty, and the glazed eyes with immortal lustre,

---

[26] Edwin T. Winkler, "Religion and Astronomy," *Baptist Quarterly*, 5 (1871), 58–74:58.

and the voice that was once so dear, that was once so frozen by the chills of death, is melted into immortal melodies."[27]

The Congregationalist pastor Enoch Fitch Burr (1818–1907) promoted pluralist ideas in a number of books and journal articles. He went even beyond Brewster and Winkler's notion of redeemed human souls living on other planets in eternity when he declared that even "God, his holy angels, . . . the spirits of saved men, . . . Satan, the evil angels, and the lost souls . . . have their proper homes on glorious materialisms *somewhere* out yonder in the profound of space."[28]

In 1862, the Scottish Presbyterian pastor William Leitch (1818–64), principal of Queen's College in Kingston, Ontario, published *God's Glory in the Heavens.* Though he accepted the possibility of ETI, he dismissed both multiple divine incarnations and cosmic redemptive consequences of Christ's work on Earth. That left him, he concluded, with only one option in the matter of salvation for extraterrestrials: Only earthlings need to be saved. "The universe is a great harp, and each orb a string of that harp; but one string, at least is untuned. . . . One great end [purpose] of redemption is to re-adjust this jarring string of our world." Scripture allows us to say, then, that even though our planet is not the "*material* centre of the universe . . . it is still the *spiritual* centre."[29]

---

[27] Winkler, 72.

[28] Enoch Fitch Burr, *Celestial Empires* (New York, 1885), 263–64.

[29] William Leitch, *God's Glory in the Heavens*, 3rd ed. (London, 1867), 329.

The Pluralist Dogma Is Challenged

Like John Foster, most of the contemporary commentators on Chalmers's book treated the existence of ETI as an established fact, reflecting Newman's assessment of the dogmatic quality of that assumption. But Foster made one particularly telling comment: "We think that, excepting to minds repugnant to magnificent ideas, the probability that the other orbs of our system are inhabited worlds, must appear so great, that a direct revelation from heaven declaring the fact, would make but very little difference in our assurance of it."[30]

We can well imagine, then, the uproar that ensued in 1853 when a Cambridge professor of minerology and moral philosophy, Reverend William Whewell (1794–1866), anonymously published an articulate and extended attack on the pluralist position. *Of the Plurality of Worlds: An Essay* shocked those who embraced the existence of ETI by challenging the common pluralist arguments as faulty in their science and dangerous to religion.[31] Ironically, Whewell had been for many years a proponent of ETI. But apparently, in the period around 1850, he had come to conclude that belief in ETI was not easily reconciled to certain essential tenets of the Christian faith.[32]

---

[30] [Foster], *Eclectic Review*, 212.

[31] William Whewell, *Of the Plurality of Worlds: A Facsimile of the First Edition of 1853; Plus Previously Published Material Excised by the Author Just Before the Book Went to Press; and Whewell's Dialogue Rebutting His Critics, reprinted from the Second Edition* (Chicago: University of Chicago Press, 2001).

[32] Crowe, *Extraterrestrial Life Debate, 1750–1900*, 265; Crowe, *Extraterrestrial Life Debate: Antiquity to 1915*, 333.

Word spread quickly that the anonymous volume was Whewell's work. The controversy intensified because of his reputation as a man of great scientific and philosophical learning, as well as an Anglican priest and defender of orthodoxy. The book enjoyed at least five English and two American editions, generating such furious debate that it provoked a wide array of responses: by 1859, twenty books, more than fifty articles and reviews, and a host of other literature, such as sections of books and correspondence. A number of prominent figures took part in the discussion.[33]

Describing the impact of Whewell's work some fourteen years after its publication, one American professor of astronomy and mathematics observed it was "like a bomb-shell thrown into an army resting on its victorious march."[34]

Whewell's Arguments against ETI

In his preface, Whewell pointed out that "it will be a curious, but not a very wonderful event, if it should now be deemed as blameable to doubt the existence of the inhabitants of the Planets and Stars as, three centuries ago, it was held heretical to teach that doctrine." He also noted that Scripture makes no mention of a doctrine of ETI and that for most of Christian history, believers have felt no need for such an idea.[35]

Whewell's arguments in the pages that followed are not easily summarized. Among his most essential positions are these: First, the unique and divinely privileged status of Earth's inhabitants, as affirmed by the Christian revelation,

[33] Crowe, *Extraterrestrial Life Debate: Antiquity to 1915*, 333.

[34] Quoted in Crowe, *Extraterrestrial Life Debate, 1750–1900*, 359.

[35] Whewell, *Of the Plurality of Worlds*, 13–14.

must be preserved. We have a special relationship with God; we are made in His image, spiritual beings with unique intellectual capabilities whose divinely intended destiny is eternal life in heaven.[36]

At the same time, the incarnation of God the Son as a human being on our planet, for our sake alone, suffering and dying for our race, is a unique event: "The earth, thus selected as the theatre of such a scheme of Teaching and Redemption, can not, in the eyes of anyone who accepts this Christian faith, be regarded as being on a level with any other domiciles. It is the Stage of the Great Drama of God's Mercy and Man's Salvation, the Sanctuary of the Universe; the Holy Land of Creation; the Royal Abode, for a time at least, of the Eternal King."[37]

In agreement with Paine, Whewell considered the idea of God's Son dying endlessly on countless planets as incompatible with Christian doctrine. But unlike Paine, this incompatibility led him to reject, not the Christian faith, but rather the plurality of inhabited worlds.

As we have seen, ETI promoters had long cited in their favor the principle of plenitude—the claim that God must surely fill all worlds throughout the universe with intelligent inhabitants, lest He waste such vastness of space. When Whewell challenged this claim, he employed recent discoveries in geology. Earth's geological history demonstrates that God did not intend it to be, for every moment of its existence through time, inhabited by intelligent life. Human

---

[36] Michael Ruse, "Introduction," in Whewell, *Of the Plurality of Worlds*, 14.

[37] Whewell, *Of the Plurality of Worlds*, 44.

history is only an instant in that long terrestrial timespan. So why should we think that intelligent life should fill the rest of the cosmos?[38]

As Whewell had insisted in another of his works, geology points upward. It teaches us that human beings are different from other creatures, different in kind and not just in form. Our unique origins are apparently miraculous, outside the usual course of nature. We should not then expect such a miracle to be repeated throughout the cosmos.

Whewell went on to offer arguments against ETI gathered from the field of astronomy. Based on what was actually known at that time about other planets, he insisted, little reason could be found to assume that the conditions favorable for life here are present on other globes. What was definitely known about Jupiter and Saturn, for example, demonstrated that they would be inhospitable to creatures like ourselves. And the heavenly body closest to us, subject to our most careful observation, is a moon that shows no signs of habitation.[39]

In Whewell's day, most astronomers assumed that the fixed stars, like our sun, were the centers of their own planetary systems. But no actual evidence of that arrangement had yet been observed, so Whewell insisted that we must not argue for a plurality of inhabited worlds based on such an assumption.[40]

---

[38] Whewell, 103.
[39] Whewell, 168–86.
[40] Whewell, 140–66.

"The Ill-Educated and Ill-Regulated Mind"

The response to Whewell's contrarian stand in the ETI debate was swift and largely predictable. Some commentators were thoughtful and respectful; others, mocking and sarcastic. Representing the latter sort, an anonymous writer in the *London Daily News* of October, 1854, called him "this knight-errant of nursery notions."[41] While in our own day, belief in extraterrestrials is often dismissed by intellectual elites as childish and naïve, in mid-nineteenth-century England, it was those who rejected ETI who were viewed that way.

Perhaps Whewell's most fervent opponent, the evangelical Scottish scientist Sir David Brewster (1781–1868), responded with *ad hominem* insults: "To conceive any one material globe . . . to have no living occupants, or not in a state of preparation to be occupied, seems to us one of those notions which could be harbored only in the ill-educated and ill-regulated mind,—a mind without faith and without hope; but to conceive a whole universe of moving and revolving worlds in such a category, indicates, in our apprehension, a mind dead to feeling and shorn of reason."

That "a man of high mental attainment, and professing the Christian faith," should take such a stand is "a most marvelous" event, he sneered. Brewster concluded that if he were among those who thought the end of the world was near, he would count Whewell's work as a sign of the Second Coming, "among the lying wonders [see 2 Th 2:9] which are to characterize the latter times."[42]

---

[41] Quoted in Crowe, *Extraterrestrial Life Debate: Antiquity to 1915*, 355.

[42] Quoted in Crowe, 355–56.

Brewster's case for ETI, of course, was much more extensive than mere *ad hominem* attacks. Among the more interesting of his arguments against Whewell from Scripture was his interpretation of Isaiah 45:12 (King James Version): "For thus saith the LORD that created the heavens, God himself that formed the earth, and made it; he hath established it, created it not in vain, he formed it to be inhabited." For Brewster, this statement implied that planets created without inhabitants would have been created in vain. He concluded that the biblical prophets knew about the existence of extraterrestrial intelligences.[43]

Brewster's response to Whewell also included novel speculations about intelligent races on Earth before Adam and inhabitants of Jupiter whose intellects far exceed that of Isaac Newton. He declared that life after death for believers will be lived on the star systems; a Christian should view the celestial bodies "as the hallowed spots in which his immortal existence is to run."[44]

However, Thomas Henry Huxley (1825–95), the English biologist who became a leading proponent of evolutionary theory, would have none of this talk, for or against ETI. He scorned the entire debate as "a hot controversy . . . broken out upon that most hyper-hypothetical of speculations, 'the Plurality of Worlds.' . . . The subject is essentially unfitted for discussion. Surely there are sufficiently wide fields of investigation whose cultivation will yield results which *can* be tested."[45]

---

[43] David Brewster, *More Worlds Than One* (London, 1870), 9–14.

[44] Brewster, 258.

[45] Brewster, 360–61.

The Effects of Darwinism on the ETI Debate

Huxley's dismissive remarks are ironic in that the scientific theories he so vigorously defended were themselves often of the sort that could hardly be tested. In any case, his skepticism foreshadows the impact on the extraterrestrial debates that the new biological theories would come to have in the last half of the nineteenth century. The evolutionary notions of the British naturalists Charles Darwin (1809–82) and Alfred Russel Wallace (1823–1913), who had independently conceived the theory of evolution by natural selection, were focused on the development of terrestrial life forms. But they had implications for the possible development of extraterrestrial forms as well.

In the revolutionary aftermath of Darwin's *On the Origin of Species* (1859), biologists began to insist that the development of intelligent life on Earth depended on rather fragile conditions. Though Darwin himself had little to say about the possibility of other inhabited worlds, Wallace explicitly entered the ETI debate. In a book entitled *Man's Place in the Universe* (1904), he argued against astronomers' attempts to seek signs of ETI, because the emergence of intelligence, he believed, was highly improbable.[46]

These and other developments in science through the end of the nineteenth century began to press against the once-common assumption that extraterrestrial intelligence was a reality, even a commonplace. Evolution seemed to be a highly specialized process with extreme sensitivity to environmental circumstances and conditions. The more details

---

[46] Wilkinson, *Search for Extraterrestrial Intelligence*, 27.

that emerged about the temperatures and composition of other planets in our solar system, the more certain it seemed that life as we know it could not be sustained there. Other planets might circle other stars, but they were most likely uninhabited.[47]

In fact, the very notion that most other stars had their own planetary systems came to be challenged. Such "exoplanets" had not yet actually been observed directly, and new theories about planetary formation suggested that planets were far rarer than once thought. This led to further division in the scientific community over the issue of intelligent extraterrestrials.

As some observers have noted, in the following century and ours, those scientists who have been strong proponents of ETI's existence have tended to be astronomers and physicists. They are most often moved by the possibilities presented by such a vast cosmos. Those who have argued against that possibility have tended to be specialists in evolutionary biology. They are most often influenced by the unlikely circumstances required for intelligent life to emerge.[48]

A more detailed analysis of the evolving science surrounding the ETI debate, with accompanying technological developments in the search for alien life forms, is beyond our scope here. We should simply note that new scientific research has provided grist for arguments on both sides of the issue. Not surprisingly, theological debaters of the topic

---

[47] Wilkinson, 27.
[48] Wilkinson, 32, 62.

have made use, as always, of whatever scientific evidence they can find to support their views.[49]

Before we conclude our historical survey with a look at the ETI conversation in the twentieth century and our own still-young century, a few Catholic writers of the late nineteenth century deserve our attention, for they made valuable and intriguing contributions to the ETI debate on Catholic terms as poets and priests.

---

[49] Wilkinson has a PhD in theoretical astrophysics as well as a PhD in systematic theology. His work provides an admirable exploration of both scientific and theological developments in the ETI conversation.

7

"Globes of Gold or Diamond"

Voices of Catholic Poets and Priests

"If [the idea of a plurality of worlds] does not enter into your astronomy, nor poetry, nor philosophy, nor religion, nor hopes, nor conjectures concerning eternal life . . . , and if, in the face of these grandiose characters and these fundamental traits of the visible work of God, you behold without seeing, without comprehending, without suspecting the possibility of intelligence, then, oh! then, I pity you!"

—Fr. Auguste Gratry[1]

WHILE THE NINETEENTH-CENTURY astronomers and biologists furiously debated, a number of Catholic poets and priests offered their own distinctive insights and speculations in the ETI conversation, shaped deeply by Sacred Scripture and Sacred Tradition. They differed in their conclusions about whether other intelligent races had fallen, and whether God had become incarnate on multiple planets. Several even offered speculations about a destiny of redeemed earthlings among the stars, with unusual biblical interpretations to support the

---

[1]   Auguste Gratry (1805–72), priest of the Oratory who was elected to the French Academy; quoted in Crowe, *Extraterrestrial Life Debate, 1750–1900* (1986), 414.

idea. The majority we will review here, but not all, agreed that many "peopled worlds" existed, and that acceptance of such a reality was not contrary to Christian faith.

"Love's Chief Triumph"

Aubrey de Vere (1814–1902) was an English poet and convert to the Catholic faith who held a professorship under Saint John Henry Newman at the Catholic University in Dublin. His poem "The Death of Copernicus" (1889) imagined certain reflections the astronomer could have had on his deathbed.

Responding to those who claimed that because our planet is so tiny in the cosmic scheme of things, God would not have bothered to redeem its fallen inhabitants, the poet asked: "Was Earth too small to be of God created? / Why then too small to be redeemed?" And if Earth is so small, he asked, isn't it more likely that Love Himself, which in His great compassion humbles Himself to descend to those most deeply lost in sorrows, "should choose that Earth for Love's chief triumph"?[2]

De Vere chastised astronomers who thought to disprove religion with their ETI speculations. The astronomer, de Vere observed, may believe that other planets are inhabited, but it is simply a matter of faith on his part; he has no scientific proof. Even if we concede that other planets are inhabited, the astronomer cannot prove that their inhabitants are fallen. And even if they are fallen, how would the astronomer know for certain that the Son of God was not incarnate

---

[2]   Aubrey de Vere, "The Death of Copernicus," *Contemporary Review* 56 (1889): 421–30, at 424.

among them as well: "Who told him that redeeming foot divine / ne'er trod those spheres?"[3]

"Is not the Universe a whole," he asked, "with mutual influence among its parts?" The One who died in ancient Judea died for all. "The Cross brought help to vanished nations"—that is, to people such as the ancient Jews who had died before the time of Christ. And if time could not set a boundary to God's love; why should space set a boundary? We do not even know what time and space truly are; why presume that the boundaries of time and space "can bind the Unbounded," the God without boundaries?[4]

De Vere's poem thus posed a litany of questions to astronomers intended to help them learn humility. He was not denying that intelligent extraterrestrials could exist—he simply denied that their existence, in whatever state, would constitute evidence against the Christian faith.

"A Million Alien Gospels"

Alice Meynell (1847–1922) was a British poet, essayist, and critic—like de Vere, a convert to the Catholic faith. Her poem "Christ in the Universe" has often been reprinted in studies of extraterrestrial life issues.

Assuming the existence of ETI, Meynell explores the prospect of God's diverse dealings with the inhabitants of diverse planets. Vast cosmic distances between the planets prevent the aliens, for now, from knowing of the divine Incarnation on Earth, and prevent us from knowing how the Creator might have dealt with them.

---

3 De Vere, 421–30, at 424.
4 De Vere, 421–30, at 424.

Of His earth-visiting feet
None knows the secret, cherished, perilous,
The terrible, shamefast, frightened, whispered, sweet,
Heart-shattering secret of his way with us.

No planet knows that this
Our wayside planet, carrying land and wave,
Love and life multiplied, and pain and bliss,
Bears, as chief treasure, one forsaken grave.

Nor, in our little day,
May his devices with the heavens be guessed,
His pilgrimage to tread the Milky Way,
Or his bestowals there be manifest.

Yet in heaven, Meynell affirms, all the various inhabitants of the cosmos will at last meet and bear mutual testimony to God's kindness toward them:

But, in the eternities,
Doubtless we shall compare together, hear
A million alien Gospels, in what guise
He trod the Pleiades, the Lyre, the Bear.

O be prepared, my soul!
To read the inconceivable, to scan
The million forms of God those stars unroll
When, in our turn, we show to them a Man.[5]

---

[5]   Alice Meynell, "Christ in the Universe," in *The Poems of Alice Meynell* (New York: C. Scribner's Sons, 1923), 92.

The ETI Conversation among Catholic Clergy

In France in 1862, a precocious twenty-year-old, Camille Flammarion (1842–1925), caused a sensation with the publication of a pro-pluralist booklet entitled *The Plurality of Inhabited Worlds*, which placed him at the center of the ongoing debate and kept him there for sixty years. He expanded the original work from 54 pages to 570, then published a second, even larger volume on the subject. The two volumes were translated into a number of languages, so that one reviewer concluded in 1884 that the author had "done more toward popularizing the study of astronomical science than any of his contemporaries."[6]

Flammarion studied four years in a Catholic seminary as a youth but eventually left his Catholic faith and came under the influence of the socialist philosopher Jean Reynaud (1806–63). Reynaud had proposed a new religious system that included the transmigration of souls (reincarnation). He insisted that after death, the soul moves from planet to planet, being gradually perfected, an idea that Flammarion adopted enthusiastically and promoted to an ever-widening audience in his teachings about intelligent extraterrestrial life.[7]

Not surprisingly, though Reynaud claimed that his doctrine was compatible with the Christian faith, a council of Catholic bishops in 1857 rejected them explicitly. Given Flammarion's popularization of Reynaud's unorthodox ideas, and the former's eventual association with the occult spiritualist movement, a number of learned Catholic clergymen

---

[6] R. A. Sherard, "Flammarion the Astronomer," *McClure's*, 2 (May 1884), 569–77:569.

[7] Crowe, *Extraterrestrial Life Debate, 1750–1900*, 378–79.

felt compelled to respond to Flammarion's speculations and became involved in the ETI conversation on explicitly Catholic theological terms.

Père Joseph Félix (1810–91), a prominent Parisian preacher, announced in 1863 to thousands of the Catholic faithful in Notre Dame Cathedral that the plurality of worlds was most certainly compatible with Christian beliefs. He told those scientists who saw belief in ETI as a barrier to faith: "Put into the sidereal world [realm of distant stars] as many populations as you please. . . . Catholic dogma has here a tolerance that will astonish you and ought to satisfy you."[8]

"The Nations of the Sky Will Tremble"

A lengthy treatment of the topic by Monseigneur de Montignez appeared in a series of nine essays in 1865–1866 entitled *Christian Theory on the Plurality of Worlds*.[9] Rather than simply explaining that ETI was compatible with Christian faith, he insisted that the notion was supportive of such faith. Our planet, he argued, is of insignificant size and is inhabited by "probably the most disgraced" creatures in the universe. This characteristic made it the ideal place for the "annihilation of the divinity" we call the Incarnation.[10]

Christ chose "Bethlehem . . . the least among the cities of Judah" [see Micah 5:2] to be His birthplace. On the same principle, then, He chose to come to humble Earth and to

---

[8] Joseph Félix, *Le progress par le Christianisme: Conférences de Notre-Dame de Paris — Anée 1863*, 2nd ed. (Paris, 1864), 120–21.

[9] Monseigneur de Montignez, "Théorie chrétienne sur la pluralité des mondes," *Archives théologiques*, 9 (1865), quoted in Crowe, *Extraterrestrial Life Debate, 1750–1900* (1986), 411–13.

[10] De Montignez, in Crowe, 412.

make it the locale for establishing His Church and accomplishing His redemptive work: "The relative smallness of the earth acts only to strengthen our belief in the mystery of our redemption . . . ; the more you represent the earth as a useless point, the more you make man a stunted, weak, pitiful, disgraced being, the more you justify the preference of which he is the object."[11]

Montignez found much to praise in Flammarion's work, but he argued against his acceptance of reincarnation. Where Flammarion had called his readers to think of the human race as a "citizen of the sky," Montignez suggested instead that we are a member of a cosmic family sharing one divine Fatherhood.[12]

The monseigneur offered an intriguing array of thoughts about the moral status of ETI and its relationship to Christ. He declared, "Even though Christ came only to our planet, he is still Lord of the universe." Echoing Origen's ancient words, he insisted that "the blood which flowed from Calvary has gushed out on the universality of creation. . . .[It] has bathed not only our world, but all the worlds which roll in space."[13]

For Montignez, however, the purpose of Christ's incarnation and redemptive work was not solely or even primarily to free the race of Adam from original sin. Its universal purpose did not include saving ETI from sin, whether their own sin or the sin of Adam, in which they did not participate. Although God would have inhabitants of other worlds

---

[11] De Montignez, in Crowe, 412.

[12] De Montignez, in Crowe, 412.

[13] De Montignez, in Crowe, 412.

undergo a test, unlike humanity they would pass the test, so they would need no redemption. The problem often raised by opponents of Christian faith—that so few are saved—"disappears if the human race is considered as only a minimal and infinitely limited fraction among the universal number of intelligent creatures."[14]

Montignez also insisted that the existence of ETI is supported by many passages from Scripture; in fact it actually helps us to understand more clearly some of these passages. For example, he interpreted the one lost sheep of the hundred, in the Gospel parable, as the human race, requiring the special care of the Good Shepherd (see Lk 15:3–7).

"Without the plurality of worlds," Montignez explained, "each chapter of the prophets and almost every verse of the psalms is an enigma full of obscurity and mystery." For the proper interpretation of such passages, he insisted, several principles must be kept in mind.

One is the solidarity and communion of earthlings with ETI. Another is that those earthlings who are saved will finally attain a true royalty, governing inhabitants of other planets—a privilege granted because the Son of God took on human flesh. Montignez found Psalm 8 to be particularly relevant to this truth: "God has elevated man almost to the equal of the angel; . . . he has set him to the government of his works; . . . he has subdued everything under his feet."[15]

Montignez also interpreted Psalm 2 in this context:

---

[14] De Montignez, in Crowe, 412.
[15] De Montignez, in Crowe, 412–13.

[This psalm is] less a scene of the earth . . . than a complete drama of which the acts are unfolded in the skies. It becomes more and more apparent . . . that there is up there, for the celestial people, a harsh test to undergo. The submission of the heart to the supremacy of Jesus Christ and to that of man deified; the elevation to the first rank of the most small and the last of creation; the descent of the grand and robust under the sceptre of a ruler of small origin. The nations of the sky will tremble, but they will submit.[16]

This particular notion of the "test" undergone by ETI actually echoes a similar notion in Catholic tradition: that the divine test of the angels, which Lucifer and a third of the heavenly hosts failed, consisted in their being presented with the prospect of one day having to adore a human being—the Son of God made flesh—and their unwillingness to do so. According to other speculations, they failed the test when they were shown that they would one day have to recognize a human being as their queen: the Blessed Virgin Mary, the Queen Mother of Jesus, the King of the Universe.[17]

"Beautiful and Grandiose"

Father Louis Lescoeur, an Oratorian, in *The Future Life* (1872), found it necessary to remind his readers that "the hypothesis of a plurality of worlds, which one today tries to twist noisily in the guise of serious arguments against Christian

---

[16] De Montignez, in Crowe, 412–13.
[17] W. Kent, "Devil," in *The Catholic Encyclopedia* (New York: Robert Appleton Company, 1908), http://www.newadvent.org/cathen/04764a.htm.

theology, has never been condemned by it." Abbé François Moigno (1804–84), a scientific author, editor, and translator of numerous works, wrote about the relations of science and religion in his multivolume *The Splendors of the Faith* (1877–79). In responding to Flammarion's claim that ETI and Christian belief were incompatible, he noted that he had received approval from "the Commission of the Roman Index to declare formally [to Flammarion] that the creation and the redemption are by no means an obstacle to the existence of other worlds, of other suns, of other planets, etc., etc."[18]

Abbé Léger-Marie Pioger repeatedly promoted the notion that intelligent extraterrestrial life is a reality in *The Christian Dogma and the Plurality of Inhabited Worlds* (1893) and his five-volume *The Splendors of Astronomy*, about "worlds other than our own" (1883–84). He quoted several other prominent French clerics who were pluralists, and wrote lyrically that the doctrine of the plurality of worlds "transfigures the universe [and] is the most beautiful and grandiose expression of the divine work." [19]

Abbé Jean Boudon vigorously opposed the antireligious notions that Flammarion and others had promoted. In 1875, he published *Adam at His Origin, King and Unique Mediator of All the Planetary Universe* to argue that "the fault of the first man [Adam] decided the fate of all the universe." After the second coming of Christ, the human race "will be recognized as having been created to be the sole king and mediator of all

---

[18] Both Lescoeur and Moigno quoted in Crowe, *Extraterrestrial Life Debate, 1750–1900*, 414.

[19] Quoted in Crowe, *Extraterrestrial Life Debate, 1750–1900*, 414.

the visible universe." Boudon's primary concern was to maintain the primacy of humankind in the cosmos.[20]

Varying Kinds of Perfection

In 1894, the priest-theologian Father Théophile Ortolan (b. 1861) published *Astronomy and Theology*, which won a prize awarded for apologetic writings from the *Institut Catholique* in Paris. He argued the compatibility of the plurality doctrine and Christian faith by offering pluralist interpretations of Scripture, such as the one lost sheep passage cited by Montignez, as well as Jesus's words that in His Father's house are "many rooms" (Jn 14:2).

Ortolan went on to claim that various passages in the writings of Origen and Saint Basil may contain a "pressentiment" of pluralist teaching, and added finally that "the Congregation of the Index, consulted on this point, has officially responded that there is not" any opposition between ETI belief and the Christian faith. In short, he appealed to the threefold authority of Scripture, Tradition, and the Magisterium to make his case.[21]

Ortolan offered a number of replies to the question of why Christ would come only to Earth. Either the inhabitants of other planets may benefit from this Incarnation, or perhaps they have no need of redemption. As for the end of the world, he suggested that our planet's destruction will probably not involve the conflagration of the entire cosmos.[22]

---

[20] Quoted in Crowe, *Extraterrestrial Life Debate, 1750–1900*, 416.
[21] Quoted in Crowe, 417–18.
[22] Quoted in Crowe, 417–18.

Contrary to the common pluralist notion among Christians that inhabited worlds best reflect God's greatness, Ortolan believed that most planets are uninhabited. Yet he was convinced that even lifeless worlds may display God's glory by exhibiting their own particular kind of perfection. "Would it be illogical to suppose . . . that certain stars have been created to represent in space, the mineral world in a more or less grand perfection, in others, the plant world, still others will have animal life, and others finally intellectual life?" Ortolan speculated, for example, that some planets might display God's beauty by being pure "globes of gold or diamond."[23]

Clerical Voices in Spain, Italy, and Beyond

Catholic priests who entered the plurality conversation were by no means all from France. Niceto Alonso Perujo (1841–90), a prominent Spanish cleric, published in 1877 a book with the impressive title *The Plurality of Inhabited Worlds Against the Catholic Faith. A study in which is examined the habitation of the stars in relation to Catholic dogmas and is demonstrated its perfect harmony with them, and is refuted many errors of Mr. Flammarion.* Father Perujo's primary concern was to defend Christian belief against Flammarion and others who opposed it on the grounds of a plurality of worlds.[24]

---

[23] Quoted in Crowe, 417–18. Interestingly enough, astronomers in 2004 discovered a planet circling a nearby star in our Milky Way galaxy that appears to be made primarily of diamond; see Clara Moskowitz, "Super-Earth Planet Likely Made of Diamond," SPACE.com, October 11, 2012, https://www.space.com/18011-super-earth-planet-diamond-world.html.

[24] Niceto Alonso Perujo, *La pluralidad de mundos habitados ante le fé católica. Estudio en que se examina la habitacion de los astros en relacion*

In Italy, for more than two decades the pluralist position was promoted by the prolific Fr. Angelo Secchi (1818–78), the director of the Roman College Observatory and the most prominent Italian astrophysicist of his day. In 1856, he noted in a work about the new observatory: "It is with a sweet sentiment that man thinks of these worlds without number, where each star is a sun which, as minister of the divine bounty, distributes life and goodness to the other innumerable beings, blessed by the hand of the Omnipotent."[25]

Secchi's two important works in spectroscopic research, published in 1877, were cited by Catholic pluralists around the world. His study had convinced him that:

> The creation, contemplated by the astronomer, is not a simple mass of incandescent matter; it is a wonderful organism where when the incandescence ceases, life commences. Even though it may not be accessible to our telescope, by analogy with our globe, we are able to conclude that it exists in the others. The atmospheric conditions of the other planets which, in certain points, is so similar to ours as that of the stars is similar to that of the sun, persuades us that these bodies are in a state similar to that of our system, or are traversing one of the periods that we have already traversed or that we will traverse some day.[26]

---

con los dogmas católicos, se demestrua su perfecta armonia con estos, y se refutan muchose errores de Mr. Flammarion (Madrid, 1877).

[25] Angelo Secchi, *Descrizione del nuevo osservatorio del collegio romano* (Rome, 1856), 158.

[26] Angelo Secchi, *Les étoiles*, v. II (Paris, 1879), 189.

Pope Pius IX was Secchi's patron and friend. Some have speculated that their relationship, in addition to Secchi's eminence as a scientist and eloquence as a writer, may have led to reticence among those in Rome who might otherwise have sought to oppose the notion of extraterrestrial intelligences.[27]

Star Worlds

The priest and seminary professor Joseph Pohle (1852–1922) was born in Germany and educated in Italy, where Secchi taught him astronomy. (His first book was a biography of Secchi.) Pohle taught in Switzerland, England, and Prussia before he joined the founding faculty of the Catholic University of America in Washington, DC, in 1889. A few years later, he returned to Germany to teach, where he wrote a twelve-volume *Textbook of Dogmatics* (1902–5).[28]

Though Pohle was known among German and American seminarians primarily for his theological textbook, in Germany he was recognized as a leading proponent of pluralism. His *Star Worlds and Their Inhabitants* (1884–85) combined science and history with metaphysics and theology to consider the probability for inhabitants in various celestial bodies, including those of our solar system.[29]

Pohle admitted that he could provide no metaphysical proofs for extraterrestrial life. Yet he offered four arguments that the existence of ETI is probable. First, God made the universe for His own glory. Though the unconscious physical

---

[27] Crowe, *Extraterrestrial Life Debate, 1750–1900*, 422–23.

[28] Crowe, 430–31.

[29] Crowe, 431.

creation glorifies Him simply by its excellence (known to theologians as "objective glory"), rational beings are able to offer Him a higher form of glory by virtue of their intellect and free will ("formal glory"). Thus he considered it "suitable to the highest purpose of the world that the habitable heavenly bodies be populated with creatures that utilize the physical splendors of their worlds for the glorification of their Creator."[30]

Second, he declared that the universe displays a high degree of perfection. Echoing the observations of Saint Thomas Aquinas (and Secchi as well), he insisted that a cosmos widely populated with intelligent creatures is more perfect than one merely occupied by "unadorned deserted wastelands."[31]

Third, Pohle observed that God has displayed His wisdom and omnipotence in populating the Earth with a great diversity of creatures. We can conclude, then, that He has acted in a similar way on other planets.[32]

Finally, the inhabitants of our planet abound in evil. So it seems highly probable, Pohl surmised, that God would populate other planets with intelligent creatures better disposed to give Him glory.[33]

---

[30] Joseph Pohle, *Die Sternwelten und ihre Bewohner*, 2nd ed. (Cologne, 1899), 415.
[31] Pohle, 416.
[32] Pohle, 427.
[33] Pohle, 428.

"Many Other Means to Remit a Sin"

We might have expected the author of a textbook in dog-matic theology to have given considerable attention to the implications of ETI for Christology, soteriology, eschatology, and anthropology (as noted in our introduction.) But most of his commentary on these issues is summed up simply in these words from his final paragraph:

> Concerning the dogma of the Redemption of fallen men through the God-Man Christ, it is not necessary to assume as probable also the fall of species on other celestial bodies. No reason . . . obliges us to think others as evil as ourselves. However, even if the evil of sin had gained its pernicious entry into those worlds, so it would not follow from it that also there an Incarnation and Redemption would have to take place. God has at his disposal many other means to remit a sin that weighs either on an individual or on an entire species.[34]

For Pohle, then, neither multiple incarnations nor universal effects of the Incarnation on Earth would be necessary to redeem fallen extraterrestrials. God has other ways to offer salvation to ETI who are not of the earthly race of Adam.

Pohle's *Star Worlds* went through seven editions, reaching a wide audience throughout Europe. It also provoked considerable reaction among Catholic theologians. This and the author's other pluralist works represented the most extensive study of ETI ever provided by a Catholic theologian of comparable prominence.

---

[34] Pohle, 457–58.

An example of Pohle's influence may be found in the work of Paul Schanz (1841–1905), a Catholic theologian who taught at the University of Tübingen in Germany. He cited Pohle in support of his speculations about the divine options with regard to those "other means to remit a sin." In his *Apology for Christianity*, he declared: "When it is said [in Scripture] that Christ died for all men, it means after all the men on earth and no other. . . . The Schoolmen [medieval Scholastic philosophers, such as Aquinas] taught . . . that the Incarnation was not an absolute necessity. Some, however, held that even apart from sin the Incarnation formed part of God's eternal plan; nor did several incarnations seem to them impossible."

In light of their reasoning, Schanz concluded, "Why not admit other possibilities for rational beings in other planets? Perhaps they did not fall in their progenitor and head [as humans did in Adam]; maybe they fell and were redeemed by an Incarnation of their own or in some other way?"[35]

"Craving for the Plurality of Worlds"

Father George Mary Searle (1839–1918) had been a Unitarian at Harvard who converted to the Catholic faith and began studies for the priesthood as a Paulist. When the Catholic University of America was founded in 1889, he was appointed as observatory director and was perhaps influenced by Pohle, who taught at the university for five years. The following year, Searle presented a lecture entitled "Are the Planets Inhabitable?" In that address, he admitted

---

[35] Paul Schanz, *A Christian Apology*, trans. M. F. Glancey and V. J. Schobel, 5th ed., v. I (Ratisbon, 1891), 394–95.

that he lacked "the craving for the plurality of worlds . . . which seems so general."[36]

Even so, in another paper on the topic (1892), he cautiously addressed the notion of plurality and sought to reconcile it with the Christian faith. Science can provide only evidence of the *habitability* of other worlds, he insisted, not of actual inhabitants. In response to the repeated claim that Earth is only an "insignificant little speck" in space, unworthy of God's attention, he observed that for the astronomer, distance and size are merely relative. In addition, God might well have created inhabitants of other planets, but if so, it does not necessarily follow that they would have needed their own divine incarnations.

"Capable of Redeeming Innumerable Worlds"

Other American Catholic priests entered the debate as well. Father Januarius De Concilio (1836–98), who was also a professor, pastor, and playwright, drew from the writings of Saint Thomas in his arguments. He focused on the idea that "the number of species to be created [by God] was determined by the place which each one holds in the scale of being or perfection." Those species holding higher places are greater in number than those below.[37]

The immense gap in the chain of being between humans and the angels requires, he insisted, that intermediate species exist between them, "thus to exhibit and represent a most

---

[36] George Mary Searle, "Are the Planets Inhabitable?" *Astronomical Society of the Pacific Publications*, 2 (1890): 165–77:169.
[37] Januarius De Concilio, "The Plurality of Worlds," *American Catholic Quarterly Review*, 9 (April 1884), 193–216:196, 211.

beautiful, harmonious order in the universe." Extraterrestrials, he concludes, are those intermediate species. [38]

Uninhabited worlds, De Concilio goes on to declare, would be a waste of divine power. God "must, if he would follow the requirements of wisdom, draw from the given forces to be created all the possible good in view of the end; in other words, he must use the least possible means to attain an object, and follow the fundamental law of wisdom laid down by St. Thomas."[39] (Ironically, Thomas, as we have seen, objected to the idea of a plurality of worlds, and he no doubt would have objected strenuously to the notion that God Himself *must* follow some law laid down by the good saint—or anyone else.)

Finally, De Concilio argued that extraterrestrials were created by God "in and through Christ." So they must attain their eternal destiny through Him. Christ's work on Earth, though a singular occurrence, must extend to every "species of incorporated [bodily] intelligences [that] may have fallen, and very likely did fall."[40] As he noted in a later work, "When Christ died and paid the ransom of our redemption, he included [extraterrestrials] also in that redemption, the value of which was infinite and capable of redeeming innumerable worlds." But De Concilio leaves unanswered the question of how Christ may have revealed "knowledge of himself, and of his Church," to inhabitants of other worlds.[41]

---

[38] De Concilio, 193–216:196, 211.
[39] De Concilio, 193–216:196, 211.
[40] De Concilio, 193–216:196, 211.
[41] Januarius De Concilio, *Harmony Between Science and Revelation* (1889); quoted in Crowe, *Extraterrestrial Life Debate, 1750–1900*, 456.

Several of De Concilio's arguments were criticized by Fr. Thomas Hughes (1849–1939), a Jesuit professor at St. Louis University. The ways of God are beyond our knowing, he insisted. How can we label a planet without inhabitants wasted if we cannot explain "why the drop of rain in *our* mid-ocean is not utterly wasted?" As for the chain of being, Hughes concluded that human beings are themselves a sufficient means between the material and the spiritual world; we need no extraterrestrials to fill the gap.[42]

De Concilio, Hughes suggested, placed too much value on the material universe and too little on humanity: "An earth for man's body, a universe for his soul." As one historian has noted, Hughes questioned De Concilio's "arguments more than his conclusions"; the former was "a man more inclined to the God of Job than the God of Aquinas."[43]

Clerical Contrarian Views

Not all the Catholic priestly writers of the late nineteenth century were so positive about intelligent extraterrestrial life. The Frenchman Abbé Joseph Émile Filachou (1812–90), in his *On the Plurality of Worlds* (1861), declared that the notion that there are "men or creatures of the same species of men in the stars" is "absolutely rejectable."

It "continues to lack positive proof," he observed, "rests only on the idea of the possibility of the thing in general," and "entails with it consequences incompatible with all that one admits as most rational in metaphysics, aesthetics, and

---

[42] Quoted in Crowe, *Extraterrestrial Life Debate, 1750–1900* (1986), 456.

[43] Crowe, 456.

physics." Theologically, Filachou insisted, the idea of ETI contradicts Christian faith in three regards: "the importance presupposed [in Scripture] of the role of man on earth, the supreme dignity attributed to the Divine founder of the Christian Church, and finally the grandeur attributed to the Church itself."[44]

Back across the Atlantic, the Canadian curé of Fort Kent, Maine, Abbé François Xavier Burque (1851–1923), published *Plurality of Inhabited Worlds Considered from the Negative Point of View* (1898). He had been annoyed for more than twenty years that so many Canadian seminary professors were pluralists, and Ortolan's pro-pluralist work had finally provoked him to write the contrarian view. Despite the constant interruption of his parishioners, he eventually composed a 427-page treatise.[45]

Burque offered the usual scientific objections to the probability of ETI, then followed with theological ones. He dismissed Ortolan's claims about biblical and early Christian perspectives on the subject, declaring that neither Scripture nor the Church Fathers addressed, much less supported, the pluralist position. His great objection to ETI was that "only with extreme difficulty" can its existence be reconciled with the incarnation and redemption of Christ on Earth.[46]

If extraterrestrial intelligences were to exist, Burque reasoned, they would almost certainly be morally fallen. He believed that such a scenario required either multiple incarnations and a multi-crucified Christ, which he thought contradicts the

---

[44] Quoted in Crowe, 411.

[45] Crowe, 420–21.

[46] Crowe, 420–21

book of Hebrews (see 9:25–28; 10:11–14), or else explaining how the earthly Incarnation could bring redemption to other planets. "It appears absolutely impossible to imagine how the Divine Blood which has flowed on Calvary could be . . . of some utility and efficacy for their justification."[47]

As a side note, Burque's discussion of this matter manifested the peculiar notion that God's primary goal in Christ's redemptive work was the expiation of the fallen angels' sin. To do this required that God take on a nature both physical and spiritual such as that of man, rather than the purely spiritual nature of the angels themselves. Only in this way could Christ undergo death without being annihilated.[48]

In the end, Burque allowed that proofs of extraterrestrials' existence might be found. But the teaching of the Catholic Church would not be affected: The plurality of worlds is not essential to Catholic doctrine, and the Church has never pronounced authoritatively on the subject. Proof of ETI would present Christians with new mysteries to ponder, but they already are aware that God's ways are not our ways (see Is 55:8).[49]

For one last contrary and fascinating conjecture by an American Catholic priest of the period, we should consider the thoughts proposed by a superior general of the Paulists. Father Augustine F. Hewitt (1820–97), who served on the founding faculty of Catholic University of America with Pohle and Searle, wrote a paper that appeared in *Catholic World* (1892) offering a novel theological speculation about extraterrestrials.[50]

---

[47] Crowe, 421.

[48] Crowe, 421–22.

[49] Crowe, 422.

[50] Augustine F. Hewitt, "Another Word on Other Worlds," *Catholic*

Hewitt dismissed belief in past or present worlds inhabited by ETI as "unphilosophical, untheological, and unscriptural." But he affirmed as "possible" or even "probable" the *future* existence of such extraterrestrials. Concluding that several New Testament texts reveal the uniqueness of Christ's incarnation and redemption on Earth, and that humans hold the highest place next to angels in heaven, Hewitt proposed that God will populate other worlds only after the Last Judgment.[51] These extraterrestrial species will be ruled by the resurrected saints of Earth and will face no divine test of the kinds that angels and humans experienced. Even so, they will be immortal and live in a somewhat inferior state of happiness than that of their human rulers.[52]

Hewitt claims that his speculation solves many problems in the ETI debate. Nevertheless, it "cannot be demonstrated scientifically or philosophically [nor] can we pretend that it is explicitly revealed."[53]

Catholic Lay Voices

The most prominent Catholic writers in the ETI debates of the late nineteenth century were clerics. But at least two laymen published works on the subject that deserve mention, not least of all because of some unusual ideas they advanced.

Jules Boiteux, a director of several French foundries, declared that he wrote "in the spirit of an orthodox Catholic." He eagerly joined the conversation with a massive work of sixty-two *Letters to a Materialist on the Plurality of Inhabited*

World, 56 (October 1892),18–26:18–19.
[51] Hewitt, 18–26:18–19.
[52] Hewitt, 18–26:18–19.
[53] Hewitt, 18–26:18–19.

Worlds (1876). Boiteux assembled an impressive array of scientific information—from astronomy, meteorology, geology, and biology—that allowed him to argue for the frailty of life on this planet, and thus the improbability of conditions on other worlds that would be hospitable to intelligent life.[54]

This writer made no absolute claims that ETI is impossible. He concluded, rather, that "superior or intelligent life will appear only in exceptional cases." But even if we grant the existence of a few "sidereal humanities . . . is it probable that they are all equal among themselves in regard to morality?" God would probably make extraterrestrial races better than earthlings, he insisted, in order to limit the necessity for multiple redemptions.[55]

Boiteux noted that the Son of God's incarnation on Earth was intended "both to teach us his perfect law and to purify us by his sacrifice." But the first purpose, he observed, which is the only one appropriate for unfallen races, could be accomplished just as well on other planets by angels. Christ's redemptive work on Earth might have redemptive force beyond Earth, he conceded. He even noted that he was ready to accept the existence of multiple divine incarnations, if the Church should sanction it. In general, Boiteux finally concluded, "the doctrine, full of unknowns, of the plurality of worlds furnishes no positive argument against Christian dogma."[56]

---

[54] Crowe, *Extraterrestrial Life Debate, 1750–1900*, 414–15.

[55] Crowe, 415.

[56] Crowe, 415–16.

Further Speculations

A second French layman, Pierre Courbet, published in 1894 an essay in the *Cosmos Review of Science* admitting that neither science nor Scripture offers definitive evidence of ETI. But he sought to demonstrate that their existence would not stand "in contradiction with the formal teachings of Christianity."[57] One of his more distinctive speculations involved the way in which God might have tested the inhabitants of other planets.

Catholic tradition teaches that the divine test of the angels was individual, leaving each spirit fallen or unfallen according to its choice. The test of the human race, on the other hand, had more communal consequences; Adam's sin left his descendants with the stain of original sin. Courbet suggested that the divine test of extraterrestrials might be individualized like that of the angels, rather than like that of humankind.[58]

This layman also echoed the thought of some earlier writers that Christ chose Earth for His incarnation for the same reason He chose little Bethlehem for His birth: "The human race is perhaps . . . the most guilty of all [and had] the greatest need to profit directly from the redemption." But Courbet rejected the possibility of multiple incarnations, proposing alternative ways in which Christ's work on our planet could have results on other worlds.[59]

---

[57] Pierre Courbet, *"De la redemption et de la pluralité des mondes habités,"* *Cosmos*, 4th ser., 28 (May 19, 1894), 208–11; (June 2, 1894), 272–76.

[58] Courbet, (May 19, 1894), 208–11; (June 2, 1894), 272–76.

[59] Courbet, (May 19, 1894), 208–11; (June 2, 1894), 272–76.

Infants need no knowledge of the effects of baptism in order to benefit from the sacrament, he observed. So inhabitants of other planets might not need to know about the Incarnation on Earth in order to benefit from it. And if a physical connection of some sort is needed, God could arrange for an interplanetary communication.[60]

Anne Catherine Emmerich

One last Catholic voice of the nineteenth century deserves mention. The celebrated German mystic and stigmatist Blessed Anne Catherine Emmerich (1774–1824) allegedly received numerous private revelations throughout her lifetime. These reportedly included visions of planets and other celestial bodies both inhabited and uninhabited, some "awaiting a future population."

The nature of the inhabitants she saw represented a mix of intelligent beings: "holy spirits" or "good spirits"; departed "souls who, although not Christian, yet led good lives on earth"; and "planetary spirits" ("fallen spirits, but not devils"). She saw on the moon "many human figures flying from light into darkness as if hiding their shame, as if their conscience were in a bad state. . . . I never saw any worship offered to God on the moon. . . . The souls that I see hiding in darkness seem to be without suffering or joy, as if imprisoned till the Day of Judgement."[61]

These and other controversial statements in the alleged reports of Emmerich's private revelations eventually led

---

[60] Courbet, (May 19, 1894), 208–11; (June 2, 1894), 272–76.

[61] Carl E. Schmöger, *The Life of Anne Catherine Emmerich* (Rockford, Ill.: TAN Books, rep., 1976), vol. 2, 206–9.

many to question the authenticity of the documents. Whatever their actual status, however, we should note that for half a century, a number of eminent Catholic theologians who examined the documents found no reason to doubt that the existence of such creatures was in accord with a traditional Christian view of the universe.

A Near-Consensus . . . with Surprises

We have seen that Catholic voices of the nineteenth century found a near (but not complete) consensus: The existence of extraterrestrial intelligence is compatible with Church teaching and is at least possible. Along with a few poets and other laymen, a number of scholarly priests took part prominently and eagerly in the ETI conversation, speaking and writing in several countries on both sides of the Atlantic. Some of them offered surprising speculations that no doubt sparked controversy, yet enlivened the debate.

Even so, within the ETI conversation, a triumphalist form of what has been called *scientism*—the dogmatic notion that science is the only reliable source of knowledge—was manifest at the same time. In 1874, at the Belfast Meeting of the British Association for the Advancement of Science, John Tyndall (1820–93), superintendent of the Royal Institution, confidently predicted in his presidential address: "The impregnable position of science may be described in a few words. We claim, and we shall wrest from theology, the entire domain of cosmological theory."[62]

---

[62] John Tyndall, "The Belfast Address," in Tyndall, *Fragments of Science*, v. II (New York, 1901), 210.

In the years to follow, science did in fact come to dominate more than ever the conversation about a plurality of inhabited worlds. Before 1900, numerous publications about ETI made little effort to distinguish between scientific and religious views. But throughout the following century, fewer explicitly Christian voices would address the matter. A century after Tyndall's boast, the American astronomer Carl Sagan (1934–96), himself an agnostic,[63] could reasonably conclude that with regard to the history of ETI speculation, in this field as in others, "science has systematically expropriated areas which are the traditional concern of religion."[64]

---

[63] Joel Achenbach, "Carl Sagan denied being an atheist. So what did he believe? [Part 1.]" *The Washington Post*, July 10, 2014, https://www.washingtonpost.com/news/achenblog/wp/2014/07/10/carl-sagan-denied-being-an-atheist-so-what-did-he-believe-part-1/.

[64] Carl Sagan, "UFO's: The Extraterrestrial and Other Hypotheses," in Carl Sagan and Donald Menzel, eds., *UFO's — A Scientific Debate* (Ithaca: Cornell, 1972), 265–75:271.

8

"They Are Children of God as We Are"

Voices of the Twentieth Century

*"It is good for Catholics to know that the principles of
their faith are entirely compatible with the most startling
possibilities concerning life on other planets."*

—Fr. Francis J. Connell[1]

DESPITE JOHN TYNDALL'S boast about expelling religion from
cosmology, in the twentieth century at least a few theologians
and other Christian voices remained in the ETI conversation.
Yet according to one historian of the subject, "during the
twentieth century, theological explorations of contact with
extraterrestrial intelligence" were "sporadic, peripheral, and
never raised to the same level of substantial debate achieved
in the previous two centuries. . . . Most theologians would
undoubtedly have preferred to remain silent on the subject."[2]

---

[1]   Francis J. Connell, "Flying Saucers and Theology," in *The Truth About
Flying Saucers*, A. Michel, ed. (New York: Pyramid Books, 1967), 258.
[2]   Dick, *The Biological Universe*, 516–17. This book provides a detailed
overview of the ETI debate in the twentieth century, including its
theological aspects.

In the next chapter, we will note how a shift in the focus of the ETI conversation led in this century to reticence among theologians and others to speak about the subject. But for now we will survey the thoughts of those who did manage to raise their voices.

"Liveliest Speculation"

As the American astrobiologist Douglas Vakoch has noted, it was at the beginning of the "Age of Space," in the middle of the twentieth century, when a flurry of brief but provocative Christian theological speculations about ETI appeared in response to new space exploration efforts. One scientist of the period, the executive secretary of the American Rocket Society, observed that "the liveliest speculation" about ETI came from Catholic theologians.[3]

Summing up the thought of a number of these theologians writing between 1955 and 1965, Vakoch observed: "The dominant position of this group was that belief in extraterrestrial beings is consistent with both science and Christian theology. Most of those who took a position on whether such life is probable argued that it is. Moreover, it was generally agreed that if extraterrestrials exist, such beings

---

[3]   Douglas A. Vakoch, "Roman Catholic Views of Extraterrestrial Intelligence: Anticipating the Future by Examining the Past," Foundation for the Future, 2000, 167; https://www.researchgate.net/publication/320274609_Roman_Catholic_Views_of_Extraterrestrial_Intelligence. Vakoch's survey of this decade includes references to the Catholic theologians (many of them priests) Theodore J. Zubek, John P. Kleinz, Daniel C. Raible, A. Carr, J. D. Conway, James Harford, John J. Lynch, L. C. McHugh, and Angelo Perego.

would be made in the image of God with the purpose of glorifying their creator."

Even so, Vakoch noted, "There was less consensus about the extent to which such beings would be successful in this task. But in spite of differences of opinion about the nature of the relationship between extraterrestrials and God, there was most often a common framework for such speculations."[4]

Among these thinkers, the most common argument for the probable existence of ETI was the glory of God. Creatures in other worlds would glorify God not just by their very existence (reflecting His greatness, love, wisdom, and power) but also by consciously and intentionally acknowledging Him as their Creator. Some suggested that certain extraterrestrial races might even glorify God in a better way than we do. Nevertheless, at least one Jesuit writer concluded that even if we were the only rational beings in the cosmos, God would still be sufficiently glorified.[5]

Theodore J. Zubek

One of the theologians referenced by Vakoch was the American Franciscan Fr. Theodore J. Zubek. He published in 1961 a seven-page article in *The American Ecclesiastical Review* that addressed ETI, dealing systematically and concisely with several concerns that we have seen to recur in the historical conversation.

---

[4]   Vakoch, 167.
[5]   Vakoch, 167.

First, he noted that "the silence of the Bible on the structure of the universe does not exclude the possibility of life outside the earth."[6]

Second, he argued that "God could have created living beings, including rational creatures, on other planets. . . . The existence of such beings is not opposed to any truth of the natural or supernatural order."[7]

"In what relation to God would such creatures be?" Zubek asked. All such creatures throughout the cosmos, simply by virtue of their status as God's creations, would be subordinate to, and dependent on, their Creator. "This relationship is universal, absolute, and inescapable." In addition, "all rational creatures have a duty willingly to admit the divine supremacy and their subordination to God, and thus consciously to glorify God."[8]

Beyond these fundamentals, Zubek insisted, the relationship of ETI to God might vary according to His purposes for them. In a remarkably condensed and comprehensive statement, he laid out a number of possibilities for their moral and spiritual status. In some ways, their condition might resemble ours; in others, they might differ; and various extraterrestrial species might vary in their status. In fact, various individuals among the *same* species might vary in their status.

They might have been created in a purely natural state, or in a state with supernatural or preternatural gifts as we were. They might be unfallen and need no redemption. If they are fallen, they might be redeemed or unredeemed or even

---

[6] Theodore J. Zubek, "Theological Questions on Space Creatures," *The American Ecclesiastical Review* 145 (1966), 393–94.

[7] Zubek, 394.

[8] Zubek, 394–95.

incapable of redemption. God might have offered each ETI species redemption in various ways, which might or might not have involved a divine incarnation, or the ultimately cosmic effects of the Incarnation on Earth. In our theological analysis in an upcoming chapter, we will examine more closely each of these possibilities as Zubek and others have presented them.

Opposing Positions on Multiple Incarnations

As we have seen in previous chapters, among the most debated challenges to Christian faith presented by the possibility of ETI is the issue of the Incarnation. God became a Man on Earth for the sake of our redemption; could He become an ETI in another world to save another race? Would He *need* to do so, or could He redeem them some other way—or perhaps His incarnation as an Earthling could redeem even the inhabitants of other worlds?

Two twentieth-century scholars at Oxford held strongly opposing views on the issue. The British astrophysicist Edward A. Milne (1896–1950), hailed as one of the foremost pioneers of theoretical astrophysics and cosmology, asked in 1950 the critical theological question: "Was this [the Incarnation on Earth] a unique event, or has it been reenacted on each of a countless number of planets? The Christian would recoil in horror from such a conclusion. We cannot imagine the Son of God suffering vicariously on each of a myriad of planets. The Christian would avoid this conclusion by the definite supposition that our planet is in fact unique."[9]

---

[9]   E. A. Milne, "The Second Law of Thermodynamics: Evolution," in *Modern Cosmology and the Christian Idea of God* (Oxford: Oxford University Press, 1952).

Even so, with the development of radio astronomy, Milne eventually concluded that one day interstellar communication would be possible, and the good news of the unique Incarnation in our world could then be broadcast to other worlds. With the cosmic spread of the Gospel, then, "the reenactment of the tragedy of the crucifixion in other planets would be unnecessary."[10]

Milne's proposal was rejected a few years later by another Oxford scholar, E. L. Mascall (1905–93), an Anglican priest and lecturer in philosophy of religion. Mascall insisted that simple knowledge of our planet's Gospel message shared by interstellar radio communication would not be enough for the possibility of universal redemption. Instead, a union of two natures in one divine Person of the sort that took place in Jesus Christ would be required on other planets, joining the divine nature with ETI nature. "There are no conclusive *theological* reasons for rejecting the notion that, if there are, in some other part or parts of the universe than our own, rational corporeal [embodied] beings who have sinned and are in need of redemption, for those beings and for their salvation the Son of God has united (or one day will unite) to his divine Person their nature, as he has united it to ours."[11]

Mascall's emphasis on *theological* reasons is telling. Milne and others (even the skeptic Thomas Paine) had raised as their objection to multiple incarnations the horror it would provoke, presumably because multiple incarnations would

---

[10]   Milne, 153–54.
[11]   E. L. Mascall, *Christian Theology and Natural Science* (London: Ronald Press, 1956), 36–45.

lead to multiple passions and deaths of the perpetually Incarnated God.

But horror is not a valid theological reason for ruling out a possibility. If it were, then on this principle we would have to reject as well the possibility that God became incarnate on this planet, since the passion and death of Jesus Christ was also horrific.

Raible and Delano

Mascall was not alone at this time in taking this position in this particular debate. His contemporary, the American Catholic priest Daniel C. Raible, was emphatic: "Yes, it would be possible for the Second Person of the Blessed Trinity to become a member of more than one human [that is, rational] race. There is nothing at all repugnant in the idea of the same Divine Person taking on the nature of many human races."

Echoing Alice Meynell's lyrical notion of "a million alien Gospels," Mascall concluded that "conceivably, we may learn in heaven that there have been not one incarnation of God's son but many."[12]

Another American Catholic priest, Kenneth J. Delano (d. 2017), extended the incarnational possibilities even further. He concluded that not just the Son of God, but "any one or all three Divine Persons of the Holy Trinity may have been chosen to become incarnated on one or more of the other inhabited worlds in the universe." He considered this possibility much more probable than the notion of the "cosmic

---

[12] Daniel C. Raible, "Rational Life in Outer Space?" *America: National Catholic Weekly Review*, 103 (August 13, 1960), 532–35.

Adam"—the idea that Christ's saving activity on Earth has redemptive effects throughout the universe.[13]

Even so, Delano speculated, the human race might have an evangelistic mission of sorts to extraterrestrials. If we shared with them the Gospel of earthly salvation, we might inspire fallen races on other planets to seek God's redemption as well.[14]

And what of the biblical silence about ETI? An early twentieth-century writer, L. T. Townsend, had asserted in *The Stars Not Inhabited* (1914): "If he [man] is not the greatest, the grandest, the most important of created things, the one to whom all else is made to contribute, then the Bible writers have misrepresented entirely man's relation to God and the universe." Delano responded to Townsend that it would have served no moral purpose for God to reveal the existence of extraterrestrials in Scripture, so He was not obligated to do so. The dawning "Space Age" required an approach to the matter that expanded beyond a merely Earth-centered or human-centered theology.[15]

"Mankind Is Utterly Unique"

Though the majority of twentieth-century Christian (especially Catholic) writers about ETI were sympathetic to the possibility of their existence, a few voices were raised publicly in opposition to the proposal. As we will see in the next chapter, many of the ETI opponents were apparently

---

[13] Kenneth Delano, *Many Worlds, One God* (Hicksville, N.Y.: Exposition Press, 1977), 110–20.

[14] Delano, 110–20.

[15] Quoted in Delano, xv, 9.

motivated by their conviction that belief in extraterrestrial intelligence is a diabolical deception. But others based their conclusions on different grounds.

In 1960, the Catholic journalist Joseph A. Breig published in *America* magazine a piece called "Man Stands Alone." Using traditional theological, devotional, and even lyrical language, he made an appeal for the claim that human beings are unique and "priceless in the divine plan" by presenting "the electrifying extraordinariness of what we know about ourselves, both by our own observation and by divine revelation. . . . Every consideration higher than the barest logic— every instinct and feeling for poetry and artistry, and every religious sense of the divine fitness of things, argues, I think, that mankind is utterly unique and will forever remain so. If the cosmos is to be populated by thinking beings, the populating will be done by us in breathtaking migrations through space." We are unique and priceless, he insisted, because of the Incarnation that took place among us.[16]

In mystical terms, Breig speaks of the human race as "representatives to God of God's creation." In humanity,

> all the material creation, unto the farthest spiral nebula and the most distant boundaries of space, is gathered up and united with an immortal spirit destined for knowledge and love and service of the infinite Creator. . . . If I . . . lift up my mind and heart to adore and love and thank and petition my Maker and Saviour, in me the cosmos is lifted up in prayer. Not merely for myself

---

[16] Joseph A. Breig, "Man Stands Alone," in *America* 106 (November 26, 1960), 294.

do I pray, but for all my fellow men past and present and future; and for the stars known and unknown; for the planets and moons and meteors and meteorites; for the mineral and plant and animal kingdoms; for all that materially exists anywhere.[17]

We might say, then, that for Breig, humanity itself, not Christ, serves as the "cosmic Adam," the head and representative of the universe.

"The crux of the matter," Breig proposes, is this: "In the Incarnation, by taking flesh and blood and bone from us through the Virgin, God in a divinely wonderful way united to himself not only mankind, but through mankind the whole of the visible creation." And this union must be singular:

Thus we have the amazingly beautiful, and the divinely magnificent, ascent of creation from its lowest and most elementary forms into union with spirit, first in man, then in the God-Man, and through him with God, the infinite pure Spirit. We have the coming together of the finite and the infinite, of the lowest and the highest. The perfection and splendor of this divine work seem to me to leave no place for supposing that it is not unique. To me, there is a divine rightness in the concept of this singular unity of mankind, of the cosmos, and of the Creator.[18]

---

[17] Breig, 294.
[18] Breig, 294–95.

For Breig, then, multiple extraterrestrial intelligences, multiple incarnations, and—in a sentiment rarely encountered in the ETI conversation, even among Catholics—multiple Mothers of God are simply unthinkable.

Stanley L. Jaki, OB

The Hungarian-born Benedictine priest Stanley L. Jaki (1924–2009), trained both as a theologian and as a physicist, wrote extensively on the relations of modern science and the Christian faith. His rejection of the possibility of extraterrestrial intelligence seems to have been based primarily on scientific grounds. "One need not be an expert in the life sciences or in nuclear physics," he insisted, "to realize that instead of 'every likelihood' [with regard to the existence of ETI] one should talk of an improbability of well-nigh zero."[19]

With regard to theological issues in the ETI conversation, Jaki's training in both the history and the philosophy of science made him attuned to the social and cultural milieu of scientific endeavors with implications for faith. He was concerned that ETI proponents, both historically and in more recent times, often seemed eager to disprove Christian claims about the meaning and purpose of human history, most especially the Incarnation.[20]

Jaki also believed that "the ETI program" in modern times is morally subversive: "The cavalier approach of ETI

---

[19] Stanley L. Jaki, "Extraterrestrials, or Better Be Moonstruck?" in *The Limits of a Limitless Science: And Other Essays* (Wilmington, Del: ISI Books, 2000), 150.
[20] Stanley L. Jaki, *The Savior of Science* (Grand Rapids, Mich: W.B. Eerdmans, 2000), 25–30.

champions to the question of human intellect is acting in the cultural context in a most harmful way. The ETI program is a systematic devaluation of the dignity of human intellect. The ETI program is doing now on a far vaster scale . . . what had been done earlier by the popularization of mechanistic science." He went on to warn that "ETI historians who take lightly the moral relativism latent in the ETI program are so many unwitting travel guides into the land of anarchy."[21]

Réginald Garrigou-Lagrange, OP

Some twentieth-century theologians made only passing remarks about extraterrestrial intelligence, taking no firm position in the debate. The French Dominican Réginald Garrigou-Lagrange (1877–1964) was a leading Neo-Thomist theologian of his day and supervisor for the doctoral research of Pope Saint John Paul II. In his commentary on the Third Part of the *Summa* of Saint Thomas Aquinas, questions about the fitness of the Incarnation prompted Garrigou-Lagrange to offer brief observations that touched on ETI. "What must be said in reply to the objection of modern scientists, who say that the Incarnation perhaps could be admitted if the earth were the center of the universe, which it is not, for it is a planet among countless millions of heavenly bodies that are greater, namely, the stars and the nebulae?"

His reply: "Even if the world were the mathematical center of the universe, this would be no reason why God should choose it for the Incarnation. Thus Christ was not born in

---

[21] Stanley Jaki, "Extraterrestrial Intelligence and Scientific Progress," paper presented at the 1985 meeting of the History of Science Society, Bloomington, Indiana; quoted in Dick, *Biological Universe*, 526.

Jerusalem, but in Bethlehem. . . . The mathematical position of a body is a matter of less importance with reference to a supernatural mystery, which infinitely transcends the spatial order." God's choice of Earth for His incarnation did not depend on any special cosmic position, size, or other status of our planet.[22]

In any case, claims about the existence of ETI are mere conjectures, he reminded his readers. "We do not know whether there are any other heavenly bodies suitable for human habitation, which are inhabited. On this point both the positive sciences and theology can offer only hypotheses." Such conjectures carry little weight compared to the apostolic witness which assures us that Earth was in fact chosen.[23]

Not only do we lack scientific proof of intelligent extra-terrestrials, he notes; we lack as well divine revelation about their existence. "If some of the other heavenly bodies are inhabited by human beings [that is, creatures like us], God has not deemed it opportune to reveal this fact to us. Some say, if perhaps there are others inhabited, then these human beings are either in the purely natural state, or there was no case of original sin among them, or if there was, then they were regenerated in some other way than by the Incarnation. There is nothing intrinsically repugnant in all these views." Even so, "it is difficult to say," he concludes, whether these opinions can be reconciled with the reality of "the Incarnation in its relation to the human race. For [divine] revelation

---

[22] Réginald Garrigou-Lagrange, *Christ the Saviour: A Commentary on the Third Part of St. Thomas' Theological Summa* (1945), commenting on Chapter 3, Question 1, First Article.

[23] Garrigou-Lagrange.

speaks of the human race as it exists on this earth," not on other worlds.[24]

Garrigou-Lagrange went to add a statement reflecting the scriptural witness to the universal headship of Christ: "Whatever is the fact about these gratuitous hypotheses, Christ, as the incarnate Word of God, is the culmination of the whole of creation, and, just as he is the head of the angels . . . so he could be such with reference to human beings who might be living on some of the other heavenly bodies." Nevertheless, he reiterated, "concerning these things and many others, we have no knowledge, and there is no need for us to stop and discuss them."[25]

Pierre Teilhard de Chardin

The work of the French Jesuit priest Pierre Teilhard de Chardin (1881–1955), both theologian and paleontologist, was highly controversial, in theological as well as scientific circles. The Congregation for the Doctrine of the Faith and other ecclesiastical officials issued multiple condemnations of several aspects of his thought, though individual theologians and even popes have referred positively to at least some of his ideas.

Teilhard's overarching theological vision presented a cosmos evolving from matter to life to human consciousness to supreme consciousness (or the "Omega Point"). We might say that his primary focus was eschatology—the end (in the sense of the goal or *telos*) of all things. So his speculations about extraterrestrial intelligence are not surprising: This

---

[24] Garrigou-Lagrange.

[25] Garrigou-Lagrange.

upward universal ascent, he concluded, has led to intelligent life, not only on earth, but throughout the cosmos, and all the intelligent life forms are moving toward redemption.

Why would other forms of intelligent life need redemption if they are not descended from Adam on Earth and thus subject to original sin? Teilhard redefined original sin as "the essential reaction of the finite to the creative act"; the fall described in the book of Genesis is actually the appearance of death in the universe. And it did not occur only on earth; it is universal: "We can no longer derive the whole of evil from one single [human]. I must emphasize . . . that long before man[,] death existed on earth. And in the depths of the heavens, far from any moral influence of the earth, death also exists. . . . In the universe today, neither one man nor the whole of mankind can be responsible for contaminating the whole [universe]."

If sin understood in this way is a universal attribute of the entire creation, Teilhard argued, God must offer redemption to all creatures as well. But humanity could not be the sole center of redemption, nor could salvation history on Earth have any value for ETI: "The idea of an earth chosen arbitrarily from countless others as the focus of Redemption is one I cannot accept. . . . The hypothesis of a special revelation, in some million of centuries to come, teaching the inhabitants of the system of Andromeda that the Word was incarnate on Earth, is just ridiculous. All that I can entertain is the possibility of a multi-aspect Redemption which would be realized on all the stars."

Even for Teilhard, such a notion raised serious issues. "Yet all the worlds do not coincide in time! There were worlds before our own, and there will be worlds after it. . . . Unless we introduce a relativity into time we should have to admit, surely, that Christ has still to be incarnate in some as yet unformed star?"

In an attempt to maintain a strong sense of the universal centrality of Christ despite these conclusions, Teilhard proposed the activity of a third, "cosmic," nature of Christ, a nature in addition to the divine and the human natures identified in Catholic dogma. Teilhard assigned to this nature, and not to the human nature of the Word, the work of recapitulating in Him all creation and all the beings that participate in it.[26]

At this point, Teilhard confessed: "There are times when one almost despairs of being able to disentangle Catholic dogmas from the geocentrism [earth-centered orientation] in the framework of which they were born."[27] Given his attempts to redefine basic terms of traditional Christian theology almost beyond recognition, the rejection of such teaching by the Catholic Church's Magisterium should not be surprising.

Yves Congar

The French Dominican friar, priest, and theologian Yves Congar (1904–1995), appointed a cardinal toward the end of his life by Pope Saint John Paul II, is known for his quip

---

[26] Teilhard de Chardin, *"La multiplicité des mondes habités,"* in *Oeuvres* (Paris: Seuil, 1969), v. X, 282.

[27] Teilhard de Chardin, "Fall, Redemption, and Geocentrism," in *Christianity and Evolution* (New York: Harcourt, Brace Jovanovich, 1971), 36–44.

about trying to learn science from the early chapters of Genesis: "The intention of Holy Scripture is to teach us how to go to heaven, not how the heavens go." In "Has God Peopled the Stars?"—an appendix to his work *The Wide World My Parish*—he wrote: "Christian doctrine is not concerned with stars or inhabited worlds but with Heaven. . . . Revelation being silent on the matter, Christian doctrine leaves us quite free to think that there are, or are not, other inhabited worlds. . . . Biblically speaking, it is an entirely open question. . . . There is no point in being subtle about it. There is nothing in the Bible that touches the matter." Even so, he added, "theology does not see any difficulty" in the possibility of ETI.[28]

What *can* theology say, then, about this topic? First, Congar insisted, intelligent extraterrestrials would also be made in God's image and would have some natural awareness of Him as the Creator of all things. "The only certainty that theology contributes here is that, if living beings endowed with understanding exist elsewhere, they too are in God's image, for he is the creator and master of Mars or Venus just as he is of the Earth. They would then have a natural religion analogous to ours, though in forms we cannot imagine." Yet even though that natural religion would be different from ours, the difference would lie in "the particular way in which they would think and express themselves," not in its "spiritual content," which would be identical with ours.

---

[28] Yves Congar, "Has God Peopled the Stars?" Appendix 2 in *The Wide World My Parish: Salvation and Its Problems*, trans. Donald Attwater (Baltimore: Helicon Press, 1961), 184–96; available online at https://archive.org/details/thewideworldmyparish/page/n195/mode/2up. The following quotes all come from this text.

This identity of human natural religion and extraterrestrial natural religion would arise from "the soul-stirring fact" that "in whatever forms they were expressed, the affirmations of these intelligences would refer to identically the same God as do ours. . . . There is only one God, a supreme and absolutely first Being, a 'Maker of all things, visible and invisible,' as we sing in the Creed."

Second is the matter of God's intended destiny for intelligent extraterrestrials. Could such beings have been "called by God to the life of grace and a supernatural revelation"? "No other answer can be given than this: 'It is possible.' Why not? But we know nothing whatever about it: it belongs to the realm of God's inviolable and sovereign freedom."

Third, could divine incarnations other than ours on Earth have taken place on other worlds? "Could the Word of God have taken flesh there and become a Martian? . . . Or could the Father have been incarnated there, or the Holy Spirit?"

With such questions, we must tread lightly, Congar warns, for "we encroach on a sphere which God reserves to himself." But "theologians think" that "it would not be impossible, that the Word of God, or one of the Persons of the Blessed Trinity, should unite himself to any creature."

Finally, what would be the relationship of Jesus Christ to such ETI?

> Jesus Christ—*our* Christ!—is King and can but be King, of all that is created; not simply of this earth, but of the whole of God's work, of the myriad of stars shining in the vault of the heavens. . . . The personal and substantial union that God has brought about, in

Jesus Christ, between him and the human race is the highest that is possible to realize. . . . Jesus Christ is, then, at the absolute pinnacle of the whole universe, whether existing or possible, now and forever. He is its King, just as he is King of the angels (though not their Redeemer).

Ever since God's incarnation in Christ, then, he "reigns over the whole universe . . . not only (if we may put it so) from the Heaven of his Godhead, but in and through the divine manhood of Jesus Christ. What an astounding destiny for the race to which we belong!"

Karl Rahner

The German Jesuit theologian Karl Rahner (1904–84) also addressed the possibility of ETI. "This question must be raised," he insisted, "in view of the vast immensity of the material cosmos. . . . If we imagine the cosmos as a world coming to be . . . then it is really not to be taken for granted that this aim has been successful only at the tiny point [in the universe] we know as our earth."[29]

Rahner thought it likely that intelligent extraterrestrials exist, and that God, who had created them, would love them, reveal Himself to them, and communicate with them. But he concluded that the divine Incarnation in Christ on Earth was meant only for the salvation of humans. Whether intelligent creatures on other planets would even need salvation is beyond what we can know. We must not assume that

---

[29] Quoted in C. L. Fisher and D. Fergusson, "Karl Rahner and the extra-terrestrial life debate," *Heythrop Journal* 47 (2006), 275.

we can understand how the drama of good and evil might play out in other worlds, nor the ways in which God might manifest His love and grace to the creatures there.[30]

Even so, Rahner was open to the possibility of divine Incarnations on other worlds: "It cannot be proved that a multiple incarnation in different histories of salvation is absolutely unthinkable."[31]

C. S. Lewis

In addition to these Catholic theologians, we must consider the speculations of C. S. Lewis (1898–1963), a British literary scholar at Oxford and an Anglican convert from atheism. Though not a theologian by training, he wrote extensively about theological matters, and his works became enormously popular and influential on both sides of the Atlantic. Lewis thought deeply about the possibility of extraterrestrial intelligence and its implications for Christian faith. He wrote more about the subject than perhaps any other Christian theological writer of the twentieth century, offering the fruit of his reflections both in essays and in fiction.

Among his many essays, the one that treats ETI most extensively is "Religion and Rocketry" (1958).[32] Here Lewis responded primarily to a question implied by Christian belief in the Incarnation on Earth: "If we find ourselves to be but one among a million races, scattered through a million spheres, how can we, without absurd arrogance, believe ourselves to have been uniquely favoured?"

---

[30] Karl Rahner, *Foundations of Christian Faith* (New York: Seabury Press, 1978), 445–46.

[31] Quoted in Fisher and Fergusson, "Karl Rahner," 275.

[32] Lewis, "Religion and Rocketry," 87–97.

To answer this question, Lewis observed, first we need to know whether there are in fact "animals [with] what we call 'rational souls.' . . . By this I include not merely the faculty to abstract and calculate, but the apprehension of values, the power to mean by 'good' something more than 'good for me' or even 'good for my species.' If instead of asking 'Have they rational souls' you prefer to ask 'Are they spiritual animals?' I think we shall both mean pretty much the same." This distinction is critical, Lewis argued, because we should not be surprised if God treated the human race differently from races of beings that were not "spiritual animals." A divine Incarnation among them would be a Gift that such a creature would be "by its nature incapable either of desiring or of receiving."[33]

As we shall see in a later chapter, to distinguish between animals that merely think ("abstract and calculate") and animals that are "spiritual" has important implications for the ETI conversation that have rarely been discussed. Exploring the issue adequately involves defining what it means for humans to be made in the "image of God." Is the *imago Dei* simply a rational intellect and a free will? Or is it the divine gift of an immortal spirit that serves as the soul, the creature's animating principle? The definition has implications even with regard to non-human terrestrial creatures, such as the now-extinct Neanderthals and Denisovans of our planet.

Lewis pressed the point: "Even if we met them [ETI] we might not find it so easy to decide [whether they were spiritual animals]. It seems to me possible to suppose creatures so clever that they could talk, though they were, from

---

[33] Lewis, 88–89.

the theological point of view, really only animals, capable of pursuing or enjoying only natural ends." With his usual wit, Lewis noted that we sometimes meet "humans—the machine-minded and materialistic type—who *look* as if they were just that." But Christians must insist that somewhere inside such people the soul exists, "however atrophied."[34]

Yet in other worlds, he surmised, "there might be creatures genuinely spiritual, whose powers of manufacture and abstract thought were so humble that we should mistake them for mere animals. God shield them from us!"[35]

The second question to be answered, Lewis noted as others had, is whether such spiritual creatures are fallen or unfallen. Lewis used this concern to respond to those who declared that the Christian faith is wrong because "the Incarnation implies some particular merit or excellence in humanity. But of course it implies the reverse: a particular demerit and depravity."

This was a common theme in his treatment of the subject: "Perhaps of all races *we* only fell." Humanity might well be the only intelligent, embodied race in the cosmos that sinned, requiring a unique redemptive response.[36]

If, however, other extraterrestrial races are fallen, the question remains whether they have "been denied Redemption by the Incarnation and Passion of Christ. . . . For of course it is no very new idea that the eternal Son may, for all we know, have been incarnate in other worlds than earth and saved other races than ours." But multiple incarnations, Lewis

---

[34] Lewis, 89–90.

[35] Lewis, 90.

[36] Lewis, 90.

speculated, are not the only possible path to redemption for fallen ETI. "Is it certain that [an Incarnation and Passion] is the only mode of Redemption that is possible? It may be. . . . But we don't know. . . . Spiritual as well as physical conditions might differ widely in different worlds. There might be different sorts and different degrees of fallenness. We must surely believe that the divine charity is as fertile in resource as it is measureless in condescension."

The "great Physician may have applied different remedies" to different diseases or to different patients with the same disease. And we might not even recognize those remedies as such even if we should hear about them.[37]

In Lewis's essay "The Seeing Eye," he offered two more possibilities for the spiritual and moral status of intelligent extraterrestrials. One is that "we might meet a species which, like us, needed Redemption but had not been given it." Yet this situation would not provide any challenges to the Christian faith that we have not already faced throughout history in discovering new peoples who have never heard about Jesus Christ. "It would be our duty to preach the Gospel to them. For if they are rational, capable both of sin and repentance, they are our brethren, whatever they look like."[38]

Finally, Lewis suggested one last, terrifying possibility: "We might find a race which was strictly diabolical—no tiniest spark felt in them from which any goodness could ever be coaxed into the feeblest glow; all of them incurably

---

[37] Lewis, 91–92.

[38] C. S. Lewis, "The Seeing Eye," in *Christian Reflections* (Grand Rapids, Mich.: Eerdmans, 1967), 167–76. This essay originally appeared under the title "Onward, Christian Spacemen," in *Show*, 3 (Feb. 1963). The quote is on p. 175.

perverted through and through." In other words, we might encounter an intelligent race with a spiritual and moral status like the demons, but who (unlike the demons) have physical bodies.[39]

Lewis's Fictional Portrayals of the Possibilities

Lewis's celebrated *Space Trilogy* is a science fiction novel sequence exploring the possibilities of human space travel. In the first volume, *Out of the Silent Planet*[40] (1938), the protagonist, Dr. Elwin Ransom, finds himself transported to *Malacandra* (the name for Mars used by its inhabitants). There he encounters three intelligent races, very different from one another.

None of the three species have ever fallen, a possibility for ETI that Lewis raised in his essays. In the story, the author imagines how unfallen "creatures genuinely spiritual, whose powers of manufacture and abstract thought" are humble, might interact with humans. They have the kind of "natural religion" that Yves Congar proposed would be found in ETI.

Not having rebelled against God, they know Him and call Him "the Old One." They know as well about His Son, *Maleldil* the Young. Not blinded by sin, they are able to see angels (*eldil*).

The Martian races have much to teach Ransom about his own planet. They call Earth *Thulcandra*, which means "the Silent Planet." And they tell Ransom that the *Oyarsa*, or angelic ruler, of Thulcandra (each planet has one), once

---

[39] Lewis, 175–76.
[40] C. S. Lewis, *Out of the Silent Planet* (London: The Bodley Head, 1938).

rebelled against the Old One. He was of course defeated, and his planet was put under quarantine from the rest of the cosmos to protect other intelligent species from being injured or corrupted by this "Bent One" (Satan).

In the second novel of the trilogy, *Perelandra* (1943),[41] Ransom has returned to Earth a changed man, but is now sent out on a mission to the planet Venus. There he encounters the beginning of an intelligent species whose first parents (a parallel to Adam and Eve) have not yet fallen. The "Eve" figure is being sorely tempted by a demon-possessed earthling who was a central figure in the first volume, and Ransom must stop him from leading her into sin.

Ransom is ultimately successful, and the Perelandran first parents are confirmed in their goodness. They are ready now to rule over their planet and to be fruitful and multiply to fill it.

In this novel, Lewis illustrates the possibility proposed in "Religion and Rocketry" that the divine Incarnation on Earth, and subsequent events there, might affect the destiny of ETI. First, he posits that the new intelligent species on Venus, unlike the Martian races, is humanoid in appearance (though green in color). This form has now become God's preferred shape for newly created ETI because His Son has taken on a human nature and joined it to Himself, granting it a unique dignity.

Second, Lewis is imagining the seed of a cosmic interplanetary salvation history. The Perelandran first parents are able to avoid the fall from grace and prepare for a glorious future with their descendants—through the mediation of an

---

[41] C. S. Lewis, *Perelandra* (London: The Bodley Head, 1943).

earthling redeemed by the Incarnate God who had visited his planet.

Finally, we must not neglect the implications for ETI at the heart of *The Chronicles of Narnia*,[42] Lewis's famous series of seven fantasy tales for children. As we will see in a later chapter, his principal character in these stories, Aslan the Lion, was envisioned as another incarnation of Christ. Though Narnia was a world totally outside our reality rather than another planet in our universe, still the author's speculation was based on a premise envisioned by his essays as at least a possibility in our universe: multiple divine incarnations.

Venerable Andrea Beltrami, Saint Pio, Popes Saint Paul VI and John Paul II

Some final, highly intriguing references to extraterrestrial intelligence come from four unlikely twentieth-century sources: three canonized Catholic saints and a venerable (someone on the path to canonization).

The Italian Salesian Father Andrea Beltrami (1870–97), who received the Salesian habit from the founder of that order, Saint John Bosco, was declared venerable by Pope Saint Paul VI in 1966. Beltrami was reported to pray for the inhabitants of other planets. According to Msgr. Corrado Balducci (1923–2008), a member of the Vatican Curia and long-time exorcist for the Archdiocese of Rome, of the sixteen books written by Beltrami (not yet published by the

---

[42] C. S. Lewis, *The Chronicles of Narnia* (London: Geoffrey Bles, 1950–1956) includes *The Magician's Nephew; The Lion, the Witch and the Wardrobe; The Horse and His Boy; Prince Caspian; The Voyage of the Dawn Treader; The Silver Chair;* and *The Last Battle*.

postulator of his cause for canonization), one is said to deal with the topic of ETI.[43]

According to a report by Reginaldo Francisco, the French Catholic philosopher and theologian Jean Guitton once had a conversation with Pope Saint Paul VI (1897–1978) in which they discussed ETI. The pope found the possibility of extraterrestrials to be reasonable and could see how "the universal Church" would in that case include more than the human race.[44]

The celebrated Italian Capuchin priest and friar Saint Pio of Pietrelcino (Padre Pio, 1887–1968) once affirmed in private conversation the existence of extraterrestrial intelligence, including unfallen ETI. Balducci reported:

> The following dialogue is documented and officially published by the Capuchin Order:
>
> **Question:** Father [Pio], some claim that there are creatures of God on other planets, too.
>
> **Answer:** What else? Do you think they don't exist and that God's omnipotence is limited to this small planet Earth? What else? Do you think there are no other beings who love the Lord?

---

[43] Reported by Corrado Balducci in "Ufology and Theological Clarifications," remarks presented at Pescara, Italy, June 8, 2001. Available by subscription at https://www.scribd.com/document/134453494/Corrado-Balducci.

[44] Reginaldo Francisco, *"Possibilità di una redenzione cosmica,"* in *Origini, l'Universo, la Vita, l'intelligenza,* ed. F. Betorla et al. (Padua: Il Poligrafo, 1994), 121–40; quoted in Thomas F. O'Meara, *Vast Universe: Extraterrestrials and Christian Revelation* (Collegeville, Minn.: Liturgical Press, 2012), 87 n. 19.

> **Another question:** Father, I think the Earth is noth-
> ing compared to other planets and stars.
>
> **Answer:** Exactly yes, and we Earthlings are nothing,
> too. The Lord certainly did not limit his glory to this
> small Earth. On other planets other beings exist who
> did not sin and fall as we did.[45]

Saint Pio might have been expressing a personal opinion
only. But we have reason to ponder why he would speak so
confidently, almost nonchalantly, about ETI. He makes no
reference to Scripture or explicit Church teaching on the
subject to support his claims.

Perhaps we should keep in mind how first-person witnesses reported throughout this saint's life that God often
revealed to him hidden matters: future events; remote events
and conversations; secret thoughts; life experiences and
unconfessed sins of penitents in the confessional. Might the
comments of this remarkable mystic have been based upon
such divinely inspired knowledge?[46]

Finally of note in this regard is a remark by the popular
Polish Pope Saint John Paul II (1920–2005). According to a
report of his visit to the parish of *Sant'Innocenzo I Papa e San
Guido Vescovo* in Rome on November 28, 1999, the pope
had a brief but significant exchange with a child who was
attending the event. When the little one asked him, "Holy

---

[45] Don Nello Castello, *Così parlò Padre Pio*, Vicenza, Italy, 1974.

[46] The many biographies of Saint Pio are filled with such testimonies.
See, for example, Katarina Tangari, *Stories of Padre Pio* (Rockford, Ill.:
TAN Books, 1996); Renzo Allegri, *Padre Pio: Man of Hope* (Ann Arbor,
Mich.: Servant Publications, 2000); C. Bernard Ruffin, *Padre Pio: The
True Story* (Huntington, In.: Our Sunday Visitor, 1991).

Father, are there any aliens?" the saint did not respond, "We don't know," or even "If they exist, then . . ."

Instead, he replied simply, "Always remember: They are children of God as we are."[47]

―――――――――
[47] Balducci, "Ufology."

9

"Intelligent Creatures in a Billion Galaxies"

A Twenty-First-Century Renewal

of the ETI Conversation

*"There might be a number of modes of supernatural life
with God, a variety of God's more intimate life shared
with intelligent creatures in a billion galaxies."*

—Thomas O'Meara[1]

THE YEARS SURROUNDING the dawn of the third Christian millennium, and the early decades of the new century, witnessed a new blossoming of interest in ETI among Christian theologians and other writers. In the late twentieth century, a certain stigma had come to be associated with any serious public discussion of extraterrestrial intelligence. (The sociopolitical reasons for this development, as opposed to the scientific reasons discussed below, are complex; they are examined briefly in the appendix, "What About UFOs?")

---

[1]   Thomas F. O'Meara, "Christian Theology and Extraterrestrial Life," *Theological Studies* 60.1 (1995), 25.

Though dismissive attitudes toward the subject are still all too common, they have begun to fade as the scientific and broader academic communities have found reasons to re-enliven the conversation.

We should recall that, as we noted in an earlier chapter, the majority of late nineteenth-century writers about ETI tended to embrace enthusiastically the pluralist position. But in the first half of the twentieth century, among scientists a new skepticism about the possibility won the day. This development owed much to the growing influence of evolutionary biologists, who insisted that the complex circumstances required for intelligent life to emerge on Earth were unlikely to have come about on other planets. Even so, in the latter part of the century, the pendulum swung back again.

"Life Is a Cosmic Imperative!"

The English physicist and cosmologist Paul Davies (b. 1946) has recalled the drastic shift in the ETI debate among scientists between the mid-twentieth century and the present, a shift back toward a more hopeful expectation of extraterrestrial life: "When I was a student in the 1960s the prevailing scientific view was that life on earth is the product of a chemical fluke so rare it would have happened only once in the observable universe. 'Almost a miracle' was the way [the Nobel prize-winning biologist, biophysicist, and neuroscientist] Francis Crick [1916–2004] expressed it. In those days speculating about extraterrestrial life was a taboo; one might as well have professed an interest in looking for fairies."

Davies went on to quote the French biochemist Jacques Monod (1910–76), also a Nobel prizewinner: "Man at last knows that he is alone in the unfeeling immensity of the universe, out of which he emerged by chance alone."[2]

Both Crick and Monod were each an "active atheist," Davies noted. They believed that the "freak chemical event" explanation for life buttressed their rejection of the traditional Christian belief that God had directly intervened in His creation to create life through a miracle. But as Davies went on to observe, associating atheism with the claim of a "sterile universe" beyond Earth and the absence of cosmic meaning or purpose implied that a "fecund universe" would support the traditional Christian claim. "And indeed today," he concluded, "the pendulum has swung very far the other way regarding the prospects for extraterrestrial life."[3]

The newly popular confidence that the cosmos is full of life—a "biological universe"[4]—rests on the notion that life emerges out of non-life not as a matter of chance alone, as Monod insisted. Instead, it is somehow "fast-tracked" by some kind of chemical "self-organization" or through the operation of a universal "life principle" that manifests itself in complex chemical systems. Yet another Nobel prizewinner, the Belgian biochemist Christian de Duve (1917–2013), summed it up memorably: "Life is a cosmic imperative!"[5]

Ironically, most of today's "biological universe" advocates still reject the traditional Christian belief in a special divine

---

[2]   Paul Davies, "Foreword," in Ted Peters, ed., *Astrotheology: Science and Theology Meet Extraterrestrial Life*, (Eugene, Or.: Cascade Books, 2018), x–xi. Davies actually has a minor planet named in his honor, 6870 Pauldavies.

[3]   Davies, in Peters, xi.

[4]   The term was coined by Steven J. Dick; see Dick, *Biological Universe*.

[5]   Dick, *Biological Universe*.

intervention to create life. Throughout the emerging field of astrobiology,[6] as it has come to be called, we find the common assumption that "life is a thoroughly natural phenomenon, emerging from complex chemistry via a sequence of purely physical processes."[7] But a number of theologians have nevertheless found within the revitalized ETI conversation a space to explore the relevant issues in light of Christian faith, with some of them maintaining that life's beginning, wherever it may occur, does indeed involve divine intervention.

In fact, in 2009, the Vatican Observatory, the astronomical institute of the Holy See, hosted a conference on astrobiology. Fr. José Funes, SJ, a former director of the observatory, was asked why the Vatican had an interest in such a topic. He replied: "Although astrobiology is an emerging field and still a developing subject, the questions of life's origins and whether life exists elsewhere in the universe are very interesting and deserve serious consideration. These questions offer many philosophical and theological implications."[8]

---

[6] On the term "astrobiology," see Ted Peters, chapter 1, "Introducing Astrotheology," in Peters, *Astrotheology*, 5–7.

[7] Peters, *Astrotheology*, xii. For an overview of the "biological universe" perspective, see Dick, *Biological Universe*. David Wilkinson's study, *Search for Extraterrestrial Intelligence*, provides a useful survey of the relevant scientific debates, 26–82. For an overview of the divine intervention debates, see Philip Clayton, "Toward a Theory of Divine Action That Has Traction," in *Scientific Perspectives on Divine Action: Twenty Years of Challenge and Progress* (Vatican City State: Vatican Observatory Publications and Berkeley, Calif.: The Center for Theology and the Natural Sciences, 2008), 87–110.

[8] "The Vatican Ponders Extraterrestrials," *The Guardian*, November 11, 2009, http://www.theguardian.com/world/2009/nov/11/Vatican-extra-terrestrials-catholic.

Other Reasons for the New Optimism

Several other factors have contributed to the new optimism about ETI that has developed since the 1960s. First, advances in the technology of astrophysics have demonstrated ever more clearly just how vast is the universe—how many countless possibilities exist for inhabitable locales. In fact, our theoretical understanding of the cosmos now suggests that some parts of the existing universe may even lie outside the universe we can observe.

Second, additional technological advances have allowed us, beginning in 1995, to confirm the existence of exoplanets—that is, planets outside our solar system orbiting another star. The existence of nearly five thousand exoplanets has now been confirmed. Determining how many of these celestial bodies feature conditions that would support life is a more challenging matter. But the continuing discovery of new exoplanets has encouraged those who promote the notion of the biological universe.[9]

A third factor has been technological advances in fields such as radio astronomy that form part of what is called the Search for Extraterrestrial Intelligence (SETI). SETI refers to a variety of search methods for discovering indicators of ETI beyond Earth, including the monitoring of electromagnetic radiation for signs of transmissions from civilizations on other planets. Though no unmistakable signals of this sort have yet been identified, the search continues enthusiastically, with publicity generated not just through news media

---

[9] For an overview of the search for exoplanets, see Jennifer Wiseman, "Exoplanets and the Search for Life Beyond Earth," in Peters, *Astrotheology*, 124–32.

but also through the entertainment industry, such as the films *Contact* (1997), *The Dish* (2000), and *Deceived* (2002).

In fact, film, television, and video game studios, not to mention print and digital publishers, have all made a profound contribution to opening the contemporary cultural imagination to the possibility of ETI. From *War of the Worlds* to *Star Wars* and beyond, entertaining speculations about intelligent life beyond earth have prepared recent generations to accept ETI more easily.[10] A Marist Poll in February 2018 found 68 percent of Americans believe that extraterrestrial life exists, up from 52 percent in 2005. Those under the age of forty-five (74 percent) and those under the age of thirty (79 percent) were more likely to believe in ETI than those older (62 percent).[11]

One last contributing factor to this development has led to a remarkable opening up of the public conversation about ETI: Several prominent news organizations have in recent years begun reporting about UAP as a serious concern; the US government (especially the Pentagon) is signaling an unprecedented willingness to address the matter; and the US Congress has passed legislation demanding more information, accountability, and transparency from the Pentagon

---

[10] See the series of articles on various aspects of "Science fiction involving extraterrestrials" in David Darling, *The Extraterrestrial Encyclopedia: An Alphabetical Reference to All Life in the Universe* (New York: Three Rivers Press, 2000), 370–73.

[11] "Are Americans Poised for an Alien Invasion?" Marist Poll, February 12, 2018, https://maristpoll.marist.edu/wp-content/misc/usapolls/us18 0129/Complete%20Survey%20Findings_Marist%20Poll_Life_on_Ot her_Planets_February%202018.pdf.

and national intelligence agencies about UAP. (These events are addressed in the appendix, "What About UFOs?")[12]

Ted Peters and Astrotheology

The increasing number of Catholic and other Christian theologians who are now speaking and writing about extraterrestrial intelligence prevents us from offering a detailed survey of each thinker's contribution. A representative sample of those engaged in the conversation must suffice.

Ted Peters is a Lutheran theologian who serves on the Advisory Council of METI (Messaging Extraterrestrial Intelligence), a non-profit research organization that creates and transmits interstellar messages in an attempt to communicate with extraterrestrial civilizations. His extensive work in the study of the interaction of science and religion has included the development of the new field he calls astrotheology. His working definition of the term carefully distinguishes his use of it from its current meaning among "neo-pagans and New Age enthusiasts" tied to "astrology and the occult": *Astrotheology is that branch of theology which combines a critical analysis of the contemporary space sciences combined with an explication of classic doctrines such as creation and Christology for the purpose of constructing a comprehensive and meaningful understanding of our human situation within an astonishingly immense cosmos.* He sees astrotheology as a form of "a

---

[12] For a summary of these developments, see Gideon Lewis-Kraus, "How the Pentagon Started Taking UFOs Seriously: For decades, flying saucers were a punchline. Then the U.S. government got over the taboo," *The New Yorker*, April 30, 2021, https://www.newyorker.com/magazine/2021/05/10/how-the-pentagon-started-taking-ufos-seriously.

theology of nature, wherein what we know by faith is complemented and expanded by what we learn from science." In this approach to the subject, science and theology are able to "engage one another in *creative mutual interaction.*"[13]

Peters has observed that in recent times, the "majority of theologians who take up the question of extraterrestrial life . . . anticipate a future engagement with an alien civilization with both caution and excitement. They put out the welcome mat for hypothetical space neighbors." But he also observed that some contemporary Christian writers reject the notion of ETI, citing the kinds of objections we have found earlier in the ETI conversation—for example, that the Bible says nothing about intelligent life on other planets, or that ETI is incompatible "with the biblical teachings of the uniqueness of the earth and the distinct spiritual position of human beings."[14]

No "Welcome Mat"

Among others who do not "put out the welcome mat" for ETI is Catholic theologian Benjamin Wiker. After a brief overview of the historical ETI conversation and related scientific issues, he concludes in an article he penned that openness to the possibility of ETI involves "sloppy logic," non-Christian metaphysics, and the inclination "to hitch theological doctrines to the science of the day."[15] Ironically,

---

[13] See Peters, *Astrotheology,* 11–13; all emphasis is in the original.

[14] Peters, 18. The second quote in this paragraph Peters himself quotes from the website *Answers in Genesis,* "Taking Back Astronomy," http://www.answersingenesis.org/articles/tba/bible-and-modern-astronomy-2.

[15] Benjamin Wiker, "Alien Ideas," June 27, 2009, https://www.catholicity.com/commentary/wiker/06325.html. For other examples of the

with regard to his last objection, the "rare earth" scientific notion Wiker uses to bolster his position has itself (as we have noted) now been largely eclipsed by the "life as a cosmic imperative" view. Additionally, the rare earth view is largely based on principles of evolutionary biology, whose Darwinism he has sharply criticized elsewhere.[16]

Wiker is concerned that the acceptance of ETI's existence would require Christians to "rerig" their "cosmology." He concludes: "I am as prepared for the arrival of extraterrestrials as I am for that of elves, and for the same reason: All evidence points to their nonexistence, and yet it remains a very, very remote possibility—so remote that to change our central doctrines to accommodate either possibility would be folly."[17]

Some contemporary Christian writers approach the ETI conversation with a focus on UAP rather than the broader theological issues we are discussing here. When they do, they often insist that reports of unidentified flying objects, and especially claims of alien abductions, represent demonic phenomena. Timothy Dailey, seeing a "paranormal conspiracy," places UAP in the same category as ghosts, Bigfoot, shapeshifters, and other forms of "high strangeness." They

position rejecting the possibility of ETI, see Wentzel van Huyssteen, *Alone in the World: Human Uniqueness in Science and Theology* (Grand Rapids, Mich.: Eerdmans, 2006); and Ted Peters, "Fundamentalist Literature," in *Science, Theology, and Ethics* (Burlington, Vt.: Ashgate, 2003), 129–34.

[16] See Benjamin Wiker with William A. Dembski, *Moral Darwinism: How We Became Hedonists* (Westmont, Ill.: InterVarsity Press), 2002; *The Darwin Myth: The Life and Lies of Charles Darwin* (Washington, D.C.: Regnery, 2009).

[17] Wiker, "Alien Ideas."

are "messengers of deception," "a diabolical conspiracy . . . a plot to lead human hearts and souls eternally astray."[18]

In support of his position, Dailey cites UFO researcher John Keel, who was not himself a Christian writer, but observed: "The UFO manifestations seem to be, by and large, merely minor variations of the age-old demonological phenomena."[19] Those who, like Daily, arrive at the conclusion that UAP is diabolical typically refrain from addressing the general theological and scientific questions that arise when discussing the possibility of ETI.

One popular TV evangelist, Pat Robertson, has even taken the startling position that those who claim to have interacted personally with extraterrestrial visitors (known as "contactees") should be stoned to death. He apparently made such a remark in light of the Old Testament law for punishing practitioners of witchcraft, who consorted with demons.[20]

---

[18] Timothy Dailey, *The Paranormal Conspiracy: The Truth About Ghosts, Aliens, and Mysterious Beings* (Minneapolis, Minn.: Chosen, 2015), 13, 30, 47, 62.

[19] The Keel quote appears in John Keel, *Operation Trojan Horse* (New York: Putnam, 1970), 299. Similar conclusions may be found in William M. Alnor, *UFOs in the New Age: Extraterrestrial Messages and the Truth of Scripture* (Grand Rapids, Mich.: Baker, 1992); Elizabeth L. Hillstrom, Testing the Spirits (Downers Grove, Ill.: InterVarsity Press, 1995); Nick Redfern, *Final Events and the Secret Government Group on Demonic UFOs and the Afterlife* (New York: Anomalist Books, 2010). See also Brenda Denzler, *The Lure of the Edge: Scientific Passions, Religious Beliefs, and the Pursuit of UFOs* (Los Angeles: University of California Press, 2002), 124–25.

[20] Peter Robbins, "Politics, Religion, and Human Nature: Practical Problems and Roadblocks on the Path toward Official UFO Acknowledgement" (August 2004), 14, https://en.calameo.com/books/00008 21983c8a0ce09cad. See also Leviticus 20:27; Skip Porteous, "Robertson

The Catholic priest Fr. Dwight Longenecker, meanwhile, summarizes the aliens-as-demons position: "The best explanation for UFOs and alleged encounters with aliens is that fallen angels are at work in the world. . . . If they can get a people wrapped up in theories of alien visitations and extraterrestrial visitors to earth; if they can get them absorbed and fascinated by any number of paranormal phenomena and distracted from God, they will have succeeded in their diabolical mission to deceive and destroy. . . . There is such a thing as extraterrestrial intelligence," he concludes. "These creatures really are from another world: the spiritual world. They're what we call angels."[21]

As an aside, we should note that a few contemporary spiritual writers make a similar identification of ETI and angels, but they turn the equation on its head. Instead of insisting that extraterrestrials encountered today are actually (fallen) angels in disguise, they believe that the angels described in ancient Scripture were actually extraterrestrials misunderstood by those who encountered them. For these writers, ETI accounts for the mystical apparitions and miraculous events recorded in the Bible. In this "Ancient Astronaut School" of thought, as Peters calls it, "UFOs are the form which divine providence and redemption take."[22]

Advocates Stoning for UFO Enthusiasts," Freedom Writer Press Release, Great Barrington, Mass. (28 July 1997).

[21] Dwight Longenecker, "Angels and Aliens," *Catholic Answers*, June 1, 2013, https://www.catholic.com/magazine/print-edition/angels-and -aliens.

[22] Peters, *Astrotheology*, 17–18. See also Wilkinson, *Search for Extraterrestrial Intelligence*, 119–25.

Finally, we should note that not all Christian writers who doubt the existence of ETI do so on theological grounds. After an extensive analysis of the relevant issues, the British astrophysicist/theologian David Wilkinson concludes: "As of the time of this writing, current scientific insights lead me to the tentative conclusion that we are alone as intelligent life in this Milky Way galaxy. . . . However, I want to remain open to the possibility of finding evidence for ETI."[23]

Four Tasks of Astrotheology

For those who "put out the welcome mat" to ETI, Peters envisions the discipline of astrotheology as having four tasks to accomplish:

First, theologians need to "reflect on the scope of creation and settle the pesky issue of geocentrism"—that is, the assumption that the Earth is the center of all things. "It is God, not Earth, who is the center of all reality," Peters insists. "And the circumference of reality as well."[24]

Second, "the astrotheologian should set the parameters within which the ongoing debates over Christology ([theology of the] Person of Christ) and soteriology ([theology of the] Work of Christ) are carried on." These debates will continue to address questions we have seen raised in earlier centuries: What possible types of spiritual and moral status might aliens, who are presumably not descended from Adam and Eve, possess in their relationship to God? What

---

[23] Wilkinson, *Search for Extraterrestrial Intelligence*, 173.
[24] Wilkinson, 41–44. The quote in this paragraph is in italics in the original.

might be the relationship of the earthly Incarnation of God the Son to intelligent species on other planets?[25]

Third, "theologians should analyze and critique astrobiology and related space sciences, exposing extra-scientific assumptions and interpreting the larger value of the scientific enterprise." Scientists often have "mistaken images" about Christian doctrine and the disposition of contemporary Christian believers toward the possibility of ETI. These need to be corrected.[26]

In addition, astrotheologians must sometimes correct the implicit assumptions and faulty reasoning that may frame scientists' discussions about ETI. Astrobiologists may be acting upon unexamined ideological commitments if they are atheists or assume that the material universe is all that exists.[27] We might add that they may even admit that some sort of God exists, yet reject out of hand any possibility of direct divine intervention through miracles, working outside of natural processes.[28]

---

[25] Wilkinson, 45.

[26] Wilkinson, 47.

[27] Wilkinson, 47. See, for an example of such an assumption (though explicitly admitted), Steven J. Dick's statement: "I begin with the assumption that the supernatural does not exist"; "Toward a Constructive Naturalistic Cosmotheology," in Peters, *Astrotheology*, 230.

[28] For an extensive debate about the nature of divine intervention in the universe in light of current scientific theory, see the six-volume series *Scientific Perspectives on Divine Action*, published jointly by the Vatican Observatory and The Center for Theology and the Natural Sciences. Titles include *Quantum Cosmology and the Laws of Nature* (1993); *Chaos and Complexity* (1995); *Evolutionary and Molecular Biology* (1998); *Neuroscience and the Person* (1999); *Quantum Mechanics* (2001); and *Scientific Perspectives on Divine Action: Twenty Years of Challenge and Progress* (2008).

Some scientists, Peters notes, may embrace *scientism*. Quoting the Indian geochemist Rustum Roy (a Christian): "*Scientism must be destroyed.* By *scientism* I mean the absurdly reductionist belief that all truth can be learned and all reality described through science (never defined) and only through science. 'Only' is what distinguishes scientism from what all of us in mainstream science believe about science."[29] Peters concludes that scientism "amounts to a belief in science alone, *sola scientifica*, a faith that science will triumph over all other competitors."

It often includes as well a messianic view of scientific knowledge, confidence that science will save us. In the specific case of astrobiology, this false hope is often reflected in the attitude that if extraterrestrial intelligences are more advanced in science and technology than we are, they must also be more advanced spiritually and morally. They can save us from ourselves.[30]

Fourth, Peters insists, "theologians and religious intellectuals should cooperate with leaders of multiple religious traditions and scientists to address ethical issues associated with space exploration and to prepare the public for the eventuality of extraterrestrial contact." Does extraterrestrial life have intrinsic value? What ethical principles would come into consideration in interaction with intelligent life? What issues should be thoroughly examined in preparation for our encounter with ETI?[31]

---

[29] Peters, *Astrotheology*, 21.

[30] Peters, *Astrotheology*, 21; see also Peters, "Extraterrestrial Salvation and the ETI Myth," 347–77.

[31] Peters, "Extraterrestrial Salvation and the ETI Myth," 50–53.

Departures from Traditional Belief

Twenty-first-century contributors to the conversation about ETI and Christian faith display a wide diversity of religious beliefs and assumptions. On one end of the spectrum are those whose positions depart significantly from certain traditional Christian beliefs. For example, the discussion of life's origin, and its likelihood on other planets, often presumes the non-interventionist view of God's action in the universe—the notion that God works in the cosmos only through natural causes.[32]

"To many, probably most, scientists, the 'special' creation of life by God has little credibility to begin with, and thus hardly needs further challenge," writes former Notre Dame philosopher Ernan McMullin. "But there are Christians, including some serious philosophers of religion, who, though willing to allow broad scope to evolution, argue that in view of the lack of any satisfactory theoretical account of such key transitions as the origin of the first cell, it is more likely in the Christian perspective to suppose that the Creator in such cases may have intervened to bridge what might otherwise be an unbridgeable gap."[33]

---

[32] See, for example, Robert John Russell, "Discovering ETI: What Are the Philosophical and Theological Implications?" in Peters, *Astrotheology*, 80, n. 30; Ernan McMullen, "Life and Intelligence Far From Earth: Formulating Theological Issues," in Steven J. Dick, ed., *Many Worlds: The New Universe, Extraterrestrial Life & the Theological Implications* (West Conshohocken, Penn.: Templeton Press, 2000), 155–56. The majority of contributors to the latter volume seem to assume the divine non-interventionist model and present some version of pantheism as the foundation of their ETI speculations.

[33] McMullen, "Life and Intelligence," in Dick, *Many Worlds*, 157–58. See also, for example, Christian de Duve, "Lessons of Life," in Dick,

Such a position apparently rules out not only the divine special creation of life but also the special creation of the individual soul, and even the possibility of miracles. McMullin posits that Saint Augustine can be interpreted to imply that "all that the created universe needs is there from the beginning, with no need for later miraculous supplementation on the Creator's part." As McMullin admits, though, Augustine insisted on the special creation of the individual soul, and we might add that the saint certainly believed in miracles.[34]

In speculating about the possible moral and spiritual status of extraterrestrials, McMullin reflects another common departure from tradition in recent ETI discussions when he delves into the doctrine of original sin. He suggests that he is not trying "to take sides in the debate" about that doctrine and the Genesis account of the fall in Eden. Yet he seems to dismiss "a relatively literal reading of the original [creation] myth and the belief that the entire course of human history would have been radically altered had an original couple happened to choose a virtuous God-directed course."[35]

"Radically New Conceptions of God"

A few contemporary contributors to the conversation about religion and ETI leave behind any recognizable form of Christian faith but still make it their point of departure. Steven J.

Many Worlds, 5. Oliver Putz speaks of the "'moderate evolutionism' of *Humani generis*, where the human body originates in pre-existent and living matter, while the soul comes directly from God"; see Putz, "God's Self-Communication," in Peters, *Astrotheology*, 173.

[34] McMullen, "Life and Intelligence," in Dick, *Many Worlds*, 156. See Augustine, *City of God*, XII, 8.

[35] McMullen, "Life and Intelligence," in Dick, *Many Worlds*, 167–69.

Dick, who is not a theologian but an historian, offers a "naturalistic" view that he terms "cosmotheology." It begins "with the assumption that the supernatural does not exist. . . .Cosmotheology must be open to radically new conceptions of God, not necessarily the God of the ancient Near East, nor the God of human imagination, but a God grounded in cosmic evolution. It is entirely possible that beings have evolved in the natural course of the universe with many of the traits we attribute to God, including omnipotence, omniscience, and so on. . . . It seems to me," Dick concludes, "that there is no need to use the loaded term 'God' for a naturally created process or for the universe itself."[36]

The astronomer Jill Cornell Tarter, who by her own admission is "a scientist and not a student of religions," writes about "the religions of the universe." The founding director of SETI's Project Phoenix, Tarter notes that any extraterrestrial civilization we might detect or even contact through the search for extraterrestrial intelligence "will be far older than we are." Displaying a remarkably uninformed and dismissive attitude toward all earthly traditional religions, she believes that "the detected, long-lived extraterrestrials either never had, or have outgrown, organized religion. . . . Based on our poor human example of religious intolerance, the existence of an old (tens of millions of years!) stable, technological civilization therefore implies a single [ETI] religion, devoid of factions and disputes, or no religion at all. If God exists, then a single, universal religion is the obvious possibility."

---

[36] Dick, "Cosmotheology," in Peters, *Astrotheology*, 230, 232, 234. It seems difficult to justify using a term that includes "theology" (which means literally "the study of God") for such a system of speculation.

If we hear from such enlightened ETI, Tarter insists, earthly "skeptics and true believers alike will be converted to the revealed, superior religion; even if its practices are at first repugnant. . . . In the face of a demonstrably stable social organization, and superior understanding of the nature of the universe, it will be hard for humanity to resist the appeal of this universal religion and its God(s)."[37]

These two non-theologians, who nevertheless attempt to construct a kind of theology, are cited here because they illustrate Peters's cases of the need for theology to critique science. Dick provides an example of ideological commitments (though not unexamined) that severely limit the usefulness of his analysis. Tarter's position, on the other hand, offers one version of "the ETI myth."

A Traditional Thomist Perspective

At the other end of the theological spectrum stands Marie I. George, an Aristotelian-Thomist professor of philosophy at St. John's University. Her thoroughly traditional Catholic perspective challenges the views of most other Christian authors, even Catholic ones, on the topic. She states explicitly at the outset: "Another shortcoming found in some Catholic authors is that they are quite willing to countenance interpretations of doctrines such as original sin which contradict Church teachings that are stated in official Church documents. I intend to address the matter of ETI existence while standing squarely within official Church teachings as found

---

[37] Jill Cornell Tartar, "SETI and the Religions of the Universe," in Dick, *Many Worlds*, 145–47.

in the papal encyclicals, [conciliar] documents, and the *Catechism of the Catholic Church.*"

When addressing matters not defined by the Magisterium of the Catholic Church, she relies on the guidance of the Fathers and Doctors of the Church, especially the works of Saint Thomas Aquinas. As a Thomist philosopher, she includes in her arguments from reason those based on what would be most "fitting" for God to do, as opposed to what would be "pointless" or "redundant."[38]

George insists, with Saint Thomas, that "there can be no conflict between faith and reason." For this reason, "the Catholic faith has no need to make concessions as to its teachings in order to withstand attacks from those who claim that ETI existence would spell the end of traditional religion."[39]

Two other characteristics of George's work set it apart from most other authors writing about ETI and Catholic faith: First, most others fail to address clearly the contrary arguments that have commonly been offered. Second, "they generally do not consider whether the passages of Scripture of a more cosmic bearing might not shed some light on the matter."[40]

Given these concerns, George sets two goals. First is "to be more exhaustive and explicit in the treatment of adversarial arguments." Second is "to look systematically through Scripture to see whether there are not passages relevant to the debate."[41] She works toward these goals with a detailed, methodical approach that students of Saint Thomas will find familiar.

---

[38] Marie I. George, *Christianity*, 3–4; 88–89.

[39] George, 4.

[40] George, 3.

[41] George, 3.

In light of reason, Scripture, Tradition, and magisterial teaching, George is convinced that certain possibilities with regard to ETI are improbable, though not impossible, while others are in fact ruled out. The existence of ETI she considers improbable, but not incompatible with Christian faith. However, if ETI exists, she has "serious reservations" about the existence of fallen extraterrestrial intelligences. Even so, because the Church has not officially taken a position on the matter, she thinks that "a person can be a good Catholic and adhere to all that the Catholic Church teaches, and still believe in fallen ETIs."[42]

George rules out other possibilities as well: that a race of unfallen ETI could be created "for purely natural happiness" rather than a supernatural life with God; that there could exist "redeemed ETIs who were not redeemed by Christ;" and that there could be multiple divine incarnations other than the Word's incarnation as a human being on Earth.[43]

George demonstrates an admirable humility in two regards. First, she recognizes that many of her arguments must posit a probability, not a certainty. Second, she adds that if the Catholic Church should pronounce authoritatively on the ETI issue in any of its aspects, she would accept that teaching and retract any views she has offered contrary to the Church's pronouncement.[44]

---

[42] George, 24, 40.

[43] George, 19–20, 182.

[44] George, 182.

Plenitude Revisited

While Marie George considers the existence of ETI improbable, the German theologian/biologist Oliver Putz argues that "there are legitimate theological reasons why we should *expect* sentient life to exist on other planets." Drawing from the teaching of the Franciscan theologian/philosopher John Duns Scotus (1265/66–1308) and a "theology of becoming" of Karl Rahner, Putz reasons: "God as transcendent cause moves creation toward the emergence of a range of self-conscious beings capable of experiencing the transcendent and, thus, of being in personal relationship with it. The universe is bound for life[,] and once present, biological diversity will eventually lead to spiritual multiplicity."

Putz confesses that his thesis may sound "outlandish," but it makes sense in light of the very nature of God, Who "creates out of love and for creation to exist in this love. Such a God might indeed warrant creatures capable of love to emerge on more than one average blue planet in a vast universe filled with potentially billions of habitable worlds."[45]

We have seen how in earlier centuries the principle of plenitude played a role in the conversation about extraterrestrial intelligence—"the premise that due to the nature of God, everything that can be will be, including ETI." Putz sees his position as "a weak version" of this principle. Though he does "not think that God's omnipotence necessitates the creation of everything possible," he proposes that God's nature as all-good, loving, and self-giving presses creation to move

---

[45] Oliver Putz, "God's Self-Communication in a Cosmos Bound for Love," in Peters, *Astrotheology*, 161–63.

toward "multiple beings that can respond to the divine self-gift in an otherwise free process of becoming."[46]

Purely Natural Happiness?

Not surprisingly, twenty-first-century Christian writers on ETI hold a variety of positions on several other issues critical to the discussion. With regard to the possibility of ETI species created for purely natural happiness rather than a supernatural life with God, the Cistercian theologian Roch A. Kereszty would disagree with George, who rejects that possibility: "We could conceive of intelligent beings who did not sin and were not called to that intimate participation in the Son as humans and angels [are called]. Nevertheless, since they, too, are spiritual beings, they, too, can find fulfillment and happiness only in some form of personal communion with God through his Son."[47]

Can we expect ETI to be fallen or unfallen? George rejects the possibility of fallen ETI. Wilkinson offers that "our best guess is that ETIs will resemble the ambiguous human condition—good, fallen, and looking for grace."[48] O'Meara thinks that "there is no reason to think that evil exists anywhere necessarily." He opposes the notion, common among "modern philosophers, devout believers, scientists, and

---

[46] Putz, in Peters, 161–62. For a similar Franciscan perspective on ETI, see Ilia Delio, "Christ and Extraterrestrial Life," *Theology and Science*, 5:3 (2007), https://www.tandfonline.com/doi/abs/10.1080/147467007 01622008?journalCode=rtas20.

[47] Kereszty, *Jesus Christ*, 448.

[48] Wilkinson, *Search for Extraterrestrial Intelligence*, 163.

artists" that evil is "the necessary result of someone having intelligence and freedom."[49]

Multiple Divine Incarnations?

On the matter of multiple divine Incarnations, O'Meara also disagrees with George, who rules out the possibility. O'Meara asks: "Could not God become incarnate as God wished? The divine motive for fashioning a universe of galaxies is God's goodness; the same motive brings incarnation. As incarnation is an intense form of divine love, would there not be galactic forms of that love?" He concludes: "An infinite being of generosity would tend to many incarnations rather than one."[50]

The Catholic theologian Peter M. J. Hess posits not only multiple incarnations but an incarnation for *every* intelligent species in the cosmos: "If multiple societies of extraterrestrial intelligent beings on exoplanets exist, we can predict that God will [provide] or already has provided a species-specific incarnation for each planet parallel to God's incarnation in Jesus Christ on Earth."[51] Robert John Russell, a seminary theology professor and coeditor of the scholarly journal *Theology and Science*, agrees.[52]

---

[49] O'Meara, *Vast Universe*, 25–26.

[50] O'Meara, 47.

[51] Peter M. J. Hess, "Multiple Incarnations of the One Christ," in Peters, *Astrotheology*, 317.

[52] Robert John Russell, "Many Incarnations or One?" in Peters, *Astrotheology*, 303–16.

Deep Incarnation

Those theologians who reject the notion of multiple divine incarnations typically consider them unnecessary because of God's saving activity on Earth. In God's singular incarnation as a human being on our planet, He has not only joined human nature to Himself; He has joined to Himself the nature of the entire universe as well.

To make this argument, they may embrace a notion that Niels Henrik Gregersen, a Danish Lutheran theologian, has called "deep incarnation." "God's incarnation," he insists, "also reaches into the depths of material existence."[53] In the person of Jesus, God took on the matter, energy, and history of all creation, from quarks to galaxies.

Citing this perspective, Ted Peters concludes that "the one incarnation of God in the Jesus of Earth's history will suffice for the entire cosmos."[54] José G. Funes, a former Director of the Vatican Observatory, reasons that "Jesus became God-in-the flesh only once. The Incarnation is a unique event in the history of the whole universe, or even every other universe if the multiverse exists."[55]

Philosopher/theologian Joshua M. Moritz agrees: "I side with those who claim that the one incarnation of God in Christ is efficacious for all sentient creatures wherever and whenever they live." He finds a sympathetic theme of cosmic

---

[53] Niels Hendrik Gregersen, "Deep Incarnation: Why Evolutionary Continuity Matters in Christology," *Toronto Journal of Theology* 26:2 (2010), 179–87, quoted in Peters, "One Incarnation or Many?" in *Astrotheology*, 293.

[54] Peters, "One Incarnation or Many?" 295

[55] José G. Funes, "The Road Map to Other Earths: Lessons Learned and Challenges Ahead," in Peters, *Astrotheology*, 69.

redemption through Christ in Church Fathers such as Saint Athanasius, Saint Irenaeus, and the Cappadocians.[56] That ancient Patristic tradition also resonates with Fr. George Coyne, SJ, another former director of the Vatican Observatory, who embraces the idea that "all creation, even the inanimate, participates in some way in [Christ's] redemption."[57]

On this particular issue, McMullin takes the middle road. "We can see that Christian theologians would be far from agreement as to whether we should expect . . . that the Creator would become incarnate in a member of [a] distant race. Their answers could range . . . from 'yes, certainly' to 'certainly not.' My own preference would be for a cautious 'maybe.'"[58]

A Lively Renewal of the Conversation

The twenty-first century has witnessed, already in its early decades, a lively renewal of the ETI conversation within the Catholic and broader Christian community. As we have seen, a few contemporary contributors reject the possibility of intelligent extraterrestrials outright, but the majority range from a cautious openness to an enthusiastic embrace of the pluralist position. Age-old debates continue to rage over the particulars, while new scientific theories are cited to challenge traditional understandings of certain Christian beliefs.

Now that we are up to date on the centuries-long ETI conversation, we can approach our final task. The historical

---

[56] Joshua M. Moritz, "One *Imago Dei* and the Incarnation of the Eschatological Adam," in Peters, *Astrotheology*, 330–46.
[57] George Coyne, "Evolution of Intelligent Life on Earth and Possibly Elsewhere: Reflections From a Religious Tradition," in Dick, *Many Worlds*, 187.
[58] McMullen, "Life and Intelligence," in Dick, *Many Worlds*, 173.

figures we have surveyed have made us familiar with the importance and seriousness of the subject, the central questions to be addressed, and the fascinating range of possible answers to those questions. I will shift now to speak in the first person singular as I attempt, with some trepidation, to lay out the broad lines of a Catholic theology of extraterrestrial intelligence as I would propose it. Given the often-contentious nature of the subject, I pray that I can do so with proper humility, civility, discernment, and faithfulness to the authoritative Catholic tradition.

II

A Contribution to the
ETI Conversation

10

"Nothing Is Impossible with God"

Is ETI Compatible with Catholic Faith?

"The things which they . . . rule out as impossible,
[God] plainly shows to be possible; that which they
deride as unfitting, his goodness makes most fit."

—Pope Saint Leo the Great[1]

THE LIFE OF *Paul the Hermit* was written in the year 374 or 375 by Saint Jerome (c. 342–420). We read there that Saint Anthony the Great was on a journey through the desert to find Saint Paul of Thebes. Jerome offered a fascinating account of an encounter Anthony had at that time with a satyr.

Satyrs are one of many creatures portrayed by the ancients but now considered mythical. At the time, however, many of Jerome's contemporaries still believed them to be real, inhabiting the Earth alongside the human race. Jerome reported that the satyr was a manlike creature, but with "a hooked snout, horned forehead, and extremities like goats' feet."

---

[1]   Saint Leo the Great, "Sermon 26, Feast of the Nativity," in *St. Leo the Great: Sermons*, trans. Jane Freeland and Agnes Conway (Washington, D.C.: Catholic University of America Press, 1996), 3.

When Anthony asked him who he was, the rather friendly satyr replied: "I am a mortal being and one of those inhabitants of the desert whom the Gentiles deluded by various forms of error worship under the names of Fauns, Satyrs, and Incubi. I am sent to represent my tribe." Then he entreated Anthony to pray for him, because his fellows had heard that Christ had come to Earth and that the gospel was being proclaimed throughout the world.

Anthony shed tears of joy and marveled that "beasts speak of Christ." Then the satyr departed quickly.[2]

Non-Human, Non-Angelic Intelligences

This story has a particular significance for a Christian discussion of ETI. Though the satyr was not extraterrestrial (today he might be designated "other terrestrial" or "ultraterrestrial"), he represented a form of non-human, non-angelic intelligence. And Saint Jerome believed that such creatures actually existed.

Someone might respond that perhaps Jerome was simply retelling the story as he heard it without attempting to "demythologize" it, even though he did not believe in such things himself. But Jerome went on to say in his account: "Let no one scruple to believe this incident; its truth is supported by what took place when [the Emperor] Constantine was on the throne [only forty-some-odd years before, about the time Jerome was born], a matter of which the whole world was witness. For a man [creature] of that kind was brought alive to Alexandria and shown as a wonderful sight to the people. Afterwards his

---

2   Saint Jerome, *The Life of Paul the Hermit*, 8, https://www.newadvent .org/fathers/3008.htm.

lifeless body, to prevent its decay through the summer heat, was preserved in salt and brought to Antioch that the Emperor might see it."[3] Jerome thus left no doubt that he believed the creature was real and the incident truly took place.

Our point here is not to claim that satyrs are real. Our point is that Saint Jerome apparently had no problem believing in the existence of non-human, non-angelic intelligences. This is the same Jerome who was one of the best educated of the Church Fathers, the one now known as "the father of biblical scholarship." He wrote numerous scriptural commentaries and was the primary creator of the Latin Bible translation called the Vulgate, which served the Catholic Church (with some revisions) until modern times.

If anyone knew exhaustively, and embraced heartily, the Scripture and the Church's Tradition, it was Saint Jerome. And if such a brilliant, devout, and well-catechized Catholic Christian saw no conflict between his faith and the existence of intelligent creatures neither human nor angelic, we need not fear that such an openness is somehow foolish or heretical. The possibility is well worth considering as we think about intelligent life on other worlds.

My Theological Orientation

First, a few words about my theological orientation in this age-old conversation. I am a Catholic Christian who seeks to understand all of life in the light of the Catholic faith. Some may consider that my approach is characterized accordingly by "blind faith," but that simply is not the case.

---

[3]   Saint Jerome, 8.

I am a Catholic Christian not by birth, but by conviction. I was once an atheist, but my continual questioning in a pursuit of truth through reason and experience led me to become a convinced Christian. Some time later, the same pursuit led me to enter the Catholic Church. It was not at all a matter of "blind faith."

Once I was convinced that the Church speaks authoritatively for Jesus Christ, I could see how the world makes more sense than I had ever before imagined in light of her teaching. And my trust in her teaching, even when what she says is not directly accessible to my reason and experience, is a reasonable trust, not a blind one. Given this foundation, my consideration of the issues related to extraterrestrial intelligence will attempt to be faithful to the Church's Sacred Scripture, Sacred Tradition, and the definitive teaching of the Sacred Magisterium.

My Primary Goal

As I noted in the introduction, my primary goal in this work is rather focused. I am not seeking to prove that ETI exists, or that UAP are undeniable evidence that it exists. (My opinions about UAP are presented in the appendix, "What About UFOs?") My primary goal is to show that if ETI exists, that reality would not be incompatible with Catholic Christian faith. The Catholic Church could accommodate such a reality in her understanding of the world, just as she has so many other scientific discoveries and developments throughout history, and she could do so without being unfaithful to the deposit of faith she has received from her Lord.

Humility requires that we avoid speaking beyond what we can know. For this reason, much of what I propose here will have to do with possibilities rather than certainties or even probabilities. Though certain fundamentals of our faith do seem to rule out at least a few possibilities with regard to ETI, I believe that those fundamental realities actually allow for more possibilities than many have recognized.

Scientific Considerations

In this conversation, humility is essential with regard not only to theology but also to science and technology as well. I am not a scientist. Yet I know that even scientists must admit the limits of what science is capable of determining; they must avoid *scientism*, as we defined it in an earlier chapter.

They must also recognize that history shows us how scientific paradigms, especially with regard to cosmology, are fluid and speculative. Much of what was once considered "settled science" is no longer such. In a similar way, technological developments continue to amaze us. What was once thought impossible technologically is now known to be possible.

As I also noted in the introduction, for these reasons, I have not attempted to argue the existence of ETI, or even the probability of its existence, on the basis of current science. Even if scientists today agreed on such matters—and they most certainly do not—the scientists of tomorrow might move in a dramatically different direction. The same is true with regard to space travel, which enters into the conversation when we speak of the possibility of interplanetary encounter. Though we obviously lack at the present the technology to travel extreme astronomical distances within a single human lifetime, we cannot demonstrate conclusively that such travel is impossible.

If the day comes—and it may—when scientists are able to demonstrate through convincing empirical evidence that ETI exists, or even that extraterrestrials have visited the Earth, then science will have settled the issue conclusively. In the meantime, however, science cannot prove the opposite. Remember the adage: Absence of evidence is not (conclusive) evidence of absence.

Philosophical Considerations

We must note that philosophers have also made valuable contributions to the ETI discussion. As the Thomist philosopher Marie George has noted, they can clarify the proper boundaries of science and religion; make useful distinctions, especially among the different meanings of words; separate good arguments from fallacious ones; and make arguments based on natural reason.[4]

Yet again, humility is essential here, especially when philosophy overlaps theology. In the ETI debates, philosophers admit that they often must argue for probabilities, not certainties. Their arguments may involve terms whose definitions can be disputed, such as "human," or are admittedly subjective, such as "fitting" or "more perfect."

The notion of what is "fitting" or "unfitting" for God to do is especially problematic. Few among Jesus's contemporaries would have considered it "fitting" of God to become a Man, and most considered it decidedly "unfitting" for the

---

[4] George, *Christianity*, 5–6. George's analysis has been extremely helpful to me.

God-Man to suffer and die an ignominious death on the Cross. Yet that is precisely what God did.

As Pope Saint Leo the Great put it when he wrote about the divine Incarnation on Earth: "The things which they, as men, rule out as impossible, [God] plainly shows to be possible; that which they deride as unfitting, his goodness makes most fit."[5]

Those philosophical traditions that rely heavily on inductive reasoning from observation will find themselves at a disadvantage in ETI discussions, where the only observable evidence available to us presently is limited to one planet and one (human) species. Aristotle could define the human being, for example, as a "rational animal" because, within the earthly bounds of his observations, he found only one animal that seemed to have a rational intellect. That one qualifier was enough, he concluded, to distinguish the species from other animals, and thus to define it. If he had encountered extraterrestrial intelligences, however, he might well have had to redefine humans as "terrestrial rational animals," or in some other way, to distinguish them from the ETI.

Some scientists may have a similar problem: When they rely so heavily on inductive observations on Earth about the possibilities for intelligent life, they may assume that all extraterrestrial life must have certain characteristics resembling ours. Even some theologians have concluded, for example, that the moral evil on display in humankind must be characteristic of all ETI life as well. One day, philosophers, scientists, and theologians may all discover that a wider array of available inductive evidence will press them to recognize new possibilities.

---

5   Leo the Great, Sermons, 3.

Principles of Scriptural Interpretation

The witness of Scripture must be examined in any discussion of ETI in the light of Christian faith. But as Marie George has noted, many Christian theologians writing about ETI seem to have ignored Scripture. At the same time, certain principles of biblical interpretation (hermeneutics) must be considered. Here are a few of the principles I will attempt to keep in mind.

First, a basic rule of interpretation: Human language (even when conveying Divine Revelation) inevitably includes certain words with more than one possible meaning. So we cannot assume that a biblical term means the same thing in all the passages where it occurs—not only passages in various books of the Bible, but even various passages within the same book of the Bible.

Consequently, we must consider carefully the context of these terms. For example, several theological arguments about ETI that I have encountered seem to have confused the various meanings of such biblical terms as "world" and "flesh" and even "all." The resulting confusion undermines such arguments.

Second, the Scriptures were written for human beings to reveal certain truths about God, the human condition, and the redeeming activity of God on our behalf—what we call "salvation history." As the *Catechism of the Catholic Church* describes it: "The books of Scripture firmly, faithfully, and without error teach *that truth which God for the sake of our salvation*, wished to see confided to the Sacred Scriptures."[6]

---

[6] *Catechism of the Catholic Church*, 2nd ed. (Vatican City: Libreria Editrice Vaticana, 1997), par. 107; emphasis added. From here forward cited as "*CCC.*"

Our salvation does not depend on knowing the truth about the existence of ETI, so we would not expect it necessarily to appear in the Bible. The truth about angels, on the other hand, is in fact a part of our salvation history and thus included in the biblical witness.

Third, we cannot assume that the scope of every passage in Scripture is cosmic. A few particular passages do seem to be intentionally cosmic in scope, so they must be examined carefully. But most can easily be read as pertaining simply to God's dealing with the human race, the human condition, human history, or an earthly setting. Such a reading is reasonable given the focus of the Sacred Text.

Fourth, the Bible is not a catalog of everything in existence, nor is it intended to be. It has no reference to microbes or molecules, planets or pulsars, dinosaurs or duck-billed platypuses. Yet we know from science that all these things do in fact exist, so the absence of something in the biblical account is obviously no proof of non-existence.

Sacred Tradition and Magisterium

The principles for interpreting Scripture apply as well to Catholic Tradition and the Magisterium. We must keep in mind the intention, the scope, and the historical context of Divine Revelation as it comes to us through the formal pronouncements of popes and councils and is interpreted through the teaching of the Fathers and Doctors of the Church. The difference in authority between the constant and apostolic Tradition of the Church on the one hand, and the multiple traditions of belief passed down on the other hand (sometimes in tension among themselves), must also be recognized.

One authority on Catholic teaching which we have quoted, and to which we will refer often, is the *Catechism of the Catholic Church*. The *Catechism* was presented to the Church by Pope Saint John Paul II in 1994 as an "authoritative exposition of the one and perennial apostolic faith" and "a sure norm for teaching the truth" (apostolic letter *Laetamur Magnopere*). It quotes and cites numerous biblical and magisterial sources, as well as the Fathers and Doctors of the Church. The *Catechism* serves, then, as a useful and reliable summary of Catholic belief, though the Church does not hold the document to be infallible.

We need to remember as well that even the formal pronouncements of the Magisterium do not all carry the same authoritative weight. The explicit certainty of dogmatic definitions is rather limited, and various types of papal and conciliar documents possess a range of authority.[7] This variety of sources means that even though we cannot simply ignore or dismiss the Church's teaching, neither can we view every formal document of the Church (much less remarks in private papal correspondence) as infallible dogma if it is not intended to be such a document.

Finally, as I noted in the introduction, if the Catholic Church should issue a definitive statement as an instance of Divine Revelation on any of the matters discussed in the present work, I would gladly embrace that truth and abandon anything to the contrary that I have proposed. Such is my confidence in the reliability of the Church's explicitly

---

[7]   See Congregation for the Doctrine of the Faith, "Doctrinal Commentary on the Concluding Formula of the *Professio Fidei*," http://www.ewtn.com/library/CURIA/CDFADTU.HTM.

definitive teaching. But I expect that no such statement will be forthcoming; the existence of ETI is at this point a matter for science to determine, if possible. And the related theological issues arising from such a scientific determination would depend largely on the actual characteristics of the extraterrestrials we would encounter.

The Primary Question

Given these fundamentals for the discussion, we can move on to the primary question to be addressed: *Is the existence of extraterrestrial intelligence compatible with the Catholic Christian faith?*

My answer is a firm yes, though with some theological qualifications. At the broadest level, the truth that allows this possibility reflects the nature of God Himself. "With God all things are possible" (Mt 19:26). "Then Job answered the LORD, 'I know that you can do all things'" (Job 42:2).

Recall that some medieval Scholastic philosophers were publicly rebuked by the bishop of Paris for insisting that God could not make multiple worlds. After all, came the response, He is omnipotent, all-powerful. He can do as He wills.

Only two types of action, we should note, are impossible to God: First, He cannot act contrary to His own nature, which is wholly good. Second, He cannot do what is nonsense because it involves an inherent self-contradiction (such as creating a stone so heavy that He Himself cannot lift it). The *Catechism* explains (with a quote from Saint Thomas Aquinas): "We believe that his might is universal, for God who created everything also rules everything and can do everything. . . . Nothing is impossible with God, who disposes his works according to his will. He is the Lord of the universe, whose order he established and which remains wholly subject to him and at his disposal. . . . God's power is in no way arbitrary. 'In God, power, essence, will, intellect, wisdom, and justice are all identical. Nothing therefore can be in God's power which could not be in his just will or his wise intellect.'"[8]

This reality helps us to see how one possibility is ruled out by our faith: There can be no creature in existence, ETI or otherwise, that was not created by God for His glory or is not subject to God's purpose and lordship. "Worthy are you, our Lord and God, . . . for you created all things, and by your will they existed and were created" (Rv 4:11).

We should note that because God, who is Truth Himself, cannot act contrary to His own nature, His Revelation to us will be truthful and cannot contradict itself. This is why His Revelation to the human race must be considered carefully when discerning the issues surrounding ETI. It will set some boundaries for the possibilities. The challenge, however, is of course to discern the true meaning of what God has said, a task that is often difficult.

Not only is it possible for God to create extraterrestrial intelligences; we can also see how their existence could glorify Him and bring Him pleasure, just as the existence of humans and angels do. The *Catechism* declares that "the world was made for the glory of God."[9] "The heavens are telling the glory of God; and the firmament proclaims his handiwork" simply by reflecting the excellence of his wisdom, beauty, and power (Ps 19:1). How much greater, then, is what theologians

---

[8] *CCC* 268–69. The quote is from Saint Thomas, *ST*, I, 25, 5, ad 1.
[9] *CCC* 293.

have called the "formal glory of God," the knowledge and praise of His goodness by intelligent creatures.

Plenitude vs. Redundancy

Some philosophical and theological debates about the existence of ETI have focused on the notions of *plenitude* and *redundancy*. Plenitude, as we saw in earlier chapters, was the notion that—judging from God's creativity as we observe it on Earth—we would expect Him to create a vast diversity in life forms, including intelligent ones, across the universe, filling it. The more, the merrier!

As Saint Thomas concluded, such diversity is itself a reflection of God's own fullness and perfection, Who communicated His goodness through His creation. "Because [his goodness] cannot be adequately represented through one creature, he produces many and diverse creatures, so that what is lacking in one for the purpose of representing divine goodness, is filled up by others." In this way, "the whole universe more perfectly shares in and represents divine goodness" than any one creature.[10]

In reply, some skeptics of ETI would insist that the principle of redundancy would apply here instead. It would be redundant for God to create more than one embodied intelligent species, and intelligent agents do not engage in repetition without reason.

We could reply to the skeptics that God might well have His reasons (unknown to us) for creating "redundant"

---

[10] Aquinas, *Summa Contra Gentiles*, IV, 53 (hereafter SCG), quoted in George, *Christianity*, 80. George offers a useful overview of this debate in chapter 5, "Plenitude or Redundancy?" 79–89.

intelligent species throughout the universe. In any case, they would probably not be creatures exactly identical with us, and they might have varying missions and destinies in the tapestry of providence, so that they would not truly be redundant. In his imitable way, G. K. Chesterton has speculated:

> Because children have abounding vitality, because they are in spirit fierce and free, therefore they want things repeated and unchanged. They always say, "Do it again"; and the grown-up person does it again until he is nearly dead. For grown-up people are not strong enough to exult in monotony. But perhaps God is strong enough to exult in monotony. . . . It may not be automatic necessity that makes all daisies alike; it may be that God makes every daisy separately, but has never got tired of making them. It may be that he has the eternal appetite of infancy; for we have sinned and grown old, and our Father is younger than we.

"The repetition in Nature may not be a mere recurrence," Chesterton concludes; "it may be a theatrical *encore*."[11] Perhaps God simply would take pleasure in creating a multiplicity of intelligent species!

In any case, arguments about plenitude and redundancy ultimately have to do with perceived *probabilities* regarding divine action, not certainties. Since I am dealing only with possibilities here, I will not try to make either argument. Even so, if someone should try to argue that according to one of these principles, God either *must* have created ETI or

---

[11] G. K. Chesterton, *Orthodoxy* (London: John Lane, 1908), 33–34.

cannot have created ETI (some have done so), then we must reply that the argument fails: Once again, God is omnipotent and sovereign, and He can act, or not act, as He wills.

Response to Objections

As we have seen in earlier chapters, some Christian writers have answered the question about ETI existence with a firm *no*. It is impossible. We must recall again their objections to determine how we might respond.

One common objection has been that extraterrestrial intelligences (embodied ones) are not referenced in Scripture. We can respond to this concern easily by noting again that Scripture is clearly not a catalog of all things in existence. God included in Scripture truths we need for the sake of our salvation, and the existence of ETI is not among those truths.

Saint Thomas Aquinas, citing Saint Augustine, once responded to the concern raised by some that the angels are not mentioned explicitly in the Genesis creation account. He suggested that God at that time kept hidden the reality of such exalted beings because the people Moses was teaching in this setting were prone to idolatry. So knowledge of the angels at that point in salvation history might have given them an occasion to stumble. In fact, the worship of angels was a problem recognized centuries later by the first Christians (see Col 2:18).

Given that some UAP enthusiasts have embraced the notion of "our space brothers" as messianic figures come to save our planet, could we have a parallel situation with regard to extraterrestrial intelligence? Perhaps God has remained silent in His Revelation about the reality of ETI because a premature disclosure could pose a stumbling block to those who are unprepared for the knowledge.[12]

A second objection, though less common, is that belief in extraterrestrial intelligence throughout Christian history stems from sloppy logic (God *can* make ETI, therefore He *has*) and a pagan metaphysical stance (atomism). If we argue that ETI existence is simply a possibility that is compatible with Christian faith, rather than a given, the claim about sloppy logic does not apply. Meanwhile, the extensive history of the ETI debate presented in earlier chapters of the present work should lay to rest the second claim. In fact, we can easily demonstrate that it was actually the pagan (and in this particular regard, mistaken) metaphysics of Aristotle that influenced so many Christians to reject the notion of a plurality of worlds for so long.

A third objection, again less common, is that all claims about the existence of ETI have diabolical origins. As we have noted, this position seems to arise from the concerns that many alleged UAP encounters, especially claims of alien abduction, resemble phenomena of the past which have traditionally been identified as demonic in nature. Even some secular researchers have observed the similarities.[13]

Our response must be that some alleged ETI encounters do in fact appear to be diabolical in origin, with the classic characteristics of demonic visitations: physical injury and

---

[12] Aquinas, *Summa* I 61.1 obj. 1 and ad 1. Cf. *De Substantiis Separatis*, c. 17, cited in Marie I. George, "Aquinas on Intelligent Extra-Terrestrial Life," *The Thomist* 65:2 (April 2001), 239–58. I owe to George the idea for this possible parallel.

[13] See, for example, Carl Sagan, *The Demon-Haunted World: Science as a Candle in the Dark* (New York: Random House, 1995), 124.

illness; sexual molestation; intrusive, disturbing thoughts and images; and perhaps most tellingly, false "revelations" about spiritual realities. But we simply cannot generalize from such cases, if they do in fact involve the activity of fallen angels, to deny the possibility of ETI altogether, or even the possibility of ETI encounters. The reasoning we offer here is not based on the nature of any particular UAP experiences.

The Special Status of the Human Race

A fourth common objection, with several aspects, is this: The Catholic (and broader Christian) tradition teaches that humans have a special status in God's creation. The concern is that our status would be contradicted or diminished by the existence of other intelligent species. This status is characterized by several traits as summarized by the *Catechism* (with quotes from conciliar documents and a Church Father), along with certain biblical texts.

First, humans "occupy a unique place in creation" in that they bear the *imago Dei*, the "image of God," as the opening chapter of Genesis declares (Gen 1:27).[14] This divine image sets them apart from other creatures and gives them a greater dignity.

The exact nature of the divine image in the human person has long been debated.[15] Saint Thomas noted that the image of God referenced in Genesis indicated the special

---

[14] *CCC* 355.

[15] See D. J. Clines, "Humanity as the Image of God," in *On the Way to the Postmodern: Old Testament Essays, 1967–1998* (Sheffield: Sheffield Academic Press, 1998).

characteristic "by which man excels all animals," namely "reason and intellect."[16] (Compare Aristotle's definition of the human being as a "rational animal.") Such an intellect implies capacities beyond simple reasoning: consciousness, free will, conscience, memory, imagination, emotionality, creativity, and more (see Ws 9:1–3; Sir 17:1–12).

Another aspect of the divine image comes into view when the *Catechism* describes the properties of the soul in particular: It is "created immediately by God" and is "*immortal.*" Though the body dies, the soul lives forever, and one day will be "reunited with the body at the final Resurrection" of the dead.[17] "God created man for incorruption, and made him *in the image of his own eternity*" (Ws 2:23, emphasis added).

In most popular usage today, the "soul" is considered to be something possessed only by human beings. But in the Aristotelian (and thus Thomist) philosophical tradition, *soul* was the general term for the principle of life in each type of living creatures—the "root" of their vital activity. In this view, animals and even plants have a "soul" of sorts, given that they are living things, and they possess an animating principle as long as they are alive. But when they die, their particular kinds of soul cannot survive apart from the matter that makes up their bodies.[18]

On the other hand, human beings have as their soul, their principle of life, an *immortal spirit* that will never cease to exist. This immortal nature of their souls is a special gift from God,

---

[16] St. Thomas Aquinas, *ST* III, iiii, 1 ad 2.

[17] Clines, *Postmodern* , 366.

[18] See "Soul (Scholastic)," in Dagobert D. Runes, ed. *The Dictionary of Philosophy* (New York: Philosophical Library, 1942), 296; Attwater, "Soul," 470–71.

an essential aspect of His image in human beings. Human beings are ordered to, created for, called to the life of perfect blessedness in heaven with God, seeing Him Face to face for all eternity: what we call the Beatific Vision. Only a creature with an immortal spirit could have such a final destiny.

Finally, we should note that according to Catholic tradition, our first parents were granted not only supernatural grace—the very life of God within them—but also preternatural gifts. The latter gifts were above and beside the powers, capacities, and requirements of their nature, but not all of created nature. For example, they had perfect self-mastery; they were immune from suffering and death as long as they remained in friendship with God.[19]

Humankind, the Summit

A second way in which humans have a special status in creation is that we stand within a "hierarchy of creatures," as the *Catechism* calls it, where we represent "*the summit* of the Creator's work" (*CCC* 342, 343; citing Genesis chapter 1; emphasis in the original).

Third, "God created everything for man . . . 'that great and wonderful living creature, more precious in the eyes of God than all other living creatures. For him the heavens and the earth, the sea and all the rest of the creation exist."[20]

---

[19] *CCC* 376–77; Zubek, "Theological Questions," 395.
[20] *CCC* 358. Cf. The Vatican II document *Gaudium et spes* 12, 1; 24, 3; 39, 1 in *Vatican Council II: The Conciliar and Post Conciliar Documents*, vol. 1, ed. Austin Flannery, rev. ed. (Grand Rapids, Mich.: Eerdmans, 1992). The quote is from St. John Chrysostom, *In Gen. Sermo II*, 1.

Fourth, the human race thus has "dominion" over the material created world: "For you [LORD] have made him [humankind] little less than the angels, and you have crowned him with glory and honor. You have given him dominion over the works of your hands; you have put all things under his feet" (Ps 8:5–6).

Fifth, God "established him [humankind] in his friendship."[21] God knows us intimately and cares for us faithfully: "O LORD, you have searched me and known me! You know when I sit down and when I rise up; you discern my thoughts from afar" (Ps 139:1–2). Divine providence has made special provisions in caring for the human race, through His action in our salvation history—most especially, through the Incarnation of His divine Son. "And the Word became flesh and dwelt among us, full of grace and truth" (Jn 1:14).

Finally, God has a special destiny for the human race that involves all creation. "At the end of time . . . the universe itself will be renewed. . . . At that time, together with the human race, the universe itself, which is so closely related to man and which attains its destiny through him, will be perfectly established in Christ."[22]

"Then I saw a new heaven and a new earth. . . . And I saw the holy city, new Jerusalem [the Church], coming down out of heaven from God" (Rv 21:1–2). "For the creation waits with eager longing for the revealing of the sons of God . . . the creation itself will be set free from its bondage to

---

[21] *CCC* 355.
[22] *CCC* 1042. Cf. the Vatican II document *Lumen Gentium* 48 in Flannery, *Vatican Council II*.

decay and obtain the glorious liberty of the children of God" (Rom 8:19, 21).

For all these reasons, then, some Christians have concluded that ETI cannot exist because of this special human status before God. Meanwhile, some skeptics of the Christian faith have insisted that not only the possibility of ETI, but even the certainty of Earth's astronomical insignificance in terms of physical size and location, is enough to disprove the notion that the human race is uniquely significant.

Would ETI Compromise Our Special Status?

To address this objection, we must first define terms.

The word *special* can have several shades of related meaning. Those that seem relevant to the ETI discussion might be these: "distinguished by some unusual quality, especially being in some way superior"; "held in particular esteem"; "unique"; "designed for a particular purpose or occasion."[23]

The term *unique* can mean "being the only one; sole"; "unequaled"; "peculiar"; or in a weaker sense, simply "unusual."[24]

Given these meanings, we can of course see how the human race does indeed have a special, even unique, status before God among the creatures of the Earth. In the various ways just specified, humankind is sole, peculiar, unequaled, distinguished by unusual qualities, superior, held in particular esteem by God, designed for a particular purpose by God. But is the human

---

[23] "Special," *Merriam-Webster Dictionary* online, https://www.merriam-webster.com/dictionary/special.

[24] "Unique," *Merriam-Webster Dictionary* online, https://www.merriam-webster.com/dictionary/unique.

race special or even unique in these ways among *all* the creatures of the universe, or simply among all *earthly* creatures?

Focused on Our Planet

In general, I think we can say, the scope of reference for the statements here in the *Catechism*—and for the relevant biblical texts and quotes from esteemed teachers of the Church as well—is limited to Earth. Most of these texts do not seem to have a cosmic scope in mind; they are focused, rather, on the realities on our planet.

For example, recall how the *Catechism* says that one of the ways "man occupies a unique place of creation" is that he is made "in the image of God." Yet Catholic tradition teaches that angels, too, are made in God's image.[25] So the scope of the statement cannot be universal; it must be limited to earthly creatures, even though that narrower scope is not made explicit.

The words that follow bear out this conclusion by making the limited, terrestrial scope explicit: When expanding on the notion of the "image of God," the *Catechism* goes on to declare that humankind is "the only creature *on earth* that God has willed for its own sake."[26] *Gaudium et spes*, the Vatican II document being cited here, in reference to humanity's special dominion over other creatures also states explicitly that the human race "was appointed by [God] as master of all *earthly* creatures."[27]

---

[25] See Aquinas, *ST* I, q. 93, art. 3.

[26] *CCC* 356, emphasis added.

[27] Quotes are from *Gaudium et spes*, 12, 3; 24, 3; emphasis added.

We can reasonably argue, then, that such statements, omitting the words "on earth" or "earthly," do so because the entire universe is presumably not in view here. Perhaps the authors of the *Catechism* did not repeat this qualification for the sake of brevity. Such ambiguity prevents us from concluding that these statements either affirm or reject the claim that humans are the only creatures in the material universe (that is, the universe apart from the angels) who bear the image of God. The words of the *Catechism* are intended, rather, to affirm how we are related to God with a special dignity.

All Creation Exists for Humankind?

What does the *Catechism* mean when it says that "*all* the rest of creation exists" for humankind?[28] Again, the word "material" may be understood here ("material creation"—that is, creation apart from spiritual creatures), since it earlier says explicitly that God "destined all *material* creatures for the good of the human race."[29] As the associated passage in Genesis declares, heavenly bodies serve us for light, for beauty, and for "signs and for seasons" (Gn 1:14); the earth and sea provide us with food.

All these things exist for our benefit. But such a statement does not necessarily mean that all creation exists *exclusively* for humankind. The same water that quenches our thirst also quenches the thirst of the animals. Perhaps God has given light to illuminate, gravity to anchor, and matter to embody the souls of extraterrestrial intelligences just as He has for us. Must we be the only intelligent race who was

---

[28] *CCC* 368.
[29] *CCC* 353, emphasis added.

given the celestial bodies to serve "for signs and for seasons" (Gn 1:14)?

As we have seen, skeptics opposed to the Christian faith have claimed that the existence of unseen celestial bodies prove that Christians are wrong in claiming that all things exist for the benefit of the human race. But the skeptics have failed to understand that the universe, taken as a whole, benefits us by providing us a habitation, even if we occupy only a tiny spot in that habitat and are unacquainted with most of the rest. The current scientific notion of the anthropic principle suggests that cosmic structures, materials, and processes far beyond the Earth—and long before the Earth came into being—had their part to play in making ours an inhabitable globe.[30] In this sense, the entire universe, not just our planet, is our home in this life; and ETI, if it exists, could make the same claim.

Even if *all* creatures (not just material ones) exist for our benefit, by considering the angels we can see how other spiritual creatures, also made in the image of God, contribute to our good. Though God has willed the angels for their own sake (as He has us), they also serve as ministers to the human race (see Heb 1:7; Ps 91:11–12). One status does not exclude the other.

The same could be true of ETI in some way still hidden from us. If intelligent extraterrestrials exist, we are presently unaware of how they might serve (or might already have served) our good. But perhaps their contribution to our welfare would be

---

[30] See John D. Barrow and Frank J. Tipler, *The Anthropic Cosmological Principle*, 1st ed. (Oxford: Oxford University Press, 1986).

manifest in heaven, where—if they are among the blessed—their happiness would certainly redound to our own.

Marie George summarizes the significance of the relevant *Catechism* statements here: "It is not reasonable to take such statements as if they were magisterial pronouncements on ETI existence when the question is not even raised. . . . If ETIs were discovered, this would not in any way affect the human specialness or uniqueness that consists in our being the only life form created on earth in the image of God." George concludes: "To date, the Church has left open the question of whether we are the only intelligent material life form in the universe."[31]

As we have seen in our historical survey in earlier chapters, no pope or council has addressed this issue specifically and authoritatively. Occasional documents (such as Saint Augustine's and Pope Zachary's references to the Antipodes) and anecdotes (such as the condemnation of Giordano Bruno) have been presented by some historians as relevant to the issue. But again, as we have noted, on closer view we can see that they are not relevant.

The Terrestrial Scope of Related Biblical Texts

The biblical texts most often associated with the teaching about humankind's special status can also be seen as implying a limited, earthly scope. The progression of the Genesis creation account (Gn 1), in which humankind, made in the image of God, is the final, crowning achievement, suggests indeed that our race is the highpoint of God's creation as

---

[31] George, *Christianity*, 46.

described. But the other creatures specified in that creation are either inanimate matter and energy or plants and lower animals. Our human nature, with its immortal spirit, stands indeed at the summit of that limited hierarchy.

Even the sun, moon, and stars described in the passage, though not terrestrial, are inanimate in themselves and thus not equal in value to a single human being made in the image of God. To recall Thomas Baker's lyrical declaration: "There is more Beauty and contrivance [creative skill] in the Structure of the Human Body, than there is in the Glorious Body of the Sun, and more perfection in one Rational immaterial Soul, than in the whole Mass of Matter."[32]

The image of God declared in Genesis 1:27 is indeed ascribed to humankind as a special status, not ascribed to the other creatures listed. But again, the other creatures described are either inanimate matter or energy, plants, or lower animals, so of course they do not bear that image. Since the angels, who also bear the image of God, are not included here, we could reasonably conclude that ETI, also not included here, could bear the image of God as well. Given the existence of angels, for humanity to be made in God's image clearly does not exclude the presence of that image in other intelligent creatures.

Another text cited in this regard is Psalm 8, especially with regard to human dominion over other creatures. The psalmist sings of "all things" being placed by God under the feet of humankind. Yet he goes on to specify what he means by that: "sheep and oxen," "beasts of the field," "birds of the air," "fish of the sea." He is speaking not about all creatures

---

[32] Baker, *Reflections*, 98.

in the cosmos but rather all creatures lower on the earthly food chain (Ps 8:7–8).

More Questions to Ponder

We have now considered Catholic texts that speak of human specialness in several aspects: our creation in the image of God, our position at the summit of the hierarchy of creatures, our dominion over the material created world, and all creation's existence for our benefit. We still must consider those statements of the *Catechism*, Scripture, and the wider Catholic Tradition that have to do with our special relationship with God as manifest in two more regards: our salvation history and our special destiny in relation to all creation.

These concerns, which have important implications for the ETI conversation, now press us to consider the possible types of ETI spiritual and moral status; their possible relationships to God and to the work of Christ on Earth; and their possible roles in the realities we call the Last Things: death, judgment, hell, and heaven.

11

"God Shield Them from Us!"

Possibilities for the Spiritual
and Moral Status of ETI

"Now it seems to me that we must find out more than we can at present know—which is nothing—about hypothetical rational species before we can say what theological corollaries or difficulties their discovery would raise."

—C. S. Lewis[1]

SAINT AUGUSTINE WROTE to God in his *Confessions*: "You are good and all-powerful; you care for each one of us as though you care for him alone, and you care for all of us as you care for each of us."[2] Every devoted parent understands the sentiment well. No matter how different our children may be, we love each of them as if there were only one of them. Or as one father I know once said to his children, "I love each one of you the best."

---

[1] C. S. Lewis, "The Seeing Eye," in *Christian Reflections* (Grand Rapids, Mich.: Eerdmans, 1967), 174.
[2] St. Augustine, *Confessions*, III.11.19, author's translation.

As we consider the claim of the Christian faith that God has shown special favor to the human race, we need to keep this thought in mind. Does *special* favor necessarily mean *exclusive* favor? Or can a father show various *kinds* of special favor to His various children, each according to their need? And isn't it possible for a father to grant a *unique* favor to one child for the benefit of them all?

If this is possible for an earthly father, how much more so for the all-loving Father who, as Saint Augustine reminds us, is not only all-good but also *all-powerful*—and, we might add, all-knowing and all-wise. He could certainly pour out His grace upon a million races of intelligent creatures, and work them all into a grand and glorious providential plan for the universe, without somehow slighting or forgetting any one of them as He cares for them. If trillions of human hairs have been numbered (see Lk 12:7), so might also ETI hairs (if they have them).

The Image of God in Relationship with God

The first four aspects of human specialness we discussed in the previous chapter have to do primarily with our relationship to the rest of *creation*. The last two aspects of that specialness regard primarily our relationship to *God*. These are beautifully reflected in the salvation history of planet Earth, from the beginning of the human race to its final consummation. Both aspects raise important questions about the possible spiritual and moral status of various races of ETI, their relationship to Christ, and their ultimate destinies as well.

The *Catechism* focuses on the divine image as it makes possible our relationship with God and others: "Of all visible creatures only man is 'able to know and love his creator.'³ He is 'the only creature on earth that God has willed for its own sake,'⁴ and he alone is called to share, by knowledge and love, in God's own life. . . . Being in the image of God the human individual possesses the dignity of a person, who is not just something, but someone. He is capable of self-knowledge, self-possession and of freely giving himself and entering into communion with other persons."⁵

The image of God is thus a trait of the human soul, not the body. Yet the human body can be said to share in the dignity of the image of God because of the profound unity between body and soul to create a single human nature.⁶

Earth's Need for Redemption

How exactly are we human beings related to God? We are His creatures, loved by Him into existence so that we could have a share in His own life, here in this universe and ultimately with Him in heaven. "The first man was not only created good, but was also established in friendship with his Creator and in harmony with himself and with the creation around him. . . . As long as he remained in the divine intimacy, man would not have to suffer or die."⁷ The perfect happiness of our first parents' existence flowed from their relationship with God.⁸

---

³ *Gaudium* 12, 3.
⁴ *Gaudium* 24, 3.
⁵ *CCC* 356–57.
⁶ See *CCC* 364–65.
⁷ *CCC* 374, 376.
⁸ See *CCC* 384.

At this point, the human story has no element that would necessarily make talk about ETI problematic for the Catholic faith. We could easily imagine that God might love into existence other intelligent embodied races and establish them in His friendship without diminishing our own relationship with Him. There is no need for jealousy when our Father could love many intelligent species as if there were only one intelligent species!

As we know all too well, however, our first parents turned away from God through sin, rejecting His loving Fatherhood and opposing Him. They lost the original righteousness they had enjoyed, and they could not pass down to their descendants what they themselves had lost. Now "the whole of human history is marked by the original fault freely committed by our first parents."[9] "Sin came into the world through one man, and death through sin, and so death spread to all men because all men sinned" (Rom 5:12).

If the creation of the human race manifests God's special favor, how much more so His loving, merciful response to this "original sin" of our first parents. He could have destroyed the human race and started again. He could have left us in our sins to descend into the abyss. Instead, He remained faithful in spite of our faithfulness, patiently preparing the world for His saving intervention on our planet. Then, "when the time had fully come, God sent forth his Son, born of woman . . . to redeem" the human race (Gal 4:4–5).

Over the centuries, He had provided many hints about His intentions. But until it happened, who could have imagined that God Himself would become a Man, taking on our

---

[9] *CCC* 390.

weakness, like us in every way except sin (see Heb 4:15)? Who in their wildest dreams could have expected that God Himself would give His life as a sacrifice to redeem a miserable race of Earthlings?

And yet He did. "Through him all things were made. For us men and for our salvation, he came down from heaven . . . and became Man."[10] The hands of the same One who had set the galaxies spinning clung to His mother, carved wood, healed the sick, broke Bread, hung on a cross, reached out from the tomb.

Now, those who respond to His redemptive work in loving faith can fulfill the destiny He intends for them: to have a share in His divine nature; to be gathered into the supernatural life of the Blessed Trinity—Father, Son, and Holy Spirit; to know, love, enjoy, and serve their Creator and Redeemer into all eternity. "What wondrous love is this, O my soul!"[11]

Why Earth?

This startling news of the Gospel is altogether glorious for the human race. But as we saw in earlier chapters, it does raise questions for the ETI conversation. If intelligent extraterrestrials exist, were they too created in God's image? Could they have rational intellects yet not be immortal? Have they too fallen into sin?

Various answers given to these and similar questions have led some Christians to reject the possibility of extraterrestrial

---

[10] From the Nicene Creed.
[11] From the first line of the American folk hymn "Wondrous Love," first published in the 2nd ed. of *Southern Harmony* (1844).

intelligence. Meanwhile, various answers to the same questions have led skeptics to conclude that Christian claims are impossible to maintain in the light of ETI. Both camps see extraterrestrial intelligence as incompatible with Christian faith, but what each side embraces as true, the other side rejects.

We will address these issues by beginning with a basic question of the skeptics: If God were to favor a planet as Christians say He has, how can we possibly believe that He would choose Earth?

Once early astronomers began to realize just how boundless are the heavens, how numerous are the celestial bodies, and how vast the space that lies between them, they began to grasp as well the Earth's astronomical insignificance in terms of its physical size and location. Judged on these terms, our planet seems to be a tiny, insubstantial thing, like a grain of sand on the beach of an infinite ocean. It is not at the center of anything except the revolution of its own humble moon.

Isn't it a silly bit of vanity to think the Creator of the cosmos would care that much for the inhabitants of such a planet—especially given that we have rejected Him? The hard realities of astrophysics, it would seem, are enough to disprove the notion that the human race is uniquely significant.

Nevertheless, the value of a planet or its inhabitants is not determined by size or location, just as the value of a work of art does not depend on such things. Their value is determined by how precious they are to the One who has decided to buy them—or in this case, buy them back, for that is what the word "redeem" means. They are worth what the divine Buyer is willing to pay for them, and this Buyer has paid for them with His own life.

In Earth's salvation history, a pattern appears: God tends to choose what is small and insignificant to accomplish His purposes. Abraham was an obscure desert nomad. Moses was the child of slaves under a death sentence. David was a young shepherd boy. When God became incarnate on our planet, He chose to be born to a young peasant woman of an oppressed people, not the emperor's consort; in a humble stable in little Bethlehem, not a grand palace in Rome.

Recall the Gospel parable of the shepherd leaving the flock to search for the one lost sheep (Mt 18:12–14). In this light, God's choice of Earth might be the best evidence that we needed His help the most. Perhaps our insistence that He stooped down to our little planet to heal us is not vanity at all but rather a humble confession of our wretchedness.

The Scandal of Particularity

In this regard, theologians have long noted what we call the *scandal of particularity*: When God makes a particular choice of a person or nation to accomplish His purposes, isn't He excluding others? Isn't that a form of unjust favoritism?

We can only reply with the words of C. S. Lewis: "If a thing is to begin at all, it must begin at some particular time and place; and any time and place raises the question: 'why just then and just there?'"[12] Ted Peters reasons: "For something to be real everywhere it must begin somewhere. . . . Any redemptive event cannot escape particularity, even if it bears universal significance."[13] If we think particularity in itself is a scandal, we will be scandalized whatever God may do.

---

[12] Lewis, "Seeing Eye," 175.
[13] Peters, "One Incarnation or Many?" 298.

At the same time, we must confess that our knowledge of God's plans and motivations, His will and His pleasure, are limited; we encounter here a mystery. We dare not accuse Him of favoritism. For we know Him to be good and wise and just, and He knows best how to distribute His gifts throughout the cosmos. That reality should inform our discussion of the matters we must now consider.

Natural Happiness or Supernatural Happiness?

In considering the range of possibilities for the spiritual and moral status of ETI races, the first issue to address concerns at once their origins and their end. If ETI exists, has God created them all in His own image, as He created us? This means that they would possess some degree of the various capacities arising from a rational intellect that we have noted: consciousness, free will, conscience, memory, imagination, emotionality, creativity. And it would mean as well that their animating principle, their soul, is immortal, created for eternal supernatural life with God. They might even have preternatural gifts as our first parents had.

Since the angels are also created in the image of God, we know that humans are not the only intelligent creatures with this gift. So it is reasonable to expect that at least some races of ETI, if they exist, have been made in the image of God as well. As we shall see, that status would open up certain possibilities for their ultimate destiny.

Yet here is a matter to consider: Would intelligent extraterrestrials necessarily be made in the image of God as we are? More specifically, can there be an intelligent race, with the capacities resulting from reason and free will, that are ordered, not to eternal supernatural happiness with Him in the next world, but only to natural happiness?

If so, we might expect them to have what we would call a "natural" religion that intuitively recognizes their Creator and Sustainer. As Oliver Putz noted, "Self-conscious beings are already always related most intimately to God and recognize God in an unreflected manner as their when and whither."[14] But creatures of the sort we are describing would have no expectation or even awareness of the Beatific Vision, so they would be content with the natural life they live.

They might seem to us much like children. In fact, they might be something like the children who die unbaptized, as envisioned in an ancient Christian belief that has never been definitively taught by the Church: They might experience the next life as a "Limbo" of natural happiness, without the possibility of the Beatific Vision yet content in their ignorance.[15]

The possibility of rational creatures existing in a state of pure nature was either expressed or implied by Saint Augustine, Saint Thomas, and Pope Pius V.[16] It was also confirmed by the papal encyclical *Humani generis*, issued in 1950 by Pope Pius XII (1876–1958). In this important document, the pope specifically condemned the teaching of those who insist that "God . . . cannot create intellectual beings without

---

[14] Putz, "God's Self-Communication," 172.

[15] The implications of a "Limbo of the infants" (if it exists), have been debated; see George, *Christianity*, 203, n. 14.

[16] See Ludwig Ott, *Fundamentals of Catholic Dogma*, trans. Patrick Lynch (Charlotte, N.C.: TAN Books, reprint 1974), 106.

ordering and calling them to the beatific vision." Such a notion destroys "the gratuity of the supernatural order."[17]

Speculations

As we noted in chapter 8, Fr. Theodore Zubek speculated about the possibilities: "In a purely natural state, a rational creature in its reasoning power would be capable of knowing God as the First Cause and Ultimate End, and—absolutely speaking—could naturally fulfill the known will of God. However, creatures in [a] purely natural state having the use of reason and free will would be influenced by their natural appetites, many times in opposition to the known will of God."[18]

"To cope with such temptations and to use the objects of their appetites in accordance with the will of God," he adds, "they would need a sort of natural help by God."[19]

Zubek also imagined creatures in a natural order being given "extraordinary faculties of soul and body, for whom the observance of natural divine law would not be so difficult" as it would be for humanity in (hypothetically) the same state.[20]

In any case, "the achievement of the ultimate end would depend upon the fulfillment of the naturally known divine will, expressed in the natural law imprinted by God into the

---

[17] Pope Pius XII, *Humani generis* (1950), par. 26; https://www.vatican.va/content/pius-xii/en/encyclicals/documents/hf_p-xii_enc_12081950_humani-generis.html. Whether God would have created humankind, in a different order of providence, with a purely natural end has been debated; see George, *Christianity*, 203–4, n. 18.

[18] Zubek, "Theological Questions," 396.

[19] Zubek, 396.

[20] Zubek, 396.

natures of such creatures." According to whether they served Him in this life, "God would eternally reward [them] with natural happiness or punish them forever."[21]

Finally, Zubek suggested that God could endow such creatures with gifts that are not supernatural but "beyond their natural demands": "He could preternaturally enrich them with infused knowledge, with freedom from inordinate concupiscence, freedom from suffering and death, and other gifts of body and soul, without elevating them into a supernatural order, without imposing upon them a supernatural destiny and without giving them adequate means for such an end."[22]

The life of such creatures, Zubek concludes, would be "quite beautiful, and the achievement of their goal natural and easy." Over a long period of time, they might reach a high level of cultural development.[23]

Thomas F. O'Meara has concluded: "In past or future spans of a hundred million years, another planet's intelligent beings may find in their world a happy, natural life and no more; they may have in their psychological and biological energies no aspiration to life after death and no longing for fulfillment from beyond. Intelligent creatures might be free of natural disasters on their planet, from illnesses and most suffering, and yet not think of immortality." Instead, O'Meara speculates, "they might expect nothing beyond a peaceful span and cessation of life."[24]

---

[21] Zubek, 396.
[22] Zubek, 396.
[23] Zubek, 396.
[24] O'Meara, *Vast Universe*, 24.

Mortal or Immortal?

Within the possible category of intelligent creatures made only for natural happiness, we might consider as well whether some of them could have souls that, like lower animals on earth, do not live forever. Much of the contemporary conversation about ETI, even among theologians, fails to raise the issue of immortality at all, leaving the impression that perhaps some writers do not believe even in *human* immortality.[25] Some Christian philosophers, on the other hand, insist that immortality is implied as an inherent quality of any rational soul. So any form of ETI, being intelligent, would be immortal.[26]

The Fifth Lateran Council (1513–21) condemned the idea that "the intellectual soul is mortal." But theologians have debated whether that statement is simply describing the human soul as is *(de facto)*, or declaring that it *must* be that way and cannot be otherwise *(de jure)*. The latter would constitute an "essential" immortality.[27]

Saint Thomas Aquinas insists, however, that all things, including immortal souls, remain in existence only because God actively conserves them. "If God took His power away from us, all things would immediately cease to exist."[28] In

---

[25] When Russell describes the *imago Dei*, for example, he speaks of the traits we have noted (along with language, tool-making, and social organization), but he says nothing about immortality; "Discovering ETI," 80.

[26] See McMullin, "Life and Intelligence," 169–70.

[27] John Hardon, *God the Author of Nature and the Supernatural: Part Two: Creation as a Divine Fact*, Thesis V, http://www.therealpresence .org/archives/God/God_010.htm.

[28] St. Thomas Aquinas, *Commentary on Colossians*, Lecture 4; in Aquinas, *Commentary on the Letters of Saint Paul to the Philippians, Colos-*

this light, nothing God has made is inherently immortal in the sense that it would be impossible for God to annihilate it by withdrawing His power that sustains it in existence.

In any case, in the context of the theological errors of its time that were being condemned, this conciliar statement clearly refers to human souls, so the possibility of ETI souls is not even in view here.[29] Are we prepared to say that God *cannot* create an extraterrestrial rational creature whose soul is not immortal—because (as some would claim) the notion of a mortal rational soul is itself self-contradictory? If God's creative power can bring a rational ETI soul out of nothingness into existence, is He unable to reverse the process?[30]

Some theologians would say that, based on the Church's teaching that all humans are made in the image of God, we must conclude that immortality is inherent in the rational soul. I would respond that only if we define "humans" simply as "rational animals," without specifying "rational *terrestrial* animals," could we call ETI "humans," as some philosophers would do. Their rationality as intelligent creatures would make them similar to us, but we must assume that ETI races would not have the same *origin* as we do—namely, descent from our first parents on Earth. In any case, certainly we can assume that any magisterial statements issued by the

---

sians, *Thessalonians, Timothy, Titus, and Philemon,* J. Mortenson and E. Alarcón, eds.; trans F. R. Larcher (Lander, Wy: Aquinas Institute for the Study of Sacred Doctrine, 2012), 89.

[29] Henry Denzinger, *The Sources of Catholic Dogma*, trans. Roy J. Deferrari, 13th ed. (Boonville, N.Y.: Preserving Christian Publications, 2009), 738.

[30] St. Thomas argued that God can annihilate what he has created, but chooses not to; see George, *Christianity*, 202–3, n. 14.

Church about "humans" have in view the earthly creatures descended from Adam and thus would not apply to ETI.

If immortality is *not* natural to the souls of rational creatures—if, as with being ordered to the Beatific Vision, it is a supernatural and gratuitous gift of God—then God could choose to create intelligent races that are similar to us in having a rational intellect and free will, but without immortality. They would be ordered instead to natural happiness, and when they die, they would have completed their existence.

Neanderthals?

Might we already be familiar with *terrestrial* creatures with this status? I would not yet go so far (as some have) to say that apes, for example, who do not possess immortal souls, nevertheless possess what could be called a lesser form of rational intellect.[31] But what about the now-extinct Neanderthals that once roamed our planet?

Archaeologists have reasonably concluded that Neanderthals exhibited capacities we would normally designate as belonging to rational creatures. Unless we conclude (as some have) that Neanderthals must be considered human, and Adam and Eve must have been Neanderthals (or their ancestors), we seem to have in this type of creature an example of terrestrial intelligences that were nevertheless not made fully

---

[31] See Putz, "God's Self-Communication," 165; "Moral Apes, Human Uniqueness, and the Image of God," *Zygon* 44:3 (2009), 613–24; Christopher Droesser and Hakai Magazine, "The Search for Intelligent Life Heads Underwater," *The Atlantic*, October 31, 2021, https://www.theatlantic.com/science/archive/2021/10/someday-we-might-really-be-able-talk-whales/620552/; Lewis thought that dolphins might be rational; see "Seeing Eye," 174.

in the image of God, not having immortal souls. If that is the case, why not extraterrestrial intelligences as well?[32]

Separated from the Church Triumphant?

Ephesians 1:8–10 declares that at the end, God will "unite all things" in Christ. Citing that passage, Marie George has ruled out the possibility of ETIs made for natural happiness, since they could not be part of Christ's Mystical Body: "If unfallen ETIs were made for natural happiness, at the time of the Last Judgment, there would be upright intelligent beings existing in separation from the Church triumphant."[33]

I would respond that being "in Christ" is not necessarily the same thing as being part of His Mystical Body. Perhaps ETI made for natural happiness could enjoy a form of communion with Christ and with each other that differs from the Mystical Body but has its own dignity and beauty within God's providence. And if such creatures were not immortal, once they died, they would no longer be in existence at all.

In his space fiction trilogy, C. S. Lewis envisioned extraterrestrial races on Mars such as we are describing, made for natural happiness. Recall his speculation about "creatures so clever that they could talk, though they were, from the

---

[32] See William Craig, "The Historical Adam," *First Things*, October 2021, https://www.firstthings.com/article/2021/10/the-historical-adam ?fbclid=IwAR2dWQa3241dqBb2AJpfxXtEEu_3yzLyFpjgvbW6XCeSI _Mwcz8QRqlYmao. Whether Neanderthals would have been unfallen is debatable; some archaeological evidence suggests that they engaged in warfare: Nicholas R. Longrich, "Did Neanderthals Go to War With Our Ancestors?" *BBC Future*, November 2, 2020, https://www.bbc .com/future/article/20201102-did-neanderthals-go-to-war-with-our-an cestors.

[33] George, *Christianity*, 20.

theological point of view, really only animals, capable of pursuing or enjoying only natural ends."[34]

Finally, some would say that they cannot see how it would "befit" a benevolent God to create an intelligent creature ordered only to natural happiness. But as we have seen, arguments based on the "fittingness" of what God might do are subjective and problematic, given that salvation history includes actions by God that many considered "unfitting" for Him. Reading Lewis's fiction opens the mind to imagine how such a creature, favored in ways hidden to us, might fit into the loving providence of God.

Having considered the possibility of ETI ordered to natural happiness, we must consider now the possibility of races that have never fallen and thus are not damaged by sin.

Is a Fall Inevitable for ETI?

If extraterrestrial intelligence exists, what might be its moral status? Is sin inevitable for creatures with a rational intellect and free will?

Some theologians have concluded that sinfulness is almost certainly universal—that is, a given for all intelligent life in the cosmos. Robert John Russell, for example, concludes: "ETI would be tragically flawed by an ambiguous ethical and moral character even as we are. . . . I expect that ETI will experience a kind of moral dilemma that in many ways resembles the moral quagmire of terrestrial human experience."[35]

---

[34] Lewis, "Religion," 89–90. The fictional races ordered to natural happiness appear on Malacandra (Mars) in *Out of the Silent Planet*.

[35] Russell, "Many Incarnations or One? in Peters, *Astrotheology*, 305.

Such a view typically rests on the notion that the biological evolutionary process, assumed to be universal, leads
inevitably to sin. This conclusion follows, in turn, from the
assumption that the human race had no set of first parents
who were created in original justice and fell by the exercise
of their free will. Instead, it is posited, the moral sense of
our ancestors evolved slowly, and "the physical laws of the
universe seem systematically conducive to conflict."[36]

Ernan McMullin summarizes: Most religious writers on
this subject "would question the literal interpretation [of Gn
3] that links human sinfulness to a single contingent historical act on the part of a single historical ancestral couple. Many
would trace human sinfulness to a division between flesh and
spirit that has deep roots in humanity's animal ancestry."[37]

I embrace, however, the traditional Catholic teaching of
a special creation of the first human pair, allowing for an
evolutionary, divinely intended, preparation of their bodies—though not an evolution in the immortal spirits they
were given as souls, which came directly from the hand of
God.[38] (Here again we see the importance of insisting that
an immortal soul is a necessary aspect of the *imago Dei*.) As
Humani generis declares: "The Teaching Authority of the
Church does not forbid that . . . research and discussions . . .

---

[36] See, for example, Hess, "Multiple Incarnations," in Peters, *Astrotheology*, 318–21.

[37] McMullin, "Life and Intelligence," 168.

[38] I recognize, of course, that this traditional teaching has been widely
rejected, and such rejection has led to numerous problematic theological
directions. I also recognize that, given recent developments in genetics,
those who hold to the traditional teaching must account for considerable evidence that would seem to contradict its claim. I believe that such
an account can be made, though certainly not in this limited space.

take place with regard to the doctrine of evolution, in as far as it inquires into the origin of the human *body* as coming from pre-existent and living matter—for the Catholic faith obliges us to hold that *souls* are immediately created by God."[39] Both Pope Saint John Paul II and Pope Benedict XVI have offered additional insights into this notion of the convergence of special creation and evolution.[40]

Hope for the Extraterrestrials

According to traditional Catholic teaching, our first parents had an unencumbered free will, and they freely chose to reject God. This original sin, not some moral evolutionary development, led to the current moral "quagmire" of the human race. Even so, though the wretched condition we inherited from our first parents after the Fall means that "all have sinned and fall short of the glory of God" on Earth (Rom 3:23), this traditional affirmation about human origins actually offers hope for ETI: Since sin was not inevitable for our terrestrial first parents—they could have chosen otherwise—it may not be inevitable for ETI, either.

Fiction writers have sometimes noted how much more difficult it is to portray holy characters than wicked ones. Apparently, we have a hard time imagining the magnificence of a soul near the pinnacle of goodness because we see one so rarely. Perhaps the same poverty of imagination prevents

---

[39] HG 36, emphasis added.
[40] See Mark Brumley, "Who Arranged the Chances? Can Belief in Evolution Be Compatible With Catholic Faith?" *The Catholic Answer*, January/February 2006, 25–28.

us from embracing the thrilling vision of an unfallen extra-terrestrial race.

C. S. Lewis offered such a vision in his novel *Perelandra*. In an ETI parallel to the Tempter's strategy with our first parents on Earth, the mother-to-be of all intelligent creatures on Venus is tempted to disobey her Creator. But she successfully passes the divine test of obedience, is confirmed in her goodness, and goes on to reign with her husband over a gloriously unfallen world.[41]

In short, I think it more than reasonable to allow for the possibility that, even if some ETI races are fallen as we are (they too would have the freedom to choose evil), at least some could well be unfallen. In fact, as we have seen, at least a few Christian thinkers have concluded that Earthlings may well be the *only* intelligent race that has fallen. Lewis observes: "I have wondered before now whether the vast astronomical distances may not be God's quarantine precautions. They prevent the spiritual infection of a fallen species from spreading."[42]

Perhaps an unfallen ETI race exists that has yet to be tested. If they should encounter us, the example and influence of our sin might actually present them the temptation that would serve as their test. How wretched it would be for us to act in the Serpent's role in an ETI paradise![43]

---

[41] See the introduction, n. 1.

[42] Lewis, "Religion," 96. In his space science fiction trilogy, because of this quarantine, Earth is known to the inhabitants of Mars and Venus as "the Silent Planet."

[43] This is essentially the scenario envisioned in Lewis's *Perelandra*.

A Mix of Fallen and Unfallen?

We should note a third possibility in the matter of fallen and unfallen races. The angels are a (purely spiritual) form of extraterrestrial intelligence. Since they do not procreate, they had no "first parents" who underwent the divine test of obedience, and whose choice would affect all those who came later.

Instead, they all underwent their test at the same time. Some chose God and were confirmed in their goodness; others rejected God and were confirmed in their evil. Considered all together, then, still today some are fallen, and some are unfallen, and they will remain so forever.

Some Christian writers have speculated that at least some races of ETI could have a similar mixed status. According to our original definition, the extraterrestrials are embodied, so unlike the angels, they might well have had a first set of parents as we did. (ETI creation and procreation could be very different from ours.) But even then, it is within God's power to create each extraterrestrial good and then test each one individually.

Some individuals might choose as the good angels did, and some might choose as the fallen angels did. And if they were not immediately confirmed in their choice by God, some might remain in friendship with God for a portion of their lives, yet eventually choose against Him.

C. S. Lewis surveyed these possibilities as well in his speculations about the spiritual and moral status of intelligent extraterrestrials. His provocative scenario about our potential encounter with an unfallen race, based on humanity's sad history of earthly exploration, should remind us again of our need for humility in these matters: "It is interesting to wonder how things would go if [human space explorers] met an unfallen race. At first, to be sure, they'd have a grand time jeering at, duping, and exploiting its innocence; but I doubt if our half-animal cunning would long be a match for [their] godlike wisdom, selfless valor, and perfect unanimity."[44]

---

[44] Lewis, "Religion," 94.

12

"The Great Physician May Have Applied Different Remedies"

Paths to Redemption for ETI?

"We must surely believe that the divine charity is as fertile in resource as it is measureless in condescension."

—C. S. Lewis[1]

IN THE YEAR 2049, Fr. Ramon Ruiz-Sanchez, a Peruvian Jesuit, biologist, and biochemist, joins three other scientists on a space voyage to the planet Lithia. His role on the team is to serve not as a Christian missionary but as a scientist and a physician for the crew. Their mission: to determine whether the planet can be opened to human contact.

What Father Ruiz-Sanchez ultimately discovers there shakes his faith. The Lithians are friendly, intelligent reptilians who walk on two legs. Their society seems utopian, without conflict, crime, ignorance, or poverty.

Even so, the Lithians have no religion; God has no place in their thoughts or experience. How is the padre to make

---

[1] Lewis, "Religion," 92.

sense of what he observes? His personal religious views do not allow for such a possibility.

Such is the premise of the award-winning science fiction novel *A Case of Conscience* by James Blish, published in 1958. Speaking about the book, Jesuit Brother Guy Consolmagno, director of the Vatican Observatory, reportedly observed that its "theology isn't only bad theology, it's not Jesuit theology."[2] Even so, in at least one regard, the premise of the story should be thought-provoking: If ETI exists, might we expect that God's activity among them could look very different from the salvation history of Earth?

Lewis makes the point rather bluntly: "God may have other ways—how should I be able to imagine them?—of redeeming a lost world. And Redemption in that alien mode might not be easily recognizable by our missionaries, let alone by our atheists."[3]

Having considered in the last chapter the possible spiritual and moral status of intelligent extraterrestrial races, we must go on to consider the matter of their potential place in God's providential plan of redemption. If ETI exists, do they need redemption? If so, has God offered them redemption? Could ETI be redeemed through the divine Incarnation on earth, Jesus Christ? And a question for the next chapter: Could God become incarnate as an ETI?

---

[2] Grayson Clary, "Why Sci-Fi Has So Many Catholics," *The Atlantic*, November 10, 2015, https://www.theatlantic.com/technology/archive/2015/11/why-are-there-so-many-catholics-in-science-fiction/414990/.

[3] Lewis, "Seeing Eye," 175.

A Working Definition

We should begin with a working definition. What exactly does the word *redemption* mean in the Catholic Christian tradition?

The biblical Hebrew and Greek words usually translated in English as "redeem" and "redemption" have to do with the notion of rescue, deliverance, or ransom. In earlier Old Testament times, before the reality of the soul's immortality had been clarified by divine revelation, such redemption was often understood in terms of this life: the protection of individuals, or the nation, from potential adversity, or their rescue from existing adversity (e.g., Ps 25:22; 26:11; 69:18).

In the New Testament, Old Testament indicators of a more thoroughgoing and final redemption to come find their fulfillment in Jesus Christ. Ultimate deliverance from all sin, suffering, and death is offered to the entire human race through His incarnation. By His life, death, and resurrection, Christ makes possible the restoration of the human race and the world to communion with God through forgiveness and transformation, which culminates in resurrection and eternal life (see Mk 10:45; Gal 3:13; 4:4–7; Eph 1:7–10; Col 1:13–14; Ti 1:11–14; Heb 9:12; Rv 5:9).

Would ETI Need Redemption?

Would intelligent extraterrestrial races need this kind of redemption? It depends on the types of spiritual and moral status we have examined. If they were unfallen, then no. They would not know sin (nor, perhaps, suffering and death), and they would already be in friendship with God. Lewis reminded us: "There would have been no Redemption in such a world because it would not have needed redeeming. 'They that are whole need not a physician' [see Matthew 9:12]. The sheep that has never strayed need not be sought for."[4]

If an extraterrestrial race were ordered only to natural happiness, perhaps God's plan would involve the sorts of gifts that Zubek suggested could assist them in receiving their final reward. If their souls were not immortal, perhaps they would at least enjoy the types of divine intervention in this life that the ancient Israelites asked God to grant them.

Fallen ETI in Need of Redemption

Intelligent extraterrestrials who were made, like humans and angels, in the image of God, but were fallen, would of course present quite a different situation. What might the possibilities be?

First, God might not offer them redemption at all. He might simply confirm them in their evil choice, as He did the fallen angels, with no chance of reform, no chance of salvation or communion with Him. We dare not imagine how it would be to encounter such a race. They would seem to us like demons, but embodied; "generations of evil beings," Zubek speculates, "a sort of devils incarnate."[5]

Some have claimed that such a possibility would not be in keeping with God's goodness, justice, and mercy. George Coyne objects: "How could he be God and leave

---

[4] Lewis, "Seeing Eye," 175.
[5] Zubek, "Theological Questions," 398.

extraterrestrials in their sin? After all he was good to us. Why should he not be good to them?"[6]

We must reply that such a possibility is already a reality with the angelic race. So it must in fact be in keeping with God's nature. As we have noted before, we are not always in a position to determine what is "fitting" for Him to do.

If God does offer redemption to a fallen extraterrestrial race, how might He do it? Is divine incarnation the only way available to God to save a fallen intelligent race? Saint Anselm appeared to think it was the only way for humankind.[7] But Saint Thomas taught (citing Saint Augustine): "It was not necessary that God should become incarnate for the restoration of human nature. For God with his omnipotent power could have restored human nature in many other ways."[8] Both theologians thought that the Incarnation was the most fitting way, but it was not the only way.

We might reasonably conclude, then, that if Saint Augustine and Saint Thomas were speculating about fallen ETI, they would allow the possibility that God could redeem such creatures in some other way than an incarnation, though Saint Anselm would probably not. "All things are possible" with an omnipotent God, if the possibility is not contrary to His nature or inherently self-contradictory.

---

[6] Coyne, "Evolution of Intelligent Life," in Dick, *Many Worlds*, 187.

[7] See St. Anselm, *Cur Deus Homo*; https://sourcebooks.fordham.edu/basis/anselm-curdeus.asp#ACHAPTER%20XII. Note, however, that Brian Lefto would argue that a closer look at Anselm's argument actually shows him to be closer to Thomas's position: "Anselm on the Necessity of the Incarnation," *Religious Studies* 31, no. 2 (June 1995): 167–85.

[8] Thomas, *ST*, III, q. 1, art. 2, citing St. Augustine, *De Trinitate*, XII, 10.

A Wide Range of Possibilities

Lewis suggested that the wide potential variety of ETI conditions might allow for redemptive possibilities we have not begun to imagine: "Spiritual as well as physical conditions might differ widely in different worlds. There may be different sorts and different degrees of fallenness. We must surely believe that the divine charity is as fertile in resource as it is measureless in condescension. . . . To different diseases, or even to different patients sick with the same disease," Lewis reminded us, "the Great Physician may have applied different remedies; remedies which we should probably not recognize as such even if we ever heard of them."[9]

What might those remedies be? Zubek listed briefly a few possible alternatives to a Divine Incarnation for the redemption of ETI. "In the supposition of fallen space creatures God could also have applied his infinite mercy by simply forgiving the sins of such creatures. He could demand personal disposition, namely repentance, for forgiveness of sin. Or he could accept a work of a mediator, a redeemer, as the satisfaction for the sins of a whole group of space creatures, or the work of the mediator combined with the cooperation of penitent sinners."[10]

Would the mediator necessarily have to be one of the three Divine Persons of the Blessed Trinity? Zubek thought not: "The mediator . . . could have been a pure creature appointed or created for that task by God. Only if God demanded an adequate, infinite satisfaction would a divine reparative act be necessary, because no limited being can give

---

[9] Lewis, "Religion," 92.
[10] Zubek, "Theological Questions," 398.

an infinite satisfaction; absolutely speaking, even for an adequate reparation, the vicarious death of God the Redeemer would not be necessary. The full reparation could also have been performed by other means."[11] What other means? "The mere incarnation or other act of the Divine Mediator, agreed upon or accepted by the Holy Trinity, would be of infinite value and sufficient for an adequate reparation."[12]

Saint Anselm might well have wondered whether some of these options were in fact contrary to God's nature (perhaps incompatible with His justice) or inherently self-contradictory. There might even be some reason why God chose to become Man that is still hidden to us and that would prevent Him from choosing a different redemptive path for ETI. In due humility, Saint Thomas confessed that we simply may not be able to fathom all the reasons why God became Man: "There are reasons of this mystery which are incomprehensible to every created intellect."[13]

With regard to extraterrestrial redemption, Lewis also speculated with humility: "It may be that the further we were permitted to see into his [God's] councils, the more clearly we should understand that thus and not otherwise— by the birth at Bethlehem, the Cross on Calvary and the empty tomb—a fallen race could be rescued. There may be a necessity for this, unsurmountable, rooted in the very nature of God and the very nature of sin. . . . But we don't know," Lewis concluded. "At any rate, I don't know."[14]

---

[11] Zubek, 398.
[12] Zubek, 398.
[13] St. Thomas, *ST* III, q. 30, art. 2, ad 3.
[14] Lewis, "Religion," 92.

I don't know, either. For this reason, I think we must at least allow for the possibility of ETI paths to redemption apart from incarnation. Perhaps we can never know in this life unless we finally encounter intelligent extraterrestrials to find out.

How Would ETI Relate to Jesus Christ?

As we saw in earlier chapters, some theologians have suggested that fallen extraterrestrials might be able to receive redemption through the work of Jesus Christ, the divine Son of God incarnate as a human being. Perhaps His redemptive act on Earth has cosmic consequences for other intelligent races. On what grounds has this possibility been considered?

Supporters of this view—for the sake of brevity, we will call it "the cosmic Christ"—typically look to certain ancient Christian writers who spoke of the cosmic reach of the Savior's redemptive work. Often quoted is a passage from Saint Irenaeus, bishop of Lyon (c. 130–c. 202) and a Father and Doctor of the Church. In his *Proof of the Apostolic Preaching*, Irenaeus wrote: "Because he [Christ] himself is the Word of God Almighty, who in his invisible form pervades us universally, in the whole world, and encompasses both its length and breadth and height and depth—for by God's Word everything is disposed and administered—the Son of God was also crucified in these [dimensions], imprinted in the form of a cross on the universe; for he had necessarily, in becoming visible, to bring to light the universality of his cross."[15]

---

[15] St. Irenaeus, *Proof of the Apostolic Preaching*, trans. Joseph P. Smith (New York: Newman Press, 1952), 69–70, 172 n. 172.

Jesus Christ, Saint Irenaeus reminds us, is the Word of God incarnate through whom all things were made (see Jn 1:2). So the form of Christ's cross—His redemptive work—has been in some mysterious way "imprinted . . . on the universe." But the context of his words offers few clues about what exactly that "imprint" might be.

Saint Athanasius (c. 296–373), another Father and Doctor of the Church, seems to point as well toward cosmic consequences of the Incarnation on Earth when he wrote: "For the coming of the Savior in the flesh has been the ransom and salvation of all creation."[16]

Saint Gregory of Nyssa (c. 335–c. 395) is known for his tendencies toward universalism (the notion that all will be saved). Given that theological orientation, we should not be surprised to read statements in his works that lend support to the "cosmic Christ" concept. He taught, for example, that "no being will remain outside the number of the saved" and that "no being created by God will fall outside the Kingdom of God."[17]

Saint John of Damascus (c. 645–749) wrote: "The gracious will of the Father has worked out in his only-begotten Son the salvation of the whole universe" because in the Son, divinity and humanity were conjoined, and "the whole creation through humanity." Other Church Fathers spoke of the ways in which nature took part in, and was sanctified and elevated through, the various events of Christ's life on

---

[16] St. Athanasius, *Epistola ad Adelphium*, vi; https://www.catholiccultu re.org/culture/library/fathers/view.cfm?recnum=2266.

[17] St. Gregory of Nyssa, *In illud: Tunc et ipse filius*, in *Gregorii Nysenni Opera* III/2, Kenneth Downing, ed. (Leiden: Brill, 1986), 1–28.

Earth: the star of Bethlehem, the Baptism in the Jordan, the nature miracles (walking on water and multiplication of loaves and fishes), and the darkening of the sun at the Crucifixion.[18]

Relevant Scriptural Passages?

"There is deeply embedded in Christian theology," George Coyne observed, "throughout the Old and New Testament[s] but especially in St. Paul and in St. John the Evangelist, the notion of the universality of God's redemption and even the notion that all creation, even the inanimate, participates in some way in his redemption."[19]

Coyne's unspecified reference to John probably points to the first chapter of John's Gospel, when he speaks of the Word of God through whom all things were made (see Jn 1:3, 10). John writes about the role of the Word of God before He became Man, but even after the Incarnation, and when He was crucified, He still possessed that divine Nature. Coyne may also be referring to John 12:32, where Jesus says, "And I, if I be lifted up from the earth, will draw all [things or people, depending on the translation] to myself."

The Pauline passages that Coyne had in mind probably include these words to the Romans: "For the creation waits with eager longing for the revealing of the sons of God; for the creation was subjected to futility, not of its own will but by the will of him who subjected it in hope; because the creation itself will be set free from its bondage to decay and obtain the glorious liberty of the children of God. We

---

[18] See Kereszty, *Jesus Christ*, 217–19.
[19] Coyne, "Evolution of Intelligent Life," in Dick, *Many Worlds*, 187.

know," the Apostle goes on to say, "that the whole creation has been groaning with labor pains together until now" (Rom 8:19–22).

Saint Paul wrote to the Ephesians: "In him [Christ] we have redemption through his blood, the forgiveness of our trespasses, according to the riches of his grace which he lavished upon us. For he has made known to us in all wisdom and insight the mystery of his will, according to his purpose which he set forth in Christ as a plan for the fullness of time, *to unite all things in him [Christ], things in heaven and things on earth*" (Eph 1:7–10, emphasis added). The Greek word translated here as "unite" can also mean "restore," "reestablish," "sum up" or "recapitulate."

In yet another passage, Saint Paul wrote to the Colossians: "He [Christ] is the image of the invisible God, the first-born of all creation, for in him all things were created, in heaven and on earth, visible and invisible . . . all things were created through him and for him. He is before all things, and in him all things hold together. He is the head of the body, the Church. . . . For in him the fullness of God was pleased to dwell, and *through him to reconcile to himself all things, whether on earth or in heaven, making peace by the blood of his cross*" (Col 1:15–20, emphasis added). The scope of Paul's passages in these three places seem to be cosmic. Where might we turn for help in interpreting them?

What Is "Creation"?

One useful approach is to consider how teachers of the Catholic faith traditionally revered by the Church have commented on these passages. What have such commentators had to say?

Several of the Church Fathers have offered us their interpretation of Romans 8:19–22. For our purposes, the key word here is "creation." How did ancient commentators interpret it?

Saint Irenaeus, Saint Cyril of Alexandria (376–444), and Saint Jerome all seemed to take the word "creation" to mean "everything created."[20] Saint John Chrysostom interpreted the word "creation" to include (though not exclusively) the lower forms of creatures, "devoid . . . of a mind and reason."[21] On the other hand, Saint Augustine specifically rules out such things as "trees, vegetables, stones, and the like" in the Apostle's statement: "Here 'the creation' means the human race."[22]

Pelagius (c. 360–420) was an ancient writer whose theology was rejected by the Church. But his relevant remarks are useful because he noted the array of alternative interpretations of the word "creation" in this passage in the commentaries of his day. He noted that some writers say it means the "whole creation." Others say it refers only to the "angelic, rational creation." Still others say it refers to Adam and Eve, or to "all who were righteous up to the coming of Christ."[23]

---

[20] St. Irenaeus, *Against Heresies*; St. Cyril of Alexandria, *Explanation of the Letter to the Romans*; St. Jerome, *Homilies on the Psalms*, quoted in *Ancient Christian Commentary on Scripture: New Testament VI: Romans*, Gerald Bray, ed. (Downers Grove, Ill.: InterVarsity, 1998), 214–17.

[21] St. John Chrysostom, *Homilies on Romans 14*, quoted in Bray, *New Testament VI*, 219.

[22] St. Augustine, *Commentary on Romans*, 53, quoted in Bray, *New Testament VI*, 218.

[23] Pelagius, *Commentary on Romans*, quoted in Bray, *New Testament VI*, 215.

Some centuries later, Saint Thomas Aquinas observed that "creation" can be interpreted three ways in this passage: in the sense of righteous human beings; in the sense of human nature itself; and in the sense of "everything under God" except the angels (because the angels are already perfected). He added that even if the word is understood to mean "humankind," it includes or represents in some way the rest of created nature, "because it shares something with every creature: with the spiritual creature it shares intellect, with the animal it shares bodily life, with the corporeal creature it shares bodily existence."[24] This particular remark might be read to support the notion of the cosmic Christ, who embodies and transforms not just humankind but all creation.

What Is "All Things?"

The Church Fathers commented on Ephesians 1:7–10 as well. The key words in this passage would seem to be "to unite all things in him [Christ], things in heaven and things on earth" (v. 10). What is meant by "all things . . . in heaven"? Would it include ETI?

Saint Irenaeus concluded that the Apostle is saying "he unites humanity to Spirit and places the Spirit in humanity. . . . Christ gives the Spirit to be the head of humanity."[25] Though, as we have seen, Saint Irenaeus wrote elsewhere about

---

[24] St. Thomas Aquinas, *Commentary on Romans*, 8:658–674.

[25] St. Irenaeus, *Against Heresies*, 5, 20, 2, quoted in *Ancient Christian Commentary on Scripture: New Testament VIII: Galatians, Ephesians, Philippians*, Mark J. Edwards, ed. (Downers Grove, Ill.: InterVarsity, 1999), 109.

the Cross imprinting itself on all creation, he does not appear to connect this passage to that cosmic vision.

Marius Victorinus, a fourth-century Roman Christian philosopher who deeply influenced Saint Augustine, understood "all things" here to mean "not all things indifferently, but . . . only those that are in Christ. Others are strange [or alien] to him. It is these that are revitalized and rise again, whether in heaven or on earth."[26]

He clearly does not view salvation as universal, yet he allows that some "things in heaven" are in Christ. Are those in "heaven" the perfected saints and the unfallen angels only, or would he include ETI? It is difficult to say.

Saint John Chrysostom interpreted "all things" in this passage to mean a "summing up" of all the "providential ordering that has occurred over a long time" in (presumably Earth's) salvation history. Then he added that it could also mean "in Christ's incarnation God has given a single head to all creation, both angels and humans."[27] The creation described by the Apostle here, Saint John concludes, is "angels and humans"; neither inanimate creation nor ETI are in view. Saint Thomas concluded that in this passage, "all things in heaven" refers to "the angels."[28]

Colossians 1:15–20 prompted similar interpretations. The commentary of Saint John Chrysostom makes it clear he believed that "things on earth" here meant human beings,

---

[26] Marius Victorinus, *Epistle to the Ephesians*, 1, 1, 10, in Edwards, *New Testament VIII*, 110.

[27] St. John Chrysostom, *Homily on Ephesians* 1, 1, 10, in Edwards, *New Testament VIII*, 110.

[28] St. Thomas Aquinas, *Commentary on Ephesians*, 1:3.

and "things in heaven" meant the angels.[29] In his remarks on the same passage, Saint Thomas agrees: "The things that are in heaven," he concludes, refers to "the angels and God."[30]

For Saint John and Saint Thomas, then, "all things . . . in heaven" refers narrowly to the angels or to the angels and God. This passage clearly teaches that Christ was the eternal Son of God, and thus the Creator of all things. In that regard He would be Lord of the extraterrestrials as He is Lord of humankind, because He has created us all. But with regard to His redemptive act, these two Doctors of the Church teach that the reconciliation through Christ involved God's relationship with humans, and our relationship with angels.

This sampling of ancient and medieval commentary shows that the passages in Romans, Ephesians, and Colossians were *sometimes* interpreted in ways that *might* include a redemption of ETI (and even inanimate creation) through Christ. But other interpretations seem to have had something much more limited in view. At the very least, we must admit that these passages are not decisive scriptural evidence for a "cosmic Christ"; the key terms are simply too ambiguous.

---

[29] St. John Chrysostom, *Commentary on Colossians*, 1:19; https://sites.google.com/site/aquinasstudybible/home/colossians/st-john-chrysostom-on-colossians. This is not to say St. John taught that the fallen angels (demons) are reconciled by Christ; instead, he proposed that the good angels in heaven had become estranged from the human race because of its enmity with God: "The earth was divided from heaven, the angels had become enemies to men, through seeing the Lord insulted." But Christ, as the representative Man who ascended to heaven, reconciled them to us again.

[30] St. Thomas Aquinas, *Commentary on Colossians*, 93.

Contemporary Adherents of "the Cosmic Christ"

We have noted in chapter 9 how various contemporary theologians have described their visions of what I am calling the "cosmic Christ." J. Edgar Burns, former president of Notre Dame Seminary in New Orleans, states succinctly: "The significance of Jesus Christ extends beyond our global limits. He is the foundation stone and apex of the universe and not merely the Savior of Adam's progeny."[31]

Joshua Moritz traces the tradition of a Messiah in ancient Jewish and early Christian thought that views Him as "God's agent for the renewal of the entirety of the living creation." He makes a rather bold claim (which would necessarily redefine the traditional theological meaning of "salvation"): "Jesus came to save the whales, the dolphins, the gorillas, the chimpanzees, the Neanderthals, and even extra-terrestrial biological life."[32]

Based on the concept we earlier noted of "deep incarnation," Ted Peters insists: "The significance of God becoming flesh stretches to every nook and cranny of the physical universe, including plants and animals who do not actively or consciously share communion with God."[33]

Some might object that an earthly incarnation for the sake of the entire cosmos would elevate humankind well beyond its deserts. But we must recall that God is known to choose a particular for the sake of the universal. He chose Abraham and told him: "I will bless you . . . so that you will

---

[31] J. Edgar Bruns, "Cosmolatry," *The Catholic World* 191, no. 1 (August 1960): 286.

[32] Moritz, "One *Imago Dei*," in Peters, *Astrotheology*, 341, 343.

[33] Peters, "One Incarnation," in *Astrotheology*, 293.

be a blessing. . . . And in you, all the families of the earth shall be blessed" (Gn 12:2–3).[34]

Lewis proposed that the Incarnation on Earth might represent the beginning of a cosmic salvation history, despite Earth's humble status. "There is a hint of something like this," he suggested, in Saint Paul's words to the Romans that we noted. "It may be that Redemption, starting with us, is to work from us and through us."[35]

Responding to the objections that such a possibility smacks of favoritism and superiority for humankind, Lewis reasoned: "The general, deciding where to begin his attack, does not select the prettiest landscape or the most fertile field or the most attractive village. Christ was not born in a stable because a stable is, in itself, the most convenient or distinguished place for a maternity."[36] The plot of Lewis's novel *Perelandra* fleshes out this insight. A diabolically driven human being and a courageous, redeemed human become battling characters in the salvation history of ETI on Venus.

"One can conceive," Lewis proposed, "an extraterrestrial development of Christianity so brilliant that earth's place in the story might sink to that of a prologue"—though I would add that it would be of course a divinely glorious and essential prologue.[37]

Implications of "the Cosmic Christ"

The "cosmic Christ" position seems to have gained popularity in recent times. Its emphasis on the uniqueness,

---

[34] See "q" in the marginal notes of the RSV.
[35] Lewis, "Religion," 92–93.
[36] Lewis, 92–93.
[37] Lewis, "Seeing Eye," 175.

universality, and sufficiency of Christ's redemptive work on Earth draws from ancient roots and presses against common modern notions of Jesus as simply a good man, and redemption as primarily revelation rather than atonement.

In addition, the "cosmic Christ" concept is attractive because of its simplicity. If it reflects reality, then most of the other possibilities we have considered become irrelevant. A divine incarnation on Earth that redeems every aspect of the universe down to its molecules obviates the need for talk about ETI as fallen or unfallen, in the image of God or existing in pure nature, redeemable or irredeemable, experiencing multiple incarnations, and all the rest.

The "cosmic Christ" is also in some ways the most optimistic of propositions. The redemption of the entire cosmos would seem to be guaranteed. We need not worry that any ETI (or human beings, for that matter) would fail to achieve their divinely intended destiny.

Even so, the very simplicity and optimism of the "cosmic Christ" notion also present one of its difficulties. The writers who take this position tend to shy away from stating the obvious: The "cosmic Christ" seems to imply universal salvation (though not in Lewis's fictional scenario). This theological position is difficult to square with the Church's definitive statements about hell, as well as the overwhelming weight of Catholic Tradition (not to mention Scripture and reason) related to the subject.[38]

---

[38] See "Hell" in Ludwig Ott, *Fundamentals of Catholic Dogma*, James Canon Bastible, ed., trans. Patrick Lynch (Charlotte, N.C.: TAN Books, rep. 1974), 479–82. See also Paul Thigpen, *Saints Who Saw Hell: And Other Christian Witnesses to the Fate of the Damned* (Charlotte, N.C.: TAN Books, 2019).

How Would They Know about Christ?

Does salvation require the understanding and cooperation of free-willed intelligent creatures as an act of faith? If it does, then how would ETI profit from the Incarnation on Earth without their knowledge of the event or cooperation with the graces it would make possible for them? How could they come to have faith and participate in the life of faith? How could the earthly Incarnation make any difference in the present lives of extraterrestrials?

Given the difficulties of interplanetary communication, the likelihood that extraterrestrials in need of redemption could learn about Earth's salvation history seems extremely remote. If we should somehow find a way to make contact, we could preach the Gospel and invite them to embrace God's redemption. But even then, the interplanetary language barrier could be insurmountable, given the potentially immense difference between species in sense experience and abstract thought. We might try to communicate through the seemingly universal language of mathematics, but as Russell has noted, "mathematics . . . is hardly a theologically sufficient language."[39]

Scenarios of interplanetary contact and evangelization might turn out not to be so difficult after all if an alien species is more like us than different. In that case, the question "Would you baptize an extraterrestrial?" might actually require from us an answer. But it is merely a possibility, by no means a certainty.[40]

---

[39] Russell, "Many Incarnations," 309 n. 11.
[40] See Guy Consolmagno and Paul R. Mueller, *Would You Baptize an Extraterrestrial? And Other Questions from the Inbox at the Vatican*

Apart from the contact and evangelization scenario, perhaps God Himself could tell extraterrestrials what He has done here on our planet and how they fit into His redemptive plan. He could communicate to ETI through angels, or even divinely inspired prophets or writers, as He has done to humankind on Earth.

Another possibility: Perhaps the "cosmic Christ" scenario could be construed in such a way that it does not involve universal salvation. Perhaps the saving work of Christ on Earth leads to the transformation of all the universe *apart from* angelic, human, and ETI species, and redemption comes only to those individuals among the intelligent species who, when they pass from this life, have somehow embraced God as they understood Him instead of turning against Him. Perhaps they would gain the necessary knowledge of Christ and cooperate with the graces He offers in a revelation at the moment of death and in a subsequent private revelation in response to their implicit faith.

No Guarantees

No doubt there are parallels in the development of Catholic doctrine that are cited as a precedent for such thinking. The Second Vatican Council declared: "Those who, through no fault of their own, do not know the Gospel of Christ or his Church, but who nevertheless seek God with a sincere heart, and, moved by grace, try in their actions to do his will as they know it through the dictates of their conscience—those too may achieve eternal salvation."[41] The parallel between

---

Observatory (New York: Image, 2014).

[41] *Lumen Gentium*, 16, in Flannery, *Vatican Council II*, 367.

peoples on Earth who have never heard the Gospel, and intelligent races on other planets who know nothing of it, seems to have a certainty validity.

Nevertheless, the Church's teaching says only that such a thing is possible, not guaranteed. And according to this conciliar statement, if those in such a state of invincible ignorance are to be saved, there are certain demanding conditions they must meet. How many extraterrestrials—how many humans—would meet those conditions?

"What Is Not Assumed Is Not Healed"

Another difficulty of the "cosmic Christ" position has to do with an ancient Christian affirmation that arose because of the Apollinarian heresy.[42] Saint Gregory of Nazianzus (329–390) stated the principle succinctly: "What is not assumed is not healed, but what is united to God is saved." That is to say, whatever was not united by the Son of God to His divine nature in the Incarnation is not healed, but what was united to God in that way is saved.[43]

The heretical claim to which Saint Gregory was responding held that when the Son of God united a human nature to His divine nature in the God-Man Christ, He did not unite a *full* human nature. According to the Apollinarians, Christ had a human body. But the rational human soul—what we might call today the mind—was in Christ replaced by the divine Word.

Why was that a problem? Because the redemption, the healing, of our nature accomplished by the Incarnation

---

[42] See Kereszty, *Jesus Christ*, 229–30.
[43] St. Gregory of Nazianzus, *First Epistle to Cledonius*, Epistle 101, 7.

depended on that nature being united to the very nature of God Himself in Christ. In that divine, life-giving union we find the grace of healing and transformation. If some part of us was not united to God in Christ, then, that part of us was not healed. Yet our intellects need healing as much as the rest of us, for sin has darkened our intellects: our reasoning, our memory, our imagination, our emotions have all been damaged by sin.

In practical terms, imagine if all these capacities, so compromised by sin, had no possibility of being healed through the graces of the Incarnation. Imagine if we could not look to Christ as our perfect model because He was not fully human. Imagine if He could not be close to us during particular trials because He lacked the part of our human nature that felt and comprehended such sufferings.

"Made Like His Brethren in Every Respect"

This reality is reflected in a passage in two related (and rather extended) passages of Hebrews:

> For he who sanctifies [makes holy] and those who are sanctified *have all one origin*. . . . Since therefore the children [human beings] share in flesh and blood, he [Christ] himself *partook of the same nature*, that through death he might destroy him who has the power of death, that is, the devil, and deliver all those who through fear of death were subject to lifelong bondage. . . . Therefore he had to be *made like his brethren in every respect*, so that he might become a merciful and faithful high priest in the service of

God, to make expiation for the sins of the people. For because he himself has suffered and been tempted, he is able to help those who are tempted. . . .

Since then we have a great high priest who has passed through the heavens, Jesus, the Son of God, let us hold fast our confession. For we have not a high priest who is unable to sympathize with our weakness, but *one who in every respect has been tempted as we are, yet without sin.* Let us then with confidence draw near to the throne of grace, that we may receive mercy and find grace in time of need. (Heb 2:11, 14–18; 4:14–16; emphasis added)

Several critical points are made here. Christ had to be fully one of us for several reasons:

He had to have *the same nature we have* in order to *sanctify* us—to make us holy, to heal and transform us.

He had to be *made like us in every respect* so that he could *serve as our representative* (high priest) before God to offer Himself as a sacrifice for us.

He had to *share our human nature* in order to *win His redemptive victory on our behalf.*

His human nature allowed Him to *suffer, to be weak, and even to be tempted to sin as we are,* so He knows our situation intimately and extends mercy to us accordingly.

For all these reasons, we can draw close to Him in confidence.

A Human Christ Would Be Alien to ETI

How could Christ do any of these things for intelligent extraterrestrials by taking a (human) nature that is alien to them? He would not be one of them, their representative, who acts as their merciful priest, offers Himself as their sacrifice to the Father, and wins victory on their behalf. How could they draw close to Him in their suffering, or even in their joy?

An ETI race might experience physical pleasures and pains through senses that are utterly alien to us. They could suffer from certain trials of the intellect—terrors, doubts, dilemmas, confusion—that have never gripped a human mind. They could be tempted in ways we can never fathom. In the midst of all these experiences, how would they find consolation in an alien Savior from Earth?

Saint Thomas, in writing about the benefits of God's becoming a Man to reconcile us to Himself, to restore our friendship with Him, noted: "Since friendship consists in a certain equality, those that are unequal as to many things do not seem to be able to be united in friendship. Therefore to the end that there would be a more familiar friendship between man and God, it was expedient for man that God would be man, because naturally man is a friend to man, and thus, when we know God visibly, we are taken up in an invisible love."[44] How might extraterrestrials' friendship with God be achieved if He drew near to them as an alien human?

Marie George has observed that "this point especially strikes home when one considers how many devotions are

---

[44] St. Thomas, *Summa contra gentiles*, IV, 54; quoted in George, *Christianity*, 99.

addressed to Christ's Sacred Humanity. . . . It would be hard, if not impossible, to fully appreciate the sufferings of a savior of an alien race and to feel the same degree of love towards him that we spontaneously feel towards a savior of our own race. . . . The ideal savior both understands us as a result of his own experience, and can be understood by us in terms of our experience, rather than through extrapolation or guessing."[45]

Consider, for example, devotion to the Sacred Heart of Jesus, so deeply meaningful to those of us humans who find in it a glorious consolation. Yet it might offer little meaning to an alien species whose alien bodies might have no heart.

All these considerations press us to consider next what for some might be a startling possibility: Could God become incarnate as an intelligent extraterrestrial?

---

[45] George, *Christianity*, 99.

13

"A Million Alien Gospels"

Multiple Incarnations for ETI?

"But, in the eternities,
Doubtless we shall compare together, hear
A million alien Gospels, in what guise
He trod the Pleiades, the Lyre, the Bear."

—Alice Meynell[1]

ASLAN THE LION has become a beloved fictional character to millions, both children and adults, ever since the publication of the fantasy series *The Chronicles of Narnia* by C. S. Lewis. Most readers have probably viewed the lion as an allegorical figure of Christ: He creates the world of Narnia, he dies on behalf of a sinner and rises again, and in the end, he judges all the creatures of that fanciful world.

Yet Lewis was adamant that this is a mistaken way of understanding his now-famous leonine character. Instead, he insisted, "Aslan . . . is an invention giving an imaginary answer to the question, 'What might Christ become like if there really were a world like Narnia and *he* chose to be

---

[1] Meynell, *Poems*, 92.

incarnate and die and rise again in that world as *he* actually has done in ours?' This is not allegory at all."[2]

In this light, Aslan might prompt us to consider: Given the problematic implications of the "cosmic Christ" notion, if intelligent extraterrestrial races exist, might multiple incarnations of God in different species be possible?

Saint Thomas: Multiple Incarnations Are Possible

As we have seen, the Christian writers we have surveyed are divided on this matter, often emphatically. What insights might we gain from Saint Thomas, other historical writers, and the Church's definitive teaching about Christ? Are there scriptural passages and magisterial documents somehow relevant to the issue?

As usual, even though he never directly addressed the possibility of extraterrestrial intelligence, Saint Thomas offered an insight that is relevant to this particular matter. In reply to the question of whether God could have become incarnate as a *human* more than once, he concluded that God certainly could have done so (though He had chosen not to do so).

The Son of God, Saint Thomas reasoned, is one divine Person Who united to Himself in Jesus Christ a single human nature. But as God, He of course has the power to unite to Himself a second human nature if He chooses; otherwise, His power would be limited, which we know is not true. For this reason, "the divine Person is able to assume [unite to

---

[2]   Lewis writing to Mrs. Hook, Dec. 29, 1958, in *Lewis: Collected Letters*, vol. 3 (San Francisco: Harper Collins, 2007), 1004–5; quoted in Paul Brazier, "C. S. Lewis: The Question of Multiple Incarnations," *Heythrop Journal* LV (2014), 393.

himself], in addition to a human nature that has already been assumed, another numerically different human nature."[3]

If this is the case for divine incarnations on Earth, the principle would seem to hold for incarnations on other planets as well. The conclusion, of course, is not that God has *certainly* done so, but rather that it is certainly *possible* for Him to do so.

The Hypostatic Union

Understanding Saint Thomas's position and the debates about multiple ETI incarnations requires that we look briefly at what Christian theologians have called the *hypostatic union*. The term *hypostatic* comes from the Greek word *hypostasis*, which means a "person" or "individual." The *hypostatic union* is the union of the two distinct natures of God and humanity, without "mixture," in the one divine Person of Jesus Christ.[4]

Christ is both true God and true Man. In His divine nature, He is of the same substance as God the Father; in His human nature, He is of the same substance as humans. These two natures are inseparably united in one divine Person, and that Person is the eternal Son of God, the Second Person of the Trinity.

This reality about the Incarnation, though in many ways a mystery, nevertheless came to be more fully clarified through ancient theological debates about how it is that Jesus Christ could be both God and Man. We have already seen how the Apollinarian heresy misunderstood this reality, claiming

---

[3] St. Thomas, *ST*, III 3.7 See also *ST* III 3.7 ad 2.
[4] See Ott, *Fundamentals*, 144–46.

that Jesus Christ was fully God but not fully human. The Nestorian heresy, which also arose in the ancient Church, erroneously held that there are not two *natures* but two *persons* in Christ. The divine Son of God was one *Person*, the Nestorians claimed, and the man Jesus was a second *person*, distinct from Him.[5]

Accordingly, the Nestorians insisted, for example, that the man Jesus, not the divine Son of God, was born to Mary, suffered, and died on the cross. (For this reason, they refused to call Mary "the Mother of God"; she was only "the Mother of Christ" or "the Mother of Man.") They attributed Our Lord's divine characteristics (such as His miracles) to one Person, the Son of God, and His human characteristics to a different person, the man Jesus.

The Church responded, however, that Mary did not give birth solely to a human nature separate from her Son's divine nature. She gave birth to a single Person, the divine Son of God, who had taken on a human nature as well. Because Jesus Christ was one Person, the Church insisted, we can attribute to that one Person all that He did and experienced: God the Son was born, hungered, wept, bled, suffered, and died.

Why is all this important to the ETI conversation? First, if the Nestorians were correct, to speak of multiple incarnations would mean that God had joined to Himself multiple persons, human and extraterrestrial. In fact, some of the language used by contemporary theologians in this debate sounds vaguely Nestorian in its view of Christ.[6] But the kind

---

[5]   See Kereszty, *Jesus Christ*, 235–39.

[6]   For example, O'Meara writes that "if there are other incarnations, Jesus of Nazareth united to the Word of God would not necessarily be

of incarnation that Saint Thomas was describing, and I am suggesting as possible in multiples, would not be like that.

Instead, I mean that the Son of God, the eternal Second Person of the Blessed Trinity, might unite to Himself the *nature* of one or more intelligent extraterrestrial races. This means we would not be talking about multiple Persons; He would be, in each incarnation, the very same divine Person, the Son of God. But that one divine Person would have joined to Himself numerically distinct, multiple natures of created rational races, and made them His own, in the kind of hypostatic union that Saint Thomas was describing.

This important clarification helps us to understand that in the case of multiple ETI incarnations, we would not be talking about multiple Saviors, multiple Lords, multiple divine Persons (that is, unless we are entertaining the notion of more than one of the three divine Persons of the Trinity becoming incarnate—a possibility that, as we have seen, some theologians would not rule out). We are speaking, rather, of one Savior, one Lord, one Son of God, one Word of God, one divine Person, Who for the love of His creatures across the cosmos had united to Himself their various natures and become one of them, to be one with them as He has with us.

The *Communicatio Idiomatum*

Understanding the hypostatic union also helps us to recognize what theologians call the *communicatio idiomatum*, the "communication of properties." It refers to the mutual

---

superior to all of them"; *Vast Universe*, 90 n. 28.

exchange of divine and human properties in Christ that results from the hypostatic union. Because of this exchange, human characteristics and activities can legitimately be attributed to the Son of God, and divine characteristics and activities attributed to the Son of Man, Who is the one Lord Jesus Christ.[7]

Roch Kereszty explains: "Thus, one rightly says that God himself suffered and died in the flesh; God the Word was a small child; but one should also admit that this man from Nazareth is God's own Son, or this prophet from Galilee is God himself. We may speak in this way because one and the same subject [Jesus Christ] is wholly divine and wholly human, possessing the properties of both natures." We see this mutual attribution at work in Scripture, and it serves as an important principle of scriptural interpretation.

For example, in 1 Corinthians 2:8, Saint Paul speaks of how "the Lord of glory" (Christ as God) was "crucified" (Christ as man). Saint Peter preached to Jesus's adversaries after the Resurrection: "You . . . killed [Christ as Man] the Author of Life [Christ as God]" (Acts 3:15). In John 8:58, Jesus (Christ as Man) declares: "Before Abraham was, I AM" (Christ as God)." The same principle is displayed in the statements of the Apostles' Creed, which attributes to the divine Son of God the human properties of conception, birth, suffering, crucifixion, dying, and being buried.

---

[7] See Ott, *Fundamentals*, 160–61.

Does Scripture Rule Out Multiple Incarnations?

God has the power to become incarnate more than once, but perhaps He has chosen not to do so. Are there scriptural passages that seem to point this direction—that rule out the possibility of multiple incarnations?

Some biblical commentators would say yes. Certain passages, they conclude, speak of the incarnation of God among humankind, Jesus Christ, in a cosmic context as the Lord of *all*, not just Lord of humans and angels. That would seem to rule out a second, "rival" incarnation. How might the principle of *communicatio idiomatum* help us interpret these passages?

We have already identified several biblical texts that seem to present Christ this way. One of them, the passage in Romans about how "the whole creation has been groaning with labor pains together until now" (8:19–22), we will consider in a later chapter on possible ETI paths to a final destiny.

As we have seen, two other Pauline passages could be interpreted in a "cosmic Christ" manner: Ephesians 1:10 ("to unite all things in him [Christ], things in heaven and things on earth") and Colossians 1:20 ("through him [Christ] to reconcile to himself all things, whether on earth or in heaven, making peace by the blood of his cross"). But as we have also seen, some respected interpreters have understood "all things" and "creation" in these texts to refer to something much more limited: the human race, or perhaps humankind and the angels. So we cannot conclude that they are firm evidence for a single "cosmic Christ" rather than multiple incarnations.[8]

---

[8]   There are other biblical texts in which the word "all" cannot be taken absolutely. For example, St. Paul declared that "all have sinned

Contrived Interpretation?

I recognize that some writers object to the idea that words in Scripture such as "all" can be interpreted narrowly as "all *humans*" rather than "all creatures." Marie George has observed: "One could argue that a qualification of this sort is understood but left unstated because Scripture is ordered to human salvation. I find this line of interpretation contrived."[9]

I can only respond: Saint Thomas and several of the other respected Christian commentators we have noted apparently did not find this approach contrived, since they provide us examples of such interpretation. They accepted the possibility that the words "creation" and "all things" in the scriptural texts we have examined were not meant absolutely; instead, they could be narrowly interpreted as applying only to humans and angels.

If Scripture is ordered to human salvation, then we should not expect it to tell us about the existence of intelligent extraterrestrials or even to have them in view. Consider this (admittedly crude) analogy.

Jesus once told a parable about the Kingdom of God in which He said that "the mustard seed is the smallest of all seeds" (Mt 13:31–32). Taken as an absolute statement, it is false; smaller seeds exist on earth that were unknown to His listeners. (For example, the seed of one type of jewel orchid is microscopic, only five hundredths of a millimeter in length.)

---

and fall short of the glory of God" (Romans 3:23). But not *all* human beings (understood as "without exception") have sinned; Christ was a human being, but He never sinned, nor did the human being who was His mother.

[9] George, *Christianity*, 38.

But assuming (as I think we must) that Christ Himself was not ignorant of such seeds, we can say that He intentionally limited the scope of what He told them to accommodate their ignorance—and to focus their attention. Telling them about the existence of the tinier but (to them) unknown seed was not necessary to the point He wished to make about their salvation. It would have complicated a rather simple parable for Him to say, "There is a seed you know nothing about that is actually the smallest seed of all, so tiny that you cannot even see it, and that seed grows into a large tree."

"Wait a minute!" they might interrupt him. "Never mind about the Kingdom! How can there be a seed so small that it cannot be seen?"

If that is indeed the case, we can interpret the words that He did say with what was (to Him) an understood but unstated qualifier: "The mustard seed is the smallest of all seeds [that you know about]."

In a similar way, perhaps Christ could say to us: "There are actually intelligent races on other planets that you know nothing about, so far away that you cannot even see them. But since knowledge of their existence is not necessary for your salvation, I speak in these passages of my Word only about the plan of redemption on this planet."

Christ as Lord of All Creation

Certain verses in Colossians indicate that Christ is not only redeemer but also Creator and Lord of all creation:

> He [God the Father] has delivered us from the domin-
> ion of darkness and transferred us to the kingdom of
> his beloved Son, in whom we have redemption, the
> forgiveness of sins. He is the image of the invisible
> God, the first-born of all creation, for in him all things
> were created, in heaven and on earth, visible and invis-
> ible . . . all things were created through him and for
> him. He is before all things, and in him all things hold
> together. He is the head of the body, the Church; he
> is the beginning, the first-born from the dead, that in
> everything he might be pre-eminent. (Col 1:13–18)

If the Apostle is saying all this about Christ, then how could such things be said about anyone else? An ETI incarnation could be seen as a rival to Christ, or as someone sharing what we know to be His unique prerogatives.

Here the reality of the *communicatio idiomatum* can help us understand the meaning. Consider how Saint Paul's original audience might have been scandalized by what he said. How could all the things he declared about Jesus Christ, a human being Who had been their contemporary, possibly be true? How could Jesus of Nazareth, born only a few decades before, be "the first-born of all creation"? How could all things have been created "in him" and "through him" and "for him"? How could all things "hold together in him"? How could he be "pre-eminent" in everything?[10]

---

[10] We should note here that St. Thomas understood the phrase "in everything pre-eminent" in this passage in a limited way; he thought it referred to the "gifts and glory he [Christ] has given the human race." In support of this interpretation, he quoted Sirach 24:9–10, which specifies preeminence in the sense of rule over all the nations and peoples of the Earth. Even so, the rest of the passage certainly speaks of a cosmic preeminence.

The answer: The Person who is Jesus Christ is the eternal, omnipotent Second Person of the Blessed Trinity—God's "beloved Son," as Saint Paul specifies in verse 13—Who has become a human being. According to the "communication of properties," the Apostle can speak of the Man, Jesus Christ, in these terms because these attributes arise from His second, divine nature; they can be legitimately attributed to this divine Person who has also united to Himself a human nature that is His own.

As we have noted, when we consider the possibility of multiple ETI incarnations, we are speaking of the same Person, the divine Son of God, Who has united Himself to various intelligent extraterrestrial *natures*, not ETI *individuals*. We are not speaking of multiple Lords but rather of the one Lord of all creation. If that is indeed the case, then all that the Apostle says about Christ as the universal Creator and Lord, for whom all things were created and in whom all things hold together, would apply as well to His incarnation as an ETI. The various incarnations would not represent rival claimants to His universal throne; they would all be the same King of the universe. The reality of the *communicatio idiomatum* allows us to speak this way truthfully.

Every Name, Knee, and Tongue

A similar passage is found in Philippians 2:9–11: "Therefore God has highly exalted him [Christ Jesus] and bestowed on him the name which is above every name, that at the name of Jesus every knee should bow, in heaven and on earth and under the earth, and every tongue confess that Jesus Christ is Lord, to the glory of God the Father." Does "every name . . .

knee . . . tongue" include ETI? The influential second-century theologian Origen commented: "In these three appellations the whole universe is indicated."[11]

On the other hand, Saint Thomas concluded that these three words apply simply to angels and saints ("in heaven") and humans ("on earth" and "under the earth," the realm of the dead).[12] And the fifth-century bishop and theologian Theodoret (393–457) said that "tongues" here refers to "peoples."[13] Since the passage can be interpreted in more than one way, it offers no firm scriptural support with regard to a single, earthly incarnation excluding all others.

"Everything in Subjection Under Him"

Yet one more scriptural passage of this sort is Hebrews 2:8–9: "Now in putting everything in subjection under him [Christ], he [God] left nothing outside his control. As it is, we do not yet see everything in subjection to him. But we see Jesus, who for a little while was made lower than the angels, crowned with glory and honor because of the suffering of death, so that by the grace of God he might taste death for every one. For it was fitting that he, for whom and by whom all things exist, should make the pioneer of their salvation perfect through suffering."

---

[11] Origen, *On First Principles*, 1.6.2, quoted in Edwards, *New Testament VIII*, 243.

[12] St. Thomas Aquinas, *Commentary on the Letters of St. Paul to the Philippians, Colossians, Thessalonians, Timothy, Titus, and Philemon*, ed. J. Mortsensen and E. Alarcón, trans. F. R. Larcher (Lander, Wy.: Aquinas Institute for the Study of Sacred Doctrine, 2012), 31.

[13] Theodoret, *Epistle to the Philippians*, 2:11, quoted in Edwards, *New Testament VIII*, 243.

Again, we see the *communicatio idiomatum* demonstrated: Christ, though truly a Man, can be described as the One who was above the angels but "for a little while was made lower than the angels," under whom everything has been placed in subjection. And Christ, though truly God, can also be described as the One who experienced suffering and death.

As in the other biblical texts, when there is a declaration made of Christ's universal Lordship—"everything [is] in subjection under him. . . . Nothing [is] left outside his control"—that declaration is made about Christ as the divine Son of God. If there should be an ETI incarnation of the Son of God, He would be the same divine Person, so the same could be said of Him. There is no contradiction here.

The same, it seems, could be said of other passages that speak of Christ's universal Lordship, such as Our Lord's words in Matthew 28:18 and the Apostle's words in Ephesians 1:20–23.

Statements in the *Catechism*

Certain statements in the *Catechism* about Christ's role in the universal divine plan might be interpreted in a similar way.

> The mystery of Christ casts conclusive light on the mystery of creation and reveals the end for which "in the beginning God created the heavens and the earth": from the beginning, God envisaged the glory of the new creation in Christ.[14]

---

[14] *CCC* 280; see also 315. *General Catechetical Directory* 51; Gen 1:1; cf. Rom 8:18–23.

Christ's ascension into heaven signifies his participation, in his humanity, in God's power and authority. Jesus Christ is Lord: he possesses all power in heaven and on earth. He is "far above all rule and authority and power and dominion," for the Father "has put all things under his feet." Christ is Lord of the cosmos and of history. In him human history and indeed all creation are "set forth" and transcendently fulfilled.[15]

In the Symbol of the faith [that is, the Creed] the Church confesses the mystery of the Holy Trinity and the plan of God's "good pleasure" for all creation: the Father accomplishes "the mystery of his will" by giving his beloved Son and the Holy Spirit for the salvation of the world and for the glory of his name. Such is the mystery of Christ, revealed and fulfilled in history according to the wisely ordered plan that St. Paul calls the "plan of the mystery."[16]

First, I think we should note that in all these statements from the *Catechism*, whatever cosmic role and work is attributed to Christ (for example, "Lord of the cosmos") is attributed to Him because He is the "beloved Son" of God whose humanity "participates in God's power and authority" through its hypostatic union with His divine nature. As with the biblical passages we noted, any incarnation of the Son of God through uniting with an extraterrestrial nature would allow us to speak of Him in the same way without

---

[15] *CCC* 668. Eph 1:10; see also Eph 4:10; 1 Cor 15:24, 27–28.
[16] *CCC* 1066. Eph 1:9, 3:9; cf. 3:4.

contradicting what is said here. Both incarnations could be called "Lord of the cosmos" because they would be the same divine Person, not different persons.

The Cosmic Plan

Second, as part of a broader perspective, we should look at the teaching presented here about God's cosmic "plan" accomplished through Christ. If intelligent extraterrestrial races exist, then whatever God has done for them is also a part of that overarching cosmic plan. To speak of the plan's being fulfilled by Christ does not exclude the possibility that the plan is also being fulfilled by the incarnation in an ETI race of that same divine Person, "God's beloved Son."

To offer a humble analogy: Imagine the commander in chief of a vast army at war. He must execute a complex battle plan to vanquish the enemy and reclaim and rebuild the territories that the enemy has overrun and ruined. The plan requires that he himself appear on several battlefields, at some distance from one another, to lead the charge, weapons in hand, and win that particular field as a necessary action in the great war to be won.

In the comprehensive plan of engagement, victory, and restoration, it is the same commander, not multiple ones, who executes the plan in various locations. And the victory he accomplishes in each local battle is an essential part of the total plan that is carried out. The plan for winning the war has been fulfilled in each one of those battles.

We could speak much the same way about the possibility of multiple incarnations in the divine plan for the cosmos. To say the Son of God's incarnation on Earth fulfills God's plan for creation does not exclude the possibility that the Son of God's incarnation on another planet also fulfills the plan, and that each has its proper role to play in the total divine strategy.

Someone might object that the Church's teaching proclaims Christ's work on earth to be *central* to God's cosmic plan. But to say that other incarnations might be essential to the plan would not contradict that proclamation. Perhaps the battle won on our planet *was* in some way a central victory, a critical turning point, in the great cosmic war.

Even so, we might recall the ancient affirmation that "God is an infinite circle whose center is everywhere and whose circumference is nowhere."[17] Or (as we heard in an earlier chapter), as Nicholas of Cusa stated it, "God . . . is the center and circumference of all stellar regions." *Wherever* God works is actually central to His plan, because He *Himself* is always the center of His plan.

Dominus Iesus

At least two magisterial documents have been cited as evidence that the existence of multiple incarnations would be contrary to the teaching of the Church. One is the declaration *Dominus Iesus*, issued in 2000 by Cardinal Joseph Ratzinger (later Pope Benedict XVI), then-prefect for the Congregation of the Doctrine of the Faith. Such a document is not infallible, nor does it even carry the weight of a papal encyclical. But it was ratified and confirmed by Pope Saint John Paul II, and "the Declaration takes up what has been

---

[17] This quote has been misattributed to Voltaire; it is actually of ancient origin.

taught in previous magisterial documents, in order to reiterate certain truths that are part of the Church's faith" (3).

The declaration's subtitle indicates that it focuses on "the unicity [uniqueness] and salvific [saving] universality of Jesus Christ and the Church."[18] In the course of the document, we find a number of statements that speak of Christ's uniqueness and universal saving work through the Church: the "character of absolute truth and salvific universality" of "the mystery of Jesus Christ and the Church" (4); "Jesus of Nazareth, son of Mary, and he alone, is the Son and the Word of the Father" (10); "Jesus Christ, who is at the center of God's plan of salvation" (10); "Jesus Christ, Son of God, Lord and only Savior" (13); "the unique mediation of the Redeemer" (14). "Hence, those solutions that propose a salvific action of God beyond the unique mediation of Christ would be contrary to Christian and Catholic faith" (14).

To understand the scope of these references, we must keep in mind the reason the declaration was issued. The document lamented repeatedly the errors of certain Catholic theologians who had been teaching for some years that Christ was not the only way to salvation, nor the Church a necessary part of that way—*for humanity*. It did not have in view intelligent races on other planets.

To demonstrate that terrestrial scope, we need only note a few of the statements (emphasis added) that make it explicit. (Others could be cited.)

---

[18] Congregation for the Doctrine of the Faith, *Dominus iesus: On the unicity and salvific universality of Jesus Christ and the Church* (2000), https://www.vatican.va/roman_curia/congregations/cfaith/documents /rc_con_cfaith_doc_20000806_dominus-iesus_en.html.

- "The Word made flesh . . . is the source . . . as well as the fulfilment of every salvific revelation of God *to humanity*" (6).
- "Christ 'the new Adam' . . . is himself the perfect man who has restored that likeness to God *in the children of Adam*" (10).
- "The universal salvific will of God is closely connected to the sole mediation of Christ: '[God] desires all *men* to be saved. . . . For there is one God; there is also one mediator between God and *men,* the man Jesus Christ" (1 Tim 2:4–6) (13).
- "The key, the center, and the purpose of the whole of *man's history* is to be found in its Lord and Master" (13).
- "The salvific action of Jesus Christ . . . extends beyond the visible boundaries of the Church *to all humanity*" (14).
- "Jesus Christ has a significance and a value *for the human race and its history*, which are unique and singular, proper to him alone, exclusive, universal, and absolute. Jesus is, in fact, the Word of God made man for the salvation of all" (15).

One other relevant statement here may give us pause: "There is only one salvific economy of the One and Triune God, realized in the mystery of the incarnation, death, and resurrection of the Son of God, actualized with the cooperation of the Holy Spirit, and extended in its salvific value to all humanity *and to the entire universe*" (12, emphasis added). This statement does have an explicit cosmic scope and could indeed be read as support for a "cosmic Christ."

That may very well be its import. I think, however, that in light of the declaration's stated purpose and its repeated expression of a terrestrial scope, we can reasonably understand this statement in context this way: "There is only one salvific economy of the One and Triune God [for humanity], realized in the mystery of the incarnation, death, and resurrection of the Son of God, and extended in its salvific value to all humanity and to the entire universe" (12).

This way we would understand it to say that God's salvation in Christ on Earth makes a contribution to His greater redemptive plan for the cosmos. If the declaration's intention was not to rule on matters that the Church has never defined, but instead to present "what has been taught in previous magisterial documents," then it cannot be ruling out multiple incarnations; the Church has never definitively settled or even addressed that issue.

Ecclesia de Eucharistia

A second magisterial document may be of relevance here. In 2003, Pope Saint John Paul II published the encyclical letter *Ecclesia de Eucharistia.* In his teaching about the Eucharist, one particular passage stands out as having an explicit cosmic scope: "This varied scenario of celebrations of the Eucharist has given me a powerful experience of its universal and, so to speak, cosmic character. Yes, cosmic! Because even when it is celebrated on the humble altar of a country church, the Eucharist is always in some way celebrated *on the altar of the world.* It unites heaven and earth. It embraces and permeates all creation." Saint John Paul continues: "The Son of God became man in order to restore all creation, in one supreme act of praise, to the One who made it from nothing" (8, emphasis in the original).

If the Eucharist has a ("so to speak") "cosmic character," embracing and permeating all creation, does that imply a "cosmic Christ" in the sense of a singular incarnation whose sacrifice redeems all intelligent life in the universe? That could very well be the implication here. (Recall the private remark of the author of this document that ETI "are children of God as we are.")

Even so, this is highly mystical language, so we must tread carefully. But when we consider that the Eucharist is the Body and Blood, Soul and Divinity of the Son of God, Who is all-present throughout His creation, then perhaps we can understand Saint John Paul's meaning. What the "Word made flesh" did on Earth (and continues to do through the Eucharist) of course has cosmic consequences, playing an essential role in restoring all creation to God. But I think that does not exclude the possibility that the same Son of God has taken flesh on other planets, and His redemptive role there also plays an essential role in the cosmic plan of salvation. (Remember the commander's overarching strategy across local battlefields to win the war.)

Incarnations among Unfallen Races?

One last possibility for multiple incarnations deserves our consideration. If *unfallen* extraterrestrial races exist, might the Son of God have united their natures to His own as well?

Within the Christian tradition, two theological perspectives have developed with regard to the reasons why God became Man. On the one hand, as we have seen, theologians such as Saint Anselm have focused on the sacrifice of Christ to atone for the sins of the world. That seems to him to be the primary (perhaps the only?) reason for the Incarnation.[19]

On the other hand, we hear an alternative perspective from theologians such as the medieval Franciscan Duns Scotus (c. 1265–1308). Scotus did not at all deny that Christ's sacrifice atoned for our sins, but he believed that God had a wider intention in becoming Man, an intention that existed prior to the fall of Adam: God became Man to reveal His love.

Think of Saint Thomas's remarks about friendship that we quoted in the last chapter: "It was expedient for man that God would be man, because naturally man is a friend to man, and thus, when we know God visibly, we are taken up in an invisible love."[20]

For Scotus, God created the universe so we could have communion with Him; He created us to have friendship with Him. The Incarnation was God's way of drawing near to us in love, uniting Himself to us, becoming one of us, and allowing us in response to know Him and draw near to Him in love. Christ's sacrifice was part of the divine plan to reconcile the human race to Himself, because the human race was fallen. But even if we had never fallen, he insisted, God would still have become One of us because of His love.[21]

---

[19] See St. Anselm, *Cur Deus Homo.*

[20] St. Thomas, *Summa contra gentiles*, IV, 54; quoted in George, *Christianity*, 99.

[21] For a useful analysis of Scotus and St. Bonaventure on this matter, see Delio, "Christ and Extraterrestrial Life."

What if Scotus (like Saint Bonaventure, who held a similar view[22]) is correct? What if sin is not a necessary condition in a world for God to enter it? If an unfallen extraterrestrial race exists, then we could easily imagine the Word taking on their flesh and dwelling among them as well, full of grace and truth (see Jn 1:14).

Why Not?

E. L. Mascall summed up the possibility of multiple ETI incarnations in this way: "[If, as the Church teaches,] the Incarnation takes place not by the conversion of the Godhead into flesh but by the taking up of manhood into God, there seems to be no fundamental reason why, in addition to human nature being hypostatically united to the Person of the divine Word, other finite rational natures should not be united to that person too."

As theologians continue to debate the issue, we would do well to imitate Mascall's humility when he further declared that he wanted to make this "suggestion . . . with all the tentativeness that is proper to a matter about which we are in almost complete ignorance."[23]

---

[22] See Delio, "Christ and Extraterrestrial Life."
[23] Mascall, *Christian Theology*, 39–40.

14

"A New Heaven and a New Earth"

Paths to a Final Destiny for ETI?

"What no eye has seen, nor ear heard, nor the heart of man conceived, . . . God has prepared for those who love him."

—1 Corinthians 1:9

To SPECULATE ABOUT the "Last Things" is at best a tricky matter.

How much easier it is to make confident statements about things that have been than about things to come. Yes, Scripture tells us about certain future events and final destinies for humankind and for the angels. But much of what it says about the subject is expressed in language not easily parsed, and it hints at a reality far beyond what we have ever known on Earth, though we may have a taste of it even now. The human mind simply cannot imagine what God has prepared (see 1 Cor 1:9).

If that is the case for the human race, how tentative must be our speculations about the ultimate destiny of intelligent extraterrestrials! And yet our study would not be complete without at least an attempt to offer some relevant thoughts.

Natural Destiny, Supernatural Destiny

In the course of discussing what we have called the possible spiritual and moral status of ETI, we have already begun, necessarily, to think about their "Last Things." For the spiritual status of an intelligent creature is determined by the ultimate purpose for which God has made it. The moral status of such a creature is determined by its response to God. And the final destiny of such a creature is determined by both these factors.

We have noted, for example, that God might have created some species of extraterrestrials purely in a state of nature, with no supernatural graces offered to them. In that case, such creatures would not in the end be able to share with us the Beatific Vision in heaven. But they could enjoy an eternity of the natural happiness for which they were intended by God.

We have also suggested that God's creatures across the cosmos might include some whose souls, though in some sense capable of rational intelligence, were nevertheless not granted the gift of immortality. Their souls, like the lower animals on Earth, would not survive after death. Yet their lives in this universe would still be a great good for them, and precious to their Creator.

But what of creatures made, as we are, in the image of God, whose souls possess all the characteristics that divine image entails? Certainly their intended final destiny would be an eternal communion with God, Face to face in heaven. If they had never fallen, or if they had fallen and received God's redemption, they would at last rest, as will the redeemed of Earth, in the arms of their Creator and Redeemer.

"The Blessed Company"

The *Catechism* speaks of "the blessed company of angels and men united in God."[1] We see the angels portrayed magnificently in the book of Revelation, where they join the saints in the worship of heaven (see Rv 4:1–11; 5:6–14). The universal Church, then, includes both intelligent species with Christ, the Son of God, as their Head: He [God] "has made him [Christ] the head over all things for the Church, which is his body, the fullness of him who fills all in all" (Eph 1:22–23).[2] As the divine Son of God, Christ naturally occupies this position.

This cosmic "fullness" of Christ's Body, the universal Church (in the broadest sense of "universal"), would certainly seem to include extraterrestrials whose final destiny is glorifying and contemplating their Creator in heaven. In Saint John's vision, he heard "every creature in heaven and on earth and under the earth and in the sea, and all therein" praising the Lamb on the throne (Rv 5:13). This statement does not necessarily include a reference to ETI, but it should prevent us from claiming that extraterrestrials would not be in that "blessed company" simply because they have not been specifically enumerated in Saint John's vision. They would easily fit into the generic category of "every creature in heaven . . . and all therein."

Would redeemed extraterrestrials need to be purged before their entrance into heaven, as most humans are purged? If

---

[1] *CCC* 336.
[2] The communion of the angels and saints is also suggested by the familiar words from the Litany of the Saints: "Blessed be God in his angels and in his saints!"

they were not yet perfected and ready to stand before the Father, it would make sense that He would make some provision for their purification so that they would be fit to stand in His immediate presence without being consumed by the blazing fire of His holiness (see Dt 4:24; 9:3; Heb 12:29). But that provision might take a form different from ours.

Thomas O'Meara offers a provocative speculation about this matter, though it is not clear from the context whether he is speaking about humans or extraterrestrials, or both: "The teaching about a purgative time and place between death and heaven found in several forms in religions is pertinent here. Some may not be ready for an intense realm of love and life. Another planet could offer the future stage of the psychologically and morally limited person. . . . Another world," O'Meara explains, "could educate them, free them, and lead them to levels of knowledge and maturity."[3] I must say that I am skeptical of that possibility.

"Groaning with Labor Pains"

A passage from Romans that we noted in an earlier chapter seems to speak of cosmic "Last Things": "For the creation waits with eager longing for the revealing of the sons of God; for the creation was subjected to futility, not of its own will but by the will of him who subjected it in hope, because the creation itself will be set free from its bondage to decay and obtain the glorious liberty of the children of God. We know," the Apostle concluded, "that the whole creation has been groaning with labor pains together until now" (Rom 8:19–22).

---

[3] O'Meara, *Vast Universe*, 59 n. 9. He seems to be presenting a variation of Herder's "golden celestial ladder" (see chapter 5).

What does Saint Paul mean here? The language is figurative, yet the intent seems clear: In some way, the perfection of creation appears to depend on the redemption of the "sons of God."

The Apostle could be referring to the way Christ's redemption breaks the curse on material creation that resulted from the fall of our first parents (see Gn 3:17–18). Or, as Saint Augustine concluded, the word "creation" means simply "humankind," since inanimate nature cannot literally "groan."

Lewis suggested that "on the conscious level, I believe that he [Saint Paul] was thinking only of our own Earth: of animal, and probably vegetable, life on Earth being 'renewed' or glorified at the glorification of man in Christ." Yet Lewis thought it possible that the Apostle's words also have a "cosmic meaning."[4]

If they do, how would that meaning relate to the speculations we have offered about ETI? One possibility is to interpret "sons of God" or "children of God" as any intelligent creatures, including extraterrestrials, who are being redeemed. But another possibility, assuming that the "sons of God" are specifically redeemed humans, is that the final completion, the perfection, of the universe requires the redemption of the human race.

The New Testament scholar C. E. B. Cranfield offers a helpful analogy: "The whole magnificent theater of the Universe, together with all its splendid properties and all the varied chorus of subhuman life, created for God's glory, is cheated of its true fulfillment so long as man, the chief actor

---

4   Lewis, "Religion and Rocketry," 93.

in the great drama of God's praise, fails to contribute his rational part . . . just as all the other players in a concerto would be frustrated of their purpose if the soloist were to fail to play his part."[5]

Cranfield is speaking narrowly of the "subhuman" creation and of redeemed human beings. But the analogy he offers also works for the universe as a whole, including ETI, if we adjust it slightly: Even if there are multiple "chief actors" who contribute their "rational part" to the great cosmic drama, and multiple "soloists" featured in the concerto, the whole universe is incomplete, its purpose frustrated, until the human race plays its part in the grand redemptive plan.

Are Humans and ETI Interconnected?

Marie George is concerned that, if intelligent extraterrestrials exist, our inability to interact with them would seem unfitting. Unlike our relationship with the angels, with whom we have long had commerce, we would be "diverse families . . . in one house, which did not communicate with each other."[6] "It is . . . impossible for the story of the universe [to] be a series of unrelated episodes."[7]

My response would be that for most of our history, almost no human beings in the Eastern Hemisphere of our globe had interaction with those in the Western Hemisphere. For countless generations they were utterly unaware of each

---

[5] C. E. B. Cranfield, "Some Observations on Romans 8:19–21," in R. Banks, ed., *Reconciliation and Hope: Essays on Atonement and Eschatology* (Grand Rapids, Mich: Eerdmans, 1974), 224–30.

[6] George, *Christianity*, 107.

[7] George, 100.

other, even though they lived in "one house," the Earth, infinitely smaller than the cosmos. And yet they were connected by their common Creator, their common humanity, their common intended destiny. They were not "unrelated episodes" in Earth's story—not only because their separate stories eventually converged in a single story, but also because, in the Author's mind, their episodes had always been part of the overall plot.

The cosmic story is not finished. But if redeemed ETI exists, our episodes will converge when we reach our final destiny. And even now, we are connected by our common Creator and common nature as made in the image of God. Who knows? We may even be connected, as some have suggested, by angelic missions between planets. And if even some of the increasingly frequent episodes of UAP turn out to have extraterrestrial origins, our interplanetary interaction may be considerably more immediate than we have realized.

We know from Scripture that the intelligent extraterrestrials we call angels assist us. If ETI exists, only God knows all the ways they may be serving us as well, and we, them. Venerable Andrea Beltrami's prayers for them would certainly have been to their benefit! Perhaps some of them know of our existence and pray for us. But even if their contribution to our welfare, and ours to them, should not be manifest until heaven, we can be certain that those extraterrestrials among the blessed will enjoy a happiness that will redound to our own.

ETI in Hell

I would be remiss to speak of ETI in heaven without considering the possibility of ETI in hell. Intelligent creatures on other planets with a free will and an immortal soul could choose to reject God and live apart from Him forever. Since He is the Source of all life, and every good thing, such permanent separation would be a horror beyond imagination for them, as it will be for human beings.[8]

Scripture portrays hell as the unending torment of both damned humans and damned angels (see Mt 25:41; Rv 20:7–15). It is not difficult to imagine that damned ETI individuals could be there as well. Yet God may well have other plans for an extraterrestrial who finally turns away from Him: Though the Church teaches us that annihilation of the wicked is not an option for our race, perhaps it may be for some on other planets. God could make creatures who have conditional immortality, whose post-mortem survival would depend on their final disposition toward Him.

Queen of the Universe

As we turn our mind toward final heavenly realities, I cannot help but think of the Blessed Virgin Mary. No Catholic perspective on extraterrestrial intelligence would seem complete without at least a brief recognition of Our Lady. I want to honor her and affirm that if ETI exists, her exalted dignity remains. Even if the Son of God has had multiple incarnations, she has borne Him on our planet and will forever be His mother, the Mother of God.

---

[8] See Thigpen, *Saints Who Saw Hell.*

We will always venerate her as Our Lady of Sorrows, Queen of Angels, Mother of Fair Love, Mystical Rose, Star of the Sea, Seat of Wisdom, and all the rest. But the one devotional title that gives me pause, should we learn that multiple divine incarnations have taken place, is her cosmic title, "Queen of the Universe."

Why is this particular title a cherished part of Catholic devotion, and how does it point to Mary's divine Son? In the monarchy of ancient Israel, descended from King David, the king often had multiple wives. This meant the title of "Queen" was usually reserved for the mother of the king (whom we would call today the "Queen Mother"). Her title in Hebrew meant literally "the Great Lady." Old Testament references to the "Great Lady" demonstrate that the King showed her high honor, and she acted as an intercessor with him on behalf of the people.

Centuries later, the archangel Gabriel announced to Mary that she would conceive a Child who was "the Son of the Most High," who would "give to him the throne of his father David" (Lk 1:32). In that declaration, the angel was announcing that she would be the Queen Mother of Christ's kingdom.

Who is the "King of the Universe," who rules over all things? The divine Son of God. So who is the Queen Mother of the Universe? His mother, the Blessed Virgin Mary.[9]

The Second Vatican Council affirms this Marian title in *Lumen Gentium*: "The Immaculate Virgin, preserved free from all guilt of original sin, on the completion of her

---

[9] See Edward Sri, "Is Mary's Queenship Biblical?" https://edwardsri .com/2014/12/27/is-marys-queenship-biblical/.

earthly sojourn, was taken up body and soul into heavenly glory, and exalted by the Lord as Queen of the universe, that she might be the more fully conformed to her Son, the Lord of lords and the conqueror of sin and death."[10] Nothing can take from her that precious title.

Mother of God, Mother of the Church

If the divine Son of God should become incarnate in extraterrestrial races, then His mother on other planets could also be rightly called the "Mother of God." He would, in fact, have several mothers—though their multiplicity would do nothing to diminish the exalted dignity of each one. The same would apply to the title "Mother of the Church," considering that the universal Church would include ETI as well.

Could there also be more than one universal Queen?

God's Son would be the universal King even if He were incarnate more than once, because each incarnation would be the same divine Person: one Lord, one Savior, one King. And we could apply that royal title to Jesus Christ and to every other incarnation, because of the *communicatio idiomatum.* But that reality does not apply to Mary. So what about *her* royal title?

We are in admittedly deep waters here, and if I offer any speculations that the Church should later rule out, I will be the first to reject them. My intention is not to dishonor my beloved Mother in any way. I am simply trying to understand what might be the implications of multiple incarnations in this regard.

---

[10] *Lumen Gentium*, 59.

Mother Most Humble

I see several possibilities here. First, we have no way of know-ing that extraterrestrial incarnations would involve biologi-cal motherhood as we understand it. Perhaps intelligent life on other planets would reproduce in a rather different way from ours, such as some kind of natural cloning, budding, or another form of asexual reproduction. Or perhaps the Son of God would take on flesh by entering an alien world fully formed and mature (though in doing so, He would lose the advantage of being in solidarity with ETI's childhood— if such creatures even *had* a childhood). In that case, Mary would be the only Mother of God and Mother of the Church.

In a similar way, perhaps the title or even the concept of a queen is unique to Earth. My own terrestrial nation and many others have no such ruler; certainly, the same could be possible on entire planets. In that case, Mary would be the sole Queen of the Universe.

Finally, even if there are multiple incarnations with mul-tiple Mothers of God and of the Church, who are also mul-tiple Queens of the Universe through the divine Majesty of their Son, the modest mother of Jesus that I know would not consider herself dishonored or diminished in any way. Nor would she view her "sisters" as rivals or be jealous of them. She is Mother Most Humble. In her perfect humility, she might well be pleased to share her dignity with mothers representing other intelligent races, who could also claim a throne as Queen of the Universe, because they too would share with her divine Son a special relationship unequalled among the race from which each one had sprung.

Meanwhile, her beloved Son would love, honor, and cherish each of His mothers as if there were only one of them.

The Particular and General Judgments

The Church teaches us that each human being will face two judgments: the individual (or particular) judgment and the general (or universal) judgment (at the Second Coming of Christ): "The New Testament speaks of judgment primarily in its aspect of the final encounter with Christ in his second coming, but also repeatedly affirms that each will be rewarded immediately after death in accordance with his works and faith."[11]

The particular judgment determines the individual's final destiny: "Each man receives his eternal retribution in his immortal soul at the very moment of his death, in a particular judgment that refers his life to Christ: either entrance into the blessedness of heaven—through purification[12] or immediately[13]—or immediate and everlasting damnation"[14].

The general judgment takes place for humanity at the end of human history: "On Judgment Day at the end of the world, Christ will come in glory to achieve the definitive triumph over good and evil, which, like the wheat and the tares, have grown up together in the course of history."[15]

---

[11] Cf. Lk 16:22; 23:43; Mt 16:26; 2 Cor 5:8; Phlm 1:23; Heb 9:27; 12:23.

[12] Cf. Council of Lyons II (1274): Denzinger, 857–58; Council of Florence (1439): Denzinger, 1304–6; Council of Trent (1563): Denzinger, 1820.

[13] Cf. Benedict XII, *Benedictus Deus* (1336): Denzinger, 1000–1001; John XII, *Ne super his* (1334): Denzinger, 990.

[14] *CCC* 1021–1022.

[15] *CCC* 681.

Though we can be certain of these judgments for human beings, we can say very little about whether any given intelligent extraterrestrial race would face such judgments, since the context of these statements seems to specify their terrestrial scope. In fact, we cannot know for sure even how or whether any given extraterrestrial race (or individual) experiences death as we know it.

The angels will accompany Christ when He returns to judge the Earth (see Mt 25:31; Lk 24:30–31; 1 Thess 4:16). Would ETI also stand with us before Christ on Judgment Day? Perhaps God has ordained that such a judgment will occur for all races, terrestrial as well as extraterrestrial, at the same time, and gather all intelligent creatures of the cosmos together on our planet.

I think it more likely, however, that if extraterrestrial species have a general Judgment Day, each planet will have its own. I say this for two reasons: First, Christ comes to *Earth* to draw *our* history to a close and judge us. It seems to be our appointed time as the terrestrial race to conclude our unique story.

Second, scientists estimate the age of the universe at many billions of years. So it seems likely that the histories of many intelligent extraterrestrial races would not coincide. There may well be planets where, by God's decree, ETI has already come and gone, or has yet to begin.

Even so, we should keep in mind that when our Day of Judgment comes on Earth, "we shall know the ultimate meaning of the whole work of creation and of the entire economy of salvation and understand the marvelous ways by

which his Providence led everything toward its final end."[16]
If races of intelligent extraterrestrials exist and are not with
us on that great and terrible day, it sounds as if we will nevertheless finally learn then about their existence and their role
in God's grand cosmic plan.

The New Heavens and New Earth

Sacred Scripture, Sacred Tradition, and the Sacred Magisterium all affirm that the ultimate destiny of the cosmos as
a whole is a grand conflagration, leading to a grand transformation. The timing of this event, or series of events, is
uncertain; it seems to follow Earth's Judgment Day, but we
cannot know how long the interval between might be: "But
the day of the Lord will come like a thief, and then the heavens will pass away with a loud noise, and the elements will
be dissolved with fire, and the earth and the works that are
upon it will be burned up. . . . But according to his [God's]
promise we wait for new heavens and a new earth in which
righteousness dwells" (2 Pt 3:10, 13).

The *Catechism* quotes the Second Vatican Council: "We
know neither the moment of the consummation of the
earth and of man, nor the way in which the universe will be
transformed."[17]

The Resurrection, Our Foretaste of Glory

In the book of Revelation, we find glorious scenes of the
perfected saints and angels worshipping around the throne

---

[16] *CCC* 1040.
[17] *CCC* 1048. *Gaudium et spes*, 39.1.

of God. We know that this scenario is taking place even now in heaven, beyond the reality we call the cosmos. But John's vision seems to speak as well of a final but mysterious convergence of that heavenly realm with the physical universe in a beautiful renewal of all things:

> Now I saw a new heaven and a new earth, for the first heaven and the first earth had passed away. . . . Then I, John, saw the holy city, new Jerusalem, coming down out of heaven from God, prepared as a bride adorned for her husband; and I heard a great voice from the throne saying, "Behold, the dwelling of God is with men. He will dwell with them, and they shall be his people, and God himself will be with them. . . . For the former things have passed away." And he who sat upon the throne said, "Behold, I make all things new." (Rv 21:1–5)

The various intelligent races across the cosmos may have their separate judgment days. But this consummation of all things is a cosmic event. It would seem, then, that the redeemed of all extraterrestrial races throughout the entire universe would dwell there with redeemed humanity in this "new heavens and new earth."

Resurrection Life

Ted Peters insists on a deep connection between the resurrection of Jesus and the ultimate transformation of the cosmos: "The first step in the promised transformation of the created order is the Easter resurrection of Jesus. . . . The first Easter resurrection amounted to . . . a fundamental alteration in the nature of nature. . . . The Christian claim is that what happened to Jesus of Nazareth on the first Easter models what will happen to the entirety of God's creation in the future."[18] In this light, perhaps the best clue about what our transformed life will be like is the body of Christ after His resurrection.

It was the same body that had lived and died on Earth; it still had the scars of His passion; His disciples could touch it; and it could still consume food. But it was now "glorious," as Saint Paul described it (see Phil 3:21), with startling capabilities: Christ could dematerialize and rematerialize; He could pass through solid objects; He could change His appearance to the point of being unrecognizable to His friends; He could ascend to heaven (see Lk 24:15–16, 31, 36–43, 50–51). His resurrected body seems to have become a radiant point of convergence between the old creation and the new creation.

The Apostle said that "the Lord Jesus Christ . . . will change our lowly body to be like his glorious body, by the power which enables him even to subject all things to himself" (Phil 3:21). He wrote at length about the resurrection of the bodies of the redeemed (see 1 Cor 15:35–50), and His description suggests that these bodies will also be part of the new creation. Perhaps these biblical passages provide us a hint of what is in store for all those who have been redeemed—both terrestrial and extraterrestrial.

"At the end of time," the *Catechism* tells us, "the Kingdom of God will come in its fullness. After the universal judgment, the righteous will reign forever with Christ,

---

[18] Peters, "One Incarnation or Many?" 299–300.

glorified in body and soul. The material universe itself will be renewed."[19] If intelligent extraterrestrial creatures exist, surely they will take part in that glorious transformation.

Tribes, Peoples, Tongues . . . Planets?

I used to speculate, with a dear Catholic friend who has now gone on to his reward, about the possibility of extraterrestrial life. We took great pleasure in imagining especially the possibility of meeting ETIs in heaven. I still recall our laughing together about how we might enter the pearly gates and find, to our surprise and delight, that in some of the "many rooms" in our Father's house (see Jn 14:2), those present looked something like the crowd of creatures in the cantina scene on Tatooine in *Star Wars*.

Saint John saw in his vision of heaven "a great multitude which no man can number from every nation, from all tribes and peoples and tongues, standing before the throne" (Rv 7:9). Perhaps my friend finally knows for sure now whether Saint John could have added to that list "all planets" as well.

---

[19] *CCC* 1042.

"The Outskirts of His Ways"

An Epilogue to the Conversation

"Behold, these are but the outskirts of his ways; and
how small a whisper do we hear of him! But the
thunder of his power who can understand?"

—Job 26:14

THE BEGINNING OF the "Age of Space" in the middle of the twentieth century, as we have seen, saw a brief surge of interest in ETI among Catholic theologians. Apparently, at least one American bishop shared their interest.

In June 1959, the Vatican commission that was preparing the agenda for the Second Vatican Council sent correspondence to all the world's bishops asking what should be discussed when they gathered. Archbishop Patrick J. O'Boyle (1896–1987) of Washington, DC, later made a cardinal, proposed that the council should make an authoritative pronouncement, "in light of the doctrines of creation and redemption," about "the possibility of intelligent life on other planets."[1]

As it turned out, the council made no such pronouncement. Perhaps the bishops considered the subject frivolous

---

[1] George Weigel, *Letters to a Young Catholic* (New York: Basic Books, 2004), 43.

or irrelevant to their purpose. Perhaps they took the matter seriously but believed, as had their predecessors, that God has not revealed to the Church His mind on this matter.

Some who write about extraterrestrial intelligence seem to be quite confident that they deal in *certainties* about the subject. Others, more modestly, speak more about *probabilities*. I have attempted (perhaps unsuccessfully) to be more modest still: I speak only of *possibilities*, beyond the few certainties in the matter provided by our Catholic faith. As the council Fathers knew, we must not presume to pronounce with certainty on matters where we have no divine authorization to speak.

We will not review here all the many specific possibilities we have explored. Instead, I wish to emphasize the overarching thesis I have argued: *The possibility that extraterrestrial intelligence exists is no threat to the Catholic, nor wider Christian, faith. We can remain faithful to the Church's magisterial teaching while accommodating that possibility.*

Why Is All This Important?

Some have wondered why I would spend so much time thinking about extraterrestrial realities when we face today so many urgently pressing terrestrial realities. If you have been patient enough to read this book to the end, I trust you will not have to be convinced that the topic is nevertheless an important one, for several reasons.

First, the public conversation about ETI and UAP is growing in significance, breadth, and seriousness in this nation and beyond. Many critics of Christian belief are using that conversation (as have others like them in the past) as an occasion to dismiss the claims of faith as contradictory, or at best irrelevant, to the possibility of intelligent life on other planets. This book reveals the many ways in which I believe they are mistaken and why they should reconsider their position.

Second, if the day should come when the world has a public, undeniable encounter with ETI, or an official disclosure of its existence, Catholics and other Christians must be prepared to assimilate that new empirical information through careful reflection and prayer. Just as their spiritual ancestors had to grapple with the theological implications of the Copernican revolution or the new encounter with peoples in the Western Hemisphere, they will have much to ponder that will require a response of "faith seeking understanding" (as Saint Anselm once called the process). And Catholic leaders, both clergy and laity, must be prepared to help them in that challenge.

Third, a public, ongoing conversation with intelligent extraterrestrials (if that can actually happen) would present opportunities to discern, if possible, their spiritual and moral status, the providential plans God might have for them, and the right kind of relationship between our races that would be implied by what we discover. Of central importance in that discovery process would be a determination of our proper response to what we find out.

What could we learn from them? What could we teach them? And more urgently, do we need to evangelize them?

Finally, I hope this present work has thoroughly demonstrated that even if we never learn the truth about extraterrestrial intelligence until the age to come, such a study

presses us to ponder questions that can draw us more deeply
into many theological and spiritual truths. The careful consideration of ETI in light of Catholic faith enriches our
understanding of God, His redemptive plan, ourselves, and
our universe.

Humility, Humility, Humility

You must forgive me if I return now, at the very end, to
the theme of humility. It may sound repetitious, but as in
so many regards, Saint Augustine is my model, who once
wrote to a friend: "If you should ask me what are the ways of
God, I would tell you that the first is humility, the second is
humility, and the third is humility."[2]

C. S. Lewis, another of my great personal mentors, sums
up my thoughts humbly and eloquently:

> This vast universe . . . may be full of life that needs
> no redemption. It may be full of life that has been
> redeemed. It may be full of things quite other than life
> that satisfy the Divine Wisdom in fashions one cannot
> conceive. We are in no position to draw up maps of
> God's psychology, and prescribe limits to his interests.
> We would not do so even for a man whom we knew
> to be greater than ourselves. The doctrines that God
> is Love and that he delights in men are positive doc-
> trines, not limiting doctrines. He is not less than this.
> What more he may be, we do not know; we know only
> that he must be more than we can conceive.[3]

---

[2] Epistle 118, to Dioscorus (a.d. 410), 3.22.
[3] C. S. Lewis, "Dogma and the Universe," in *Undeceptions: Essays on*

We should expect, then, Lewis concluded, that most of God's expansive creation should be beyond our comprehension. Down all these paths we have explored at most what Job called "the outskirts of his ways."

Theology and Ethics (London: Geoffrey Bles, 1971), 21.

What about UFOS?

Thoughts about Unidentified Flying Objects

*"What was once a ticket to the political loony bin
has leaped off Hollywood screens and out of science-
fiction novels and into the national conversation."*

—Michael Rosenwald

ON AUGUST 19, 1949, Saints Peter and Paul Catholic Church
in Norwood, Ohio, began a three-night parish fundraising
carnival. To grab the attention of the community, the event
featured an army surplus searchlight beamed up into the
night sky, operated by Sgt. Donald R. Berger of the University of Cincinnati's Reserve Officers' Training Corps. As
a result, parishioners and their guests had their eyes turned
toward the heavens.

What they saw there took them quite by surprise.

Around 8:15 p.m., the searchlight came across a "glowing
disc," seen by the sergeant, the parish pastor, Father Gregory
Miller, and others. This was, in fact, only the first occurrence
of the anomalous phenomenon: On nine occasions between
August 1949 and March 1950, UFOs (Unidentified Flying
Objects) were seen over the church, witnessed as well by local
residents not associated with the parish, including the mayor.

In one of these sightings, two groups of five triangular objects were observed emerging from the disc. One of the witnesses that night was Father Cletus Miller, Father Gregory's brother. Interestingly enough, he was at that time dean of the *Institutum Divi Thomae*—a graduate research institute established by the Archdiocese of Cincinnati, one of whose goals was to demonstrate that there is "no conflict between religion and science." Father Cletus reported that the triangular objects were shaped "like the apex of Indiana arrowheads."

Father Gregory reportedly possessed film of the object taken by Sgt. Davidson during the October 23 sighting. That film was shown to a closed audience in the studios of the Cincinnati TV station WCPO. It has since vanished.

The case of the "glowing discs" over Saints Peter and Paul remains unsolved.[1]

Multiplied Sightings around the World

These sightings of anomalous objects in the skies over Norwood were by no means unique. In fact, the mid-twentieth century saw a highly publicized increase in the sightings of UFOs (aka UAP, for "Unidentified Aerial Phenomena"). Hundreds of reports of such phenomena throughout the world, some no doubt legendary, can be found in accounts dating all the way back to the centuries before Christ, with aerial objects described as "airships," "glowing disks," "flying shields," and much more.[2] But reports of puzzling and

---

[1] See Nick Repatrizone, "Close Encounters: A priest and a mysterious U.F.O. sighting," *America* magazine, July 27, 2018.

[2] For an intriguing survey of such sightings, see Jacques Valle and Chris Aubeck, *Wonders in the Sky: Unexplained Aerial Objects from*

sometimes frightening sightings famously multiplied across the United States and around the globe beginning in the 1940s, starting with the "foo fighters," mysterious aerial lights that frequently tracked both Allied and Axis aircraft during World War II.

The American fascination with UAP that followed was heightened by a number of factors: the rapid development of aeronautics technology; Cold War tensions; a multiplication of popular science fiction novels, short stories, and films with alien invasion themes; highly publicized claims about UAP sightings and even encounters; and government attempts to ignore, dismiss, falsify, or actively suppress information related to anomalous aerial phenomena.[3]

Overviews of the Contemporary UAP Debate

Since the 1940s, countless UAP reports have been investigated and debated fiercely. Though some of the sightings have prosaic explanations, many do not. Some cases involve the kind of evidence that is difficult simply to dismiss, such as dozens of simultaneous and credible witnesses whose testimony is in full agreement, even decades after the events witnessed, and physical evidence pointing to close encounters with a craft.

Antiquity to Modern Times and Their Impact on Human Culture, History, and Beliefs (New York: Jeremy P. Tarcher/Penguin), 2009. We should note that the authors include sightings that Catholic tradition has recognized as apparitions of saints and other spiritual phenomena.

[3] My summary here is based on numerous accounts of these phenomena. For an excellent summary, see Ross Coulthart, *In Plain Sight: An investigation into UFOs and impossible science* (Harper Collins, 2021).

The history of such investigation and debate has been thoroughly documented, so I will not attempt even a summary here. For those who are interested, I highly recommend the book *In Plain Sight: An investigation into UFOs and impossible science* (Harper Collins, 2021) by Ross Coulthart, an award-winning Australian investigative journalist. Coulthart's work on this subject is thorough, comprehensive, level-headed, open-minded, and persuasive.

For those who tend to doubt the credibility or competence of UAP witnesses, I suggest especially Leslie Kean's *UFOs: Generals, Pilots, and Government Officials Go on the Record* (Harmony Books, 2010). Kean is an American investigative journalist whose work is carefully researched and compelling. Her sources, as the book's subtitle suggests, have impeccable credentials, and many of them come from nations around the world with similar stories to tell.

The Occasion for Writing This Book

In fact, it was Kean's reporting for *The New York Times* that prompted the writing of the present book. I have wanted to write on this subject for many years, but too many other subjects pressed ahead of it to demand my consideration. That is, until now.

The extraordinary events of the recent *annus horribilis*, the year 2020, were deeply unsettling: In our nation we witnessed a pandemic and a resulting economic lockdown; what is arguably the most intense, extensive social and political upheaval endured in half a century or more; the natural disasters of record-breaking hurricanes, vast wildfires, earthquakes and, yes, the threat of murder hornets. But the convergence of all these disturbing developments so riveted our national attention that yet another extraordinary media headline was all but ignored.

On July 23, *The New York Times* published a startling report by Leslie Kean and Ralph Blumenthal, both seasoned journalists. It was entitled, "No Longer in Shadows, Pentagon's U.F.O. Unit Will Make Some Findings Public." The article began: "Despite Pentagon statements that it disbanded a once-covert program to investigate unidentified flying objects, the effort remains underway—renamed and tucked inside the Office of Naval Intelligence, where officials continue to study mystifying encounters between military pilots and unidentified aerial vehicles." The journalists went on to say that this "Unidentified Aerial Phenomenon Task Force" was noted in a report of the US Senate's Select Committee on Intelligence that called for it to make some of its findings public.[4]

Though the task force was ostensibly focused on the threat that our earthly adversaries may have extremely advanced aviation technologies,

> retired officials involved with the effort—including Harry Reid, the former Senate majority leader—hope the program will seek *evidence of vehicles from other worlds*. . . . Mr. Reid, . . . who pushed for funding the earlier U.F.O. program when he was the majority leader, said *he believed that crashes of objects of unknown*

---

[4] Ralph Blumenthal and Leslie Kean, "No Longer in Shadows, Pentagon's U.F.O. Unit Will Make Some Findings Public," *The New York Times*, July 23, 2020, https://www.nytimes.com/2020/07/23/us/politics/pentagon-ufo-harry-reid-navy.html?searchResultPosition=1.

*origin may have occurred and that retrieved materials
should be studied.* 'After looking into this [Reid stated],
I came to the conclusion that there were reports—
some were substantive, some not so substantive—that
*there were actual materials that the government and the
private sector had in their possession*'" (emphasis added).[5]

Eric W. Davis, an astrophysicist who had worked as a sub-
contractor and then a consultant for the Pentagon UAP program since 2007, said that "he gave a classified briefing to
a Defense Department agency as recently as March [2020]
about *retrievals from 'off-world vehicles not made on this earth.'*
. . . Mr. Davis said he also gave classified briefings on retrievals of unexplained objects to staff members of the Senate
Armed Services Committee on Oct. 21, 2019, and to staff
members of the Senate Intelligence Committee two days
later" (emphasis added).[6]

If not for the screaming media headlines in July about
more earthly matters, a reference to "retrievals from 'off-
world vehicles not made on this earth'" would almost certainly have been front-page news. Consider: Our government
may well possess physical evidence (as many investigators
have suspected for years) of spacecraft (and their occupants?)
visiting from another world. I asked myself, shouldn't we be
talking about this matter?

---

[5]   Blumenthal and Kean, "No Longer in Shadows."
[6]   Blumenthal and Kean.

New Congressional Legislation

In December 2020, legislation was passed by the US Congress instructing the director of national intelligence to help produce an unclassified report on everything government agencies know about UAP. The House Intelligence Committee met with Navy and FBI officials on June 16, 2021, for a highly classified briefing on the full report in a "sensitive compartmented information facility." A much shorter, unclassified version was made public on June 25.[7]

Not surprisingly, the unclassified report was quite limited in its scope and reserved in its findings, with an analysis of only 143 UAP reports from government sources since 2004. Only one case could be explained. It made no suggestion of extraterrestrial origins for the 142 cases it could not explain, but neither did it rule out such origins. It *did* make the important declarations that none of these 142 cases represented secret American aircraft, and that they exhibited extraordinary maneuvering capabilities: hypersonic speeds (up to five times the speed of sound); no observable means of propulsion; and extremely rapid acceleration and abrupt change of direction—all beyond the known capabilities of human terrestrial aircraft.

In a majority of these cases, "UAP were registered across multiple sensors, to include radar, infrared, electro-optical, weapon seekers, and visual observation." In some of the cases, radio frequency energy was detected in association

---

[7] Juliegrace Brufke and Aaron Feis, "UFOs could threaten US security, pols say after Capitol Hill briefing," *New York Post*, 16 June 2021, https://nypost.com/2021/06/16/ufos-could-threaten-u-s-security-pols-say-after-briefing/.

with the UAP. A few even indicated the capability of performing "signature management"—that is, efforts to avoid detection by radar or other electronic systems, indicating intelligent control.[8]

Finally, the report called for "consistent consolidation of reports from across the federal government, standardized reporting, increased collection and analysis, and a streamlined process for screening all such reports against a broad range of relevant USG [U.S. government] data," which "will allow for a more sophisticated analysis of UAP that is likely to deepen our understanding."[9] Military personnel who witness UAP are now actually encouraged to report what they have observed. This is an important change in military policy; previously, fear of stigma and even retribution typically kept witnesses from reporting.

The US Senate Select Committee on Intelligence had access to the classified report. Among the members of that committee were Senator Kirsten Gillibrand (D-NY) and Senator Marco Rubio (R-FL), vice-chairman. Apparently, what these two legislators learned from the UAP report pressed Gillibrand to sponsor, and Rubio to cosponsor with others, an amendment to the National Defense Authorization Act for 2022, which was passed by both houses of

---

[8]   Julian E. Barnes, "U.S. Has No Explanation for Unidentified Objects and Stops Short of Ruling Out Aliens," *The New York Times*, June 25, 2021, https://www.nytimes.com/2021/06/25/us/politics/pen tagon-ufo-report.html. For the full unclassified report, see Office of the Director of National Intelligence, "Preliminary Assessment: Unidentified Aerial Phenomena," June 25, 2021, https://www.dni.gov/files/OD NI/documents/assessments/Prelimary-Assessment-UAP-20210625.pdf.
[9]   Office of the Director of National Intelligence, "Preliminary Assessment."

Congress in December 2021. The amendment called for the creation of a new joint Defense Department and Intelligence Community office focused on UAPs. This office will collect and analyze UAP data from across the many US intelligence communities; establish a science plan to test scientific theories related to UAP characteristics and performances; coordinate with federal agencies, including the FAA and NASA, as well as international allies and partners on issues related to UAPs; and provide unclassified annual reports to Congress, plus classified semiannual briefings on intelligence analysis, reported incidents, and much more.[10]

In all these ways, then, since the dawn of the twenty-first century, a new interest in the subject has emerged, and serious discussions about it are slowly growing more respectable. Because of the changes in Pentagon policy and the involvement of Congress, news coverage of the subject has become more commonplace (and less derisive and frivolous). And several foreign governments have become much more transparent about UAP sightings in their countries.[11]

---

[10] Marik Von Rennenkampff, "Sen. Gillibrand's historic legislation would revolutionize study of UFOs," *The Hill*, November 19, 2021, https://thehill.com/opinion/national-security/580698-sen-gillibrands -historic-legislation-would-revolutionize-study-of. For more details on the relevant amendment, see "Gillibrand's Groundbreaking Unidentified Aerial Phenomena Amendment Included in Final NDAA," https:// www.gillibrand.senate.gov/news/press/release/gillibrands-groundbre aking-unidentified-aerial-phenomena-amendment-included-in-final -ndaa. The legislation passed the House on December 7 and the Senate on December 15.

[11] For a summary of these developments, see Gideon Lewis-Kraus, "How the Pentagon Started Taking UFOs Seriously: For decades, flying saucers were a punchline. Then the U.S. government got over the taboo," *The New Yorker*, April 30, 2021, https://www.newyorker

As Michael Rosenwald noted in *The Washington Post*: "What was once a ticket to the political loony bin has leaped off Hollywood screens and out of science-fiction novels and into the national conversation." Former Senator Harry Reid (D-NM), who for years was instrumental in bringing the conversation into the open among government officials, recalled: "Everyone told me this would cause me nothing but trouble. But I wasn't afraid of it. And I guess time has proven me right."[12]

How Are UAP Related to the Theological Issues in This Book?

As I noted in the introduction, the UAP debate is not the focus of the present work, which seeks to examine the possibility of extraterrestrial intelligence in light of specifically Catholic, and more generally Christian, faith. Theological proposals about ETI are not dependent on whether any particular reports of UAP can be verified as authentic or debunked as misidentification or hoax.

.com/magazine/2021/05/10/how-the-pentagon-started-taking-ufos-se riously. For details about foreign government disclosures, see Coulthart, *In Plain Sight*, and Kean, *UFOs*.

[12] Michael Rosenwald, "How UFOs went from joke to national security worry in Washington," *The Washington Post*, May 23, 2021, https:// www.msn.com/en-us/news/us/how-ufo-sightings-went-from-joke-to -national-security-worry-in-washington/ar-AAKiHOp?ocid=uxbndl bing; Marik von Rennenkampff, "NASA chief Bill Nelson latest official to suggest UFOs have otherworldly origins," *The Hill*, November 1, 2021, https://thehill.com/opinion/international/579303-nasa-chief-bill -nelson-latest-official-to-suggest-ufos-have. Reid died on December 28, 2021. Not surprisingly, news outlets failed to mention in his obituaries, among his other accomplishments, his key role in the government's development of UAP study and disclosure.

Even so, as I also noted, because of recent developments, the subject may finally receive the prolonged and focused attention it deserves. If our government or another country's government should actually disclose evidence of extraterrestrial intelligence, the Church must be prepared for the challenges that would inevitably arise from such a public disclosure.

Back in 1960, an influential American think tank focusing on public policy issued a report to NASA that warned of the possibility of cultural, religious, and social disruption if the discovery of ETI should be disclosed to the public. The report suggested that civil authorities, in consultation with scientists, would need to consider withholding such information.[13]

The conclusion that civil authorities, with the cooperation of scientists, may need to hide what they know about ETI to protect an unenlightened populace seems to me rather patronizing and wrong-headed. In more recent years, other sociological studies have suggested that ETI disclosure or encounter would not at all be disruptive to most religious communities. Some of these studies have been challenged on methodological grounds, but I am unaware of any studies suggesting that the verified existence of ETI would cause

---

[13] Fred Dews, "Communication, Technology, and Extraterrestrial Life: The Advice Brookings Gave NASA About the Space Program in 1960," *Brookings Now*, May 12, 2014, https://www.brookings.edu/blog/brookings-now/2014/05/12/communications-technology-and-extraterrestrial-life-the-advice-brookings-gave-nasa-about-the-space-program-in-1960/.

enough social disruption to justify keeping the public from knowing the truth.[14]

At this point, the more likely consequence of government disclosure, after years of denial, would be a further erosion of public confidence in civil officials. Therein might lie the more likely reason for government reticence on the matter. Even so, recent developments suggest that the government's longstanding policy might be changing—not just the recent Pentagon report to the US Senate Intelligence Committee but also the US Navy's unprecedented public admission that certain leaked videos of unidentified aerial phenomena made by naval aviators, which seem to defy the laws of physics, are genuine and cannot be explained.[15]

In any case, even in the absence of major disruptions, if government officials should make a public disclosure of convincing evidence that ETI exists, the Church would need to respond to her challengers. A reasonable, understandable demonstration that Christian faith is not undermined by confirmation of extraterrestrial intelligence could go far in reassuring the Christian faithful while helping skeptics and adherents of ETI-based religions to reconsider their claims.

---

[14] On the possible effects of public disclosure of the existence of ETI, see Ted Peters, "Extraterrestrial Life and Terrestrial Religion: A Crisis?" in *Astrotheology*, 183–205; David A. Weintraub, ed., *Religions and Extraterrestrial Life: How Will We Deal With It?* (New York: Springer, 2014); Richard M. Dolan and Bryce Zabel, *A.D. After Disclosure: The People's Guide to Life After Contact* (Rochester, N.Y.: Keyhole Publishing, 2010).

[15] Alan Yuhas, "The Pentagon Released U.F.O. Videos. Don't Hold Your Breath for a Breakthrough," *The New York Times*, April 28, 2020, updated July 24, 2020, https://www.nytimes.com/2020/04/28/us/pentagon-ufo-videos.html.

If, in a more stunning development, we should witness a public, verifiable ETI encounter, and communication with the visitors became possible, the Church would need to engage in a carefully considered dialogue with our new interlocuters. In light of the possibilities we have noted in this book about ETI knowledge of their Creator, and their spiritual and moral status in relationship with Him, we would have much to teach, and perhaps much to learn.

"An Absurd Extreme of Hypercriticism"

Christian writers examining the topic of ETI since the proliferation of UAP have largely avoided that controversy, focusing instead on the theological implications of possible extraterrestrial intelligence. Even so, certain wider issues surrounding the UAP have some relevance to the theological ETI conversation.

Monsignor Corrado Balducci (1923–2008), an Italian theologian, exorcist for the Archdiocese of Rome, and member of the Roman Curia, on several occasions publicly addressed the issue of ETI in light of Catholic faith. One of his concerns was the facile dismissal of all the testimony by countless observers who have witnessed UAP, simply because they attest to extraordinary events. Balducci noted that the apostolic witness to Christ would itself have to be dismissed if we were to maintain the irrational principle that testimony to extraordinary events unexplained by science must automatically be ruled out as mistaken or fraudulent, even when the witnesses are competent, credible, and numerous.[16]

---

[16] This incident is reported by Corrado Balducci in "Ufology and Theological Clarifications," remarks presented at Pescara, Italy, June 8,

In this observation, Balducci made reference to the work of the British priest Fr. Herbert Thurston, SJ (1856–1939). This Jesuit scholar's research into paranormal phenomena a century ago encountered extraordinary events that were also frequently dismissed out of hand as fraud, simply because science could not account for the activity. Thurston quoted a Dominican priest acquaintance involved in similar research, who asked: "Is it possible . . . without falling into an absurd extreme of hypercriticism, to refuse credence to the confidences, made by word of mouth, of people whose mental balance, good faith, and high level of intelligence are beyond all question?" Such "an attitude of skepticism," Thurston noted, "would undermine the validity of all human testimony in favour of the miraculous"—and, we might add, in favor of what is merely scientifically unexplainable.[17]

I think we must return to a theme often noted in this work: the importance of *humility* in this conversation. We need humility to consider seriously the many claims of trustworthy and mentally competent individuals who insist that they have in fact witnessed what seems to be an extraterrestrial aircraft—or even that they have encountered ETI directly. In this regard, I differ from many scholars and commentators who discuss this matter. They flatly dismiss the value of such reports, reflexively questioning their veracity or even the credibility of the witnesses. But I think it would be patently presumptuous for us to take that attitude.

2001. Available by subscription at https://www.scribd.com/document/134453494/Corrado-Balducci.

[17] Herbert Thurston, *The Church and Spiritualism* (Milwaukee, Wis.: Bruce, 1933), 7–8. Thurston is today remembered primarily for his extensive contributions to *The Catholic Encyclopedia*.

We must note as well that some of the philosophical, theological, and scientific arguments against the existence of ETI are based on the presumed "fact" that they have never visited our planet. Such arguments are weakened by so much reasonable testimonial evidence to the contrary. We cannot dismiss out of hand so many testimonies by intelligent, credible witnesses simply because their experience challenges our common assumptions about our world. I am particularly sensitive to this concern as the author of several books on spiritual warfare: I have encountered a similar extreme and unwarranted skepticism toward first-person testimonies to the reality of demons.

The English philosopher John Stuart Mill once rightly noted that in debated matters, people tend to be correct in what they affirm, and wrong in what they deny. I think this principle holds true because of a common type of arrogance: The kinds of realities people deny are often excluded from consideration on the mere grounds that they themselves have not experienced such things. But if they themselves were to have a close encounter, for example, with aliens or demons, they would almost certainly change their minds.

After years of intensive study of UAP, I have several tentative conclusions and speculations to offer. Though my analysis of ETI in light of the Catholic faith does not depend on any claims about UAP, my publisher and editor have urged me to include this appendix. I agree with them that many readers interested in ETI would be disappointed, if not annoyed, if I failed to include at least a few words about the subject.

For what they are worth, here are my thoughts.[18]

A Massive Body of Compelling Evidence

First, we simply cannot dismiss what is now a massive body of UAP literature available from countless reliable sources, compiled over many decades from nations around the world: credible and competent witnesses, once-classified government documents, respected investigative journalists, highly trained pilots, and high-ranking officials of the military and other government bodies.

As we have noted, in some of the most compelling UAP cases, multiple eyewitness testimony was confirmed through our military's most advanced sensors. Such UAP exhibited beyond-next-generation technological capabilities. These include instantaneous acceleration and maneuvering; hypersonic velocity (without sonic booms); evasive action and other indicators of intelligent control; low observability (stealth technology); transmedium travel (the ability to operate in various environments, moving between space, the atmosphere, and bodies of water); and positive lift (the ability to fly without the apparent need for control surfaces, wings, or any obvious forms of propulsion).

Again, as we have noted, the Pentagon has finally confirmed that these crafts have capabilities beyond any that our nation possesses, and as far as we know, beyond any that our terrestrial adversaries possess. In fact, most of these

---

[18] I will not attempt to document each point individually. Interested readers can refer to the two books I have just cited and other sources in the bibliography as well, which provide ample evidence for these conclusions and speculations.

capabilities were apparent in many of the sightings as long ago as the 1940s, when no nation on earth could conceivably have produced them.[19]

This extensive body of startling but undeniable evidence compels me to conclude that at least some unidentified aerial phenomena have no prosaic explanation. They cannot be accounted for by any known natural phenomena or human technology.

Meanwhile, as noted in the introduction, I find unconvincing any claims that UAP cannot possibly represent interstellar travelers because the laws of physics do not allow for movement beyond the speed of light. Our understanding of physics continues to expand and evolve. The emerging science of breakthrough propulsion studies, working at the edge of known physics, suggests the serious possibility of space drives, warp drives, gravity control, and faster-than-light travel through the manipulation of space-time itself.[20]

Government Cover-Up, Intimidation, Ridicule

A second conclusion: Multiple documents obtained through the Freedom of Information Act and other sources, as well as the testimony of numerous former military and government

---

[19] Nikolas Lanum, "Ex-UFO Pentagon program chief outlines 'compelling' UFO theories and 'unique' vehicle characteristics," *FOX News*, March 23, 2021, https://www.foxnews.com/tech/ufo-theories-pentagon-chief-report.

[20] See Marc G. Mills and Eric W. Davis, eds., *Frontiers of Propulsion Science* (Reston, Va.: American Institute of Aeronautics and Astronautics, Inc., 2009); https://arc.aiaa.org/doi/book/10.2514/4.479953. See especially Davis, "Review of Gravity Control Within Newtonian and General Relativistic Physics," 175–228.

officials, convince me that for more than seventy years, the US government, especially the Pentagon, has systematically engaged in an attempted cover-up of the evidence about UAP in its possession. If made public, this evidence would disclose significant information about these unidentified phenomena. In addition, the US military and the intelligence community long engaged in a disinformation campaign involving not just secrecy and denial but also intimidation and ridicule of those who would take the subject of UAP seriously or go public with their personal UAP experiences. Until quite recently, most of the news industry has collaborated in such denial and mockery, providing only rare, dismissive, and frivolous coverage of the subject.

Speculations abound about the motives for such official policy. Almost certainly, concerns about national security were part of the mix during the Cold War. The 1960 Brookings Institute report cited earlier suggests that some officials also feared social disruption should disclosure of UAP take place. Today such concerns seem hardly worthy of such secrecy; perhaps the recent limited admissions by the Pentagon about the subject demonstrate a recognition that times have changed in that regard.

Even so, those who know the truth may still remain silent because they feel fear may spread through the public, believing that the government, especially the military, cannot protect us against whoever it is that controls such advanced technology (if indeed we need protection). In addition, some officials and former officials may fear legal repercussions if they should admit to having engaged in deceit and intimidation. Perhaps an offer of amnesty could finally open the door to full, or at least nearly full, disclosure.

Meanwhile, recall the *New York Times* report: We must consider that the military (or perhaps civilian government contractors in the aerospace industry) may in fact possess retrieved crashed UAP material, as many alleged witnesses have claimed, going all the way back to the famous Roswell, New Mexico incident of 1947. If so, then scientists and technologists have almost certainly been trying to reverse engineer the exotic technology and materials in their possession.[21]

That scenario, if true, could also help to explain the ongoing secrecy: The less our terrestrial adversaries know, the less likely they would be to engage in successful espionage or sabotage of our efforts. Even so, we should not underestimate our adversaries' intelligence-gathering capabilities, despite whatever secrecy we might try to enforce.

Perhaps for decades, a more startling theory suggests, the government has actually operated secret alliances with alien visitors or even alien colonizers. They maintain such covert arrangements because the aliens offer them advanced technology in exchange for earthly resources. Such a claim was most famously made by Haim Eshed, a retired brigadier

---

[21] See Bryce Zabel, "The Roswell UFO Crash is on the Fast Track to Disclosure," *Trail of the Saucers*, July 2, 2021, https://medium.com/on-the-trail-of-the-saucers/roswell2021-a9e209925a66; Thomas J. Carey and Donald R. Schmitt, *Witness to Roswell: Unmasking the Government's Biggest Coverup*, 2nd ed., rev. (San Francisco: Weiser, 2009); Stanton T. Friedman, *Top Secret/Majic: Operation Majestic-12 and the United States Government's UFO Cover-up*, 2nd ed. (Boston: Da Capo Press, 2005).

general in Israeli Military Intelligence who was for thirty years the head of Israel's space program.[22]

According to one religiously-oriented speculation, high-level government officials secretly traffic in demons but employ the ruse of UAP to conceal their activities.[23] Others have claimed that certain high-level figures in the intelligence community are fundamentalist Christians who want to conceal what the government knows because they believe that anything involving UAP and the paranormal is diabolical. According to Luis Elizondo, the former director of the US government's Advanced Aerospace Threat Identification Program (AATIP), these officials consider the UAP data collected to be a threat to their belief system.[24]

Whatever the reasons for a cover-up, some certainly more difficult to believe than others, the relevant point is this: Certain officials in the American government, including those in the Pentagon and national intelligence agencies,

---

[22] Aaron Reich, "Former Israeli space security chief says aliens exist, humanity not ready," *The Jerusalem Post,* December 10, 2020, https://www.jpost.com/omg/former-israeli-space-security-chief-says-aliens-exist-humanity-not-ready-651405.

[23] See, for example, William Cyrus, "NASA's Satanic Illuminati Fallen Angel Alien Agenda Exposed!! 2015," https://www.dailymotion.com/video/x36lppi.

[24] Quoted in Alejandro Rojas, "The X-Files Revealed: The Paranormal Roots of the Pentagon's UFO Program," May 15, 2019, https://www.denofgeek.com/tv/the-x-files-revealed-unidentified-history/. Elizondo has been a central figure in the recent developments moving toward increased government transparency and even disclosure with regard to UAP. He has appeared in numerous interviews; see, for example, Charlie Burton, "This man ran the Pentagon's secretive UFO programme for a decade. We had some questions," November 9, 2021, https://www.gq-magazine.co.uk/politics/article/luis-elizondo-interview-2021.

ignored or concealed important information about UAP for more than seventy years, and attempted to discredit those who sought some kind of serious analysis of the phenomena. Along with many skeptical journalists and dismissive scientists—and no doubt strengthened by hoaxers, bizarre UFO tales, and uninformed observers—these officials helped to form a culture of cynicism about ETI discussion in "enlightened" circles.

Is UAP Demonic?

A second element of the UAP story has important theological implications: As we have noted, many of the highly publicized claims to personal encounters with ETI (especially the so-called "abduction" stories) have shown certain parallels to traditional accounts of encounters with demons. Though such claims have involved only a small portion of alleged UAP sightings, a number of Christian observers have concluded that the entire UAP phenomenon is diabolically designed and executed.[25]

I think it likely that some reported UAP encounters are indeed diabolical. Alien abduction accounts reporting assault or injury of the abductee, direct manipulation of the

---

[25] See, for example, Timothy Dailey, *The Paranormal Conspiracy: The Truth About Ghosts, Aliens and Mysterious Beings* (Minneapolis, Minn.: Chosen, 2015); William M. Alnor, *UFOs in the New Age: Extraterrestrial Messages and the Truth of Scripture* (Grand Rapids, Mich.: Baker, 1992); Elizabeth L. Hillstrom, *Testing the Spirits* (Downers Grove, Ill.: InterVarsity Press, 1995); Nick Redfern, *Final Events and the Secret Government Group on Demonic UFOs and the Afterlife* (New York: Anomalist Books, 2010); Dwight Longenecker, "Angels and Aliens," May 1, 2013, https://www.catholic.com/magazine/print-edition/angels -and-aliens.

abductee's thoughts, or alleged "spiritual revelations" of an occult nature all suggest demonic involvement. In addition, at least some abductees have testified that calling on Jesus for help during an abduction experience immediately ended the encounter and kept the "aliens" from returning.[26] Some of the terrifying and violent paranormal phenomena associated with UAP at the much-publicized Skinwalker Ranch in Utah would also seem to fit this category, given especially the associations there with Native American witchcraft.[27]

Nevertheless, I believe we must not assume that diabolical activity in some cases implies such activity in all cases. The great majority of UAP reports include no elements of manipulated thoughts, spiritual "revelations," or malicious injury to witnesses (though some involve injury from what seems to be incidental exposure to radiation). At the same time, in the case of so-called "nuts-and-bolts" UAP—especially if a clearly physical object has crashed, allowing retrieval of debris—we would be hard pressed to explain why demons, who are purely spiritual beings, would need to be transported by physical vehicles.

---

[26] Nick Redfern, *The NASA Conspiracies: The Truth Behind the Moon Landings, Censored Photos, and the Face on Mars* (Pompton Plains, N.J.: New Page Books, 2011), 149–52.

[27] See Colm A. Kelleher and George Knapp, *Hunt for the Skinwalker: Science Confronts the Unexplained at a Remote Ranch in Utah* (New York: Paraview, 2005); James T. Lacatski, Colm A. Kelleher, and George Knapp, *Skinwalkers at the Pentagon: An Insiders' Account of the Secret Government UFO Program* (Henderson, Nev.: RTMA, LLC, 2021).

Parallels with Ultraterrestrials

Finally, we must recognize that the UAP "extraterrestrial hypothesis," as it is called, is only one of several possibilities frequently proposed by those who believe that many such phenomena have no prosaic explanation. They agree that many cases of UAP seem to be a function of non-human intelligence. But (ruling out good and evil angels), does this mean that UAP necessarily have extraterrestrial origins? Could they instead be *ultraterrestrial*—that is, non-human intelligent beings who inhabit our planet alongside us, largely hidden from our view?

At this point, admittedly, we move into the puzzling territory of "high strangeness." But we are not alone in taking this step; at least a few Christian thinkers have been in that territory before us. Recall, for example, Saint Jerome's account of Saint Anthony and the satyr. The brilliant and devout "father of biblical scholarship" apparently accepted, without theological objections, the existence of a least one form of ultraterrestrial that was intelligent but neither human nor diabolical.[28]

The mythology, legends, and folklore of quite different cultures around the world have long hinted that we share the planet with various kinds of "faerie folk," sometimes called "the secret commonwealth." Depending on their locale, they are variously known as satyrs and nymphs, fairies and pixies,

---

[28] Though some might point out that the word "satyr" actually appears in some English translations of the Bible (see Lv 17:7; Is 13:21; 34:14; 2 Ch 11:15), scholars debate the meanings of the Hebrew word in these passages. It could simply refer to a shaggy creature, a he-goat, a pagan idol in the form of a goat, or a demon.

leprechauns and elves, dwarfs and trolls, brownies and mene-hune and stick people.

According to one understanding of faerie folk in medieval culture, they were mortal and bodily rather than supernatural and spiritual. Their bodies, however, might be composed of matter more "subtle" than ours; they typically would live longer than humans; and they would possess some abilities that seem magical to humans because they differ from our own. They represent what the seventeenth-century Scottish folklorist and Anglican pastor Robert Kirk called "a middle nature between man and angel," and they operate in a world that is parallel to ours.[29]

In his book *The Discarded Image*, C. S. Lewis described these as a third rational and terrestrial species distinct from angels and humans. He quoted Reginald Scot's *Discoverie of Witchcraft* (1584), who insisted that "their nature is middle between heaven and hell. . . . They reign in a third kingdom, having no other judgement or doom to expect forever."[30] Though one alternative view of the faeries was that they are simply demons, Lewis suggested that this view reflected a

---

[29] Perhaps the best-known presentation of faerie stories (collected from the Scottish people) is Robert Kirk, *The Secret Commonwealth: Of Elves, Fauns, and Faeries*, first published in 1815 by Sir Walter Scott, then reedited and published in 1893 by Andrew Lang. The quote is from Kirk.

[30] See chapter VI, "The *Longaevi*," in C. S. Lewis, *The Discarded Image: An Introduction to Medieval and Renaissance Literature* (Cambridge: Cambridge University Press, 1964), 122–38. The Scot quote is on p. 135.

superstitious darkening that became the common position in post-medieval thought.[31]

Could there possibly be some kind of historical reality underlying the belief that a third rational terrestrial species, distinct from angels and humans, exists? Lewis himself seemed to take the subject seriously; in a lecture at Oxford on the subject, he even referred to someone he knew who had encountered fairies. In his description of the medieval cosmos, he relished such "marginal, fugitive creatures" who "intrude a welcome hint of wildness and uncertainty into a universe that is in danger of being too self-explanatory, too luminous."[32]

More than one contemporary commentator on UAP has suggested the possibility that modern unidentified flying "aircraft" may actually represent a new appearance of the old ultraterrestrials known to myth and legend, but now in space age garb. The very suggestion may seem little more than a fanciful whim. But it has arisen in part because today's claims of alien encounters often demonstrate clear parallels to ancient stories of "little people."

Both types of alleged creatures are frequently described as diminutive and human-like. They are often associated with glowing orbs. They can suddenly appear, disappear, and fly around. Though many times vexatious and capricious, they are rarely hostile. In fact, they are often playful, even to the

---

[31] Lewis, 138.
[32] Lewis, 122; Brinton Dickieson, "C. S. Lewis's Faerie Lecture, and a Prince Edward Island Folk Tale," *A Pilgrim in Narnia*," December 14, 2012, https://apilgriminnarnia.com/2012/12/14/kidnapped-by-fairies/.

point of playing pranks and "games" of hide and seek with those who encounter them.[33]

Luis Elizondo, former director of the US government's UAP analysis program, has speculated about UAP in a way that hints at this theory: Rather than extraterrestrials, he observed, "it's possible that it's something that has been on Earth for a very long time."[34]

Parallels with Poltergeists

A similar kind of phenomenon is encountered in accounts of poltergeists. Hollywood, with its perpetual thirst for horror stories, has portrayed the poltergeist phenomenon as consistently malicious and evil. Historical records of such phenomena do in fact demonstrate that some encounters are almost certainly diabolical and can be countered only by the ministrations of the Catholic Church.

Even so, the thorough investigations and analysis of Father Herbert Thurston, SJ (noted previously), reveal a pattern in many carefully recorded cases: Poltergeists may harass and confuse humans, and do damage to their property, but they rarely cause any serious injury to their persons. In numerous

---

[33] See, for example, Jacques Valle, *Passport to Magonia: From Folklore to Flying Saucers* (New York: Daily Grail, 2014); John A. Keel, *Operation Trojan Horse: An exhaustive study of unidentified flying objects — revealing their source and the forces that control them* (London: Abacus, 1973). I cite these two works simply as examples of this hypothesis; they are problematic in many ways because their limited secular perspective fails to distinguish genuinely supernatural and spiritual experience of the Christian tradition with other, quite different, claims of extraordinary phenomena.

[34] Quoted in Burton, "Pentagon's secretive UFO programme."

cases, in fact, they are known rather to tease and play pranks. In this way, they seem to be more akin to the faerie folk.[35]

More importantly, in many cases, the prayers, sacraments, sacramentals, relics, and rites of the Church have been incapable of halting poltergeist activity. In fact, priests who attempted to exorcise poltergeist-ridden homes were sometimes mocked by having their vestments and books torn by unseen hands or being pelted with filth that seemed to come out of nowhere. We would expect that if the entities involved were truly demonic, they would have to yield to such powerful spiritual weapons. Instead, the unseen forces acted more like mischievous school children, irreverent but not diabolical.

"Nothing more purposeless," Thurston concluded, "—one might say, nothing more childish—could be imagined than these incomprehensible displays of some Puck-like spook bent on every exasperating form of mischief. . . . To attribute them all to diabolical agency is difficult, if only because we credit the enemy of mankind with a higher level of intelligence than that which seems to prompt these outbreaks."[36]

In his book *The Church and Spiritualism*, Thurston recalled that the alleged private revelations to Blessed Anne Catherine Emmerich included the notion of "planetary spirits" who, she said, are "fallen spirits but not devils. They are very, very different from devils." These were among the claims that eventually led to controversy about the authenticity of the alleged record of her testimony, but Thurston reasoned:

---

[35] See Herbert Thurston, *Ghosts and Poltergeists*, J. H. Crehan, ed. (London: Burns Oates, 1953).

[36] Thurston, 202–3.

"My point . . . is not that these were true revelations or that she was responsible for them, but that for fifty years they were accepted as hers without protest by all sorts of eminent theologians, who believed her to have a supernatural knowledge of many mysteries hidden from mankind at large."

The theologians' initial response suggested that they considered the existence of such creatures to be possible within the bounds of a traditional Christian view of the world. "The fact seems to imply," Thurston concluded, "that we possess very little positive knowledge regarding the spiritual influences which, under certain ill-understood conditions, may possibly be able to interfere in the everyday concerns of mankind."[37]

Contemporary UAP often exhibit behaviors similar to poltergeist phenomena. The most common descriptions of how projectiles (usually stones or household objects) are moved through the air by poltergeists sound much like the typical movements of unidentified flying objects. Thurston reported: "Another peculiarity is the wavey path, quite irreconcilable with gravitational laws, which these projectiles seem to follow. They turn corners, swerve in and out, and behave, in fact, like a bird which is free to pick its own way." In addition,

---

[37] Herbert Thurston, *The Church and Spiritualism* (London: Burns Oates, 1933), 3–5, citing Schmöger, *Emmerich*, 206–7. We should note here that Emmerich's description of "planetary spirits" actually bears a strong resemblance to yet another medieval category of faerie folk as identified by Lewis: the "demoted" angels who were sympathetic to Lucifer's rebellion but did not actually join him in it; they were expelled from heaven and banned to dwell on Earth or in the airy regions above it, where they interacted with human beings. See Lewis, *Discarded Image*, 135–36.

they seem to dematerialize and rematerialize as they fly.[38] This description offers an uncanny parallel, for example, to recent accounts of UAP behavior by Navy pilots, not to mention military UAP reports from the last seven decades.[39]

The common prankster/poltergeist connection with UAP is even more obvious in settings such as the Skinwalker ranch in Utah. Prominent among the anomalous phenomena that have appeared there are flying orbs and strange aircraft, in the sky or near the ground, associated with classic prankster occurrences. At Skinwalker, for example, a seventy-pound post digger suddenly and mysteriously disappeared when the owner who was using it left it alone for a few minutes. It was later found perched in the upper branches of a tree twenty feet above the ground.[40]

"Can We Be Quite Sure?"

To sum up: With UAP, we may actually be dealing with extraordinary phenomena of various origins despite similar characteristics.

I think the extraterrestrial hypothesis best accounts for many UAP, and the diabolical hypothesis best accounts for some encounters. But humility requires that we be open to other possibilities for some of the phenomena observed: ultraterrestrials, perhaps; interdimensional beings (as some would insist) from another dimension of existence altogether that at times intersects with our own; or even time-traveling

---

[38] Thurston, *Ghosts*, 196–97.
[39] See Lewis-Kraus, "Pentagon."
[40] Kelleher, *Hunt*, 29, 81.

humans from the future (as still others have suggested). Such realities would not lie beyond the creative wisdom and power of our omniscient, omnipotent Creator.

Are we alone in the universe with God and the angels? That possibility seems to me unlikely. I believe the existence of ETI is highly probable; I can make no knowledgeable claims for faerie folk or poltergeists, interdimensionals or time travelers. But as a parting thought, I most certainly would echo Thurston's provocative challenge: "Is it even certain that there are no other intelligent beings at any time in God's universe besides these three categories of angels, demons, and human souls? I have no thought of affirming as a fact the possibility envisaged in this . . . question; I only ask, *can we be quite sure?*"[41]

---

[41] Kelleher, 2–3, emphasis added.

Bibliography

Achenbach, Joel. "Carl Sagan denied being an atheist. So what did he believe? [Part 1.]" *The Washington Post.* 10 July 2014.

Adams, John. *Diary and Autobiography of John Adams,* L. H. Butterfield, ed. New York: Atheneum, 1964.

St. Albert the Great. *Alberti Magni opera omnia.*

Alnor, William M. *UFOs in the New Age: Extraterrestrial Messages and the Truth of Scripture.* Grand Rapids, Mich.: Baker, 1992.

Ancient Christian Commentary on Scripture: New Testament VI: Romans. Gerald Bray, ed. Downers Grove, Ill.: InterVarsity, 1998.

Ancient Christian Commentary on Scripture: New Testament VIII: Galatians, Ephesians, Philippians. Mark J. Edwards, ed. Downers Grove, Ill.: InterVarsity, 1999.

St. Anselm. *Cur Deus Homo.*

"Are Americans Poised for an Alien Invasion?" Marist Poll, February 12, 2018.

Aristotle. *De Generatione Animalium.*

St. Athanasius. *Epistola ad Adelphium.*

St. Augustine. *City of God.*

———. *De Genesi ad Litteram,* vol. 41 in *Ancient Christian Writers: The Works of the Fathers in Translation.* Edited by J. Quasten, W. Burghardt, T. Lawler. Mahwah, N.J.: Paulist Press, 1982.

———. *Enchiridion.*

———. Epistle 118, to Dioscorus.

Bailey, Philip James. *Festus: A Poem.* 1st American ed. Boston: B.B. Mussey, 1845.

Baker, Thomas. *Reflections upon Learning.* London, 1699.

Balducci, Corrado. "Ufology and Theological Clarifications." Pescara, Italy, June 8, 2001.

Barker, Peter and Bernard R. Goldstein. "Theological Foundations of Kepler's Astronomy" in *Osiris*, vol. 16, *Science in Theistic Contexts*. Chicago: University of Chicago Press, 2001.

Barnes, Julian E. "U.S. Has No Explanation for Unidentified Objects and Stops Short of Ruling Out Aliens." *The New York Times,* 25 June 2021.

Barrow, John D. and Frank J. Tipler. *The Anthropic Cosmological Principle.* 1st ed. Oxford: Oxford University Press, 1986.

St. Basil. *Exegetical Homilies.* Translated by Agnes Clare Way, CDP. Washington, D.C.: Catholic University Press, 1963, Homily 3.

Bentley, Richard. "A Confutation of Atheism from the Origin and Frame of the World." London, 1693, in *Isaac Newton's Papers and Letters on Natural Philosophy.* Edited by Bernard Cohen. Cambridge, Mass.: Harvard University Press, 1958.

Berkeley, George. *Works of Berkeley.* London: Nelson, 1950.

Blumenthal, Ralph and Kean Leslie. "No Longer in Shadows, Pentagon's U.F.O. Unit Will Make Some Findings Public." *The New York Times,* 23 July 2020.

Borel, Pierre. *A New Treatise.*

Boscovich, Roger Joseph. *A Theory of Natural Philosophy.* Translated by J. M. Child Cambridge. Mass.: Harvard University Press, 1966.

Boss, Valentin. *Newton and Russia: The Early Influences 1698–1796.* Cambridge, Mass: Harvard University Press, 1972.

Brazier, Paul. "C. S. Lewis: The Question of Multiple Incarnations." *Heythrop Journal* LV (2014), 393.

Breig, Joseph A. "Man Stands Alone." *America* 106 (November 26, 1960), 294.

Brewster, David. *Memoirs of Life, Writings, and Discoveries of Sir Isaac Newton.* Edinburgh, 1855.

———. *More Worlds Than One.* London, 1870.

Brufke, Juliegrace and Feis, Aaron. "UFOs could threaten US security, pols say after Capitol Hill briefing." *New York Post,* 16 June 2021.

Brumley, Mark. "Who Arranged the Chances? Can Belief in Evolution Be Compatible With Catholic Faith?" *The Catholic Answer,* January/February 2006, 25–28.

Bruno, Giordano. *On the Infinite Universe and Worlds.* Third Dialogue, Translated by Dorothea Waley Singer. New York: Henry Schuman, 1950.

Bruns, J. Edgar. "Cosmolatry." *The Catholic World* 191:1 August 1960.

Burr, Enoch Fitch. *Celestial Empires.* New York, 1885.

Burton, Charlie. "This man ran the Pentagon's secretive UFO programme for a decade. We had some questions." *Gentlemen's Quarterly,* November 9, 2021, https://www.gq-magazine.co.uk/politics/article/luis-elizondo-interview-2021.

Burton, Robert. *Anatomy of Melancholy.* London: John C. Nimmo, 1893; reprint New York, 1973.

Cadonicci, Giovanni. *Confutazione teologica-fisica del sistema di Gulgielmo Derham inglese, che vuole tutti i planeti de creature ragionevoli, come la terra, abitati.* Brescia, 1760.

Campanella, Tommaso. "The Defense of Galileo." Translated by Grant McColley. *Smith College Studies in History,* 22, nos. 3 and 4, 1937, 66–67.

Carey, Thomas J. and Donald R. Schmitt. *Witness to Roswell: Unmasking the Government's Biggest Coverup.* 2nd ed., rev. San Francisco: Weiser, 2009.

Castello, Don Nello. *Così parlò Padre Pio*. Vicenza, Italy, 1974.

Catechism of the Catholic Church. 2nd ed. Vatican City: Libreria Editrice Vaticana, 1997.

Chalmers, Thomas. *A Series of Discourses on the Christian Revelation Viewed in Connection with the Modern Astronomy*. New York: American Tract Society, 1850.

Chesterton, G. K. *Orthodoxy*. London: John Lane, 1908.

Clary, Grayson. "Why Sci-Fi Has So Many Catholics." *The Atlantic* 10 November 2015.

Clayton, Philip. "Toward a Theory of Divine Action That Has Traction," in *Scientific Perspectives on Divine Action: Twenty Years of Challenge and Progress*. Vatican City State: Vatican Observatory Publications and Berkeley, Calif.: The Center for Theology and the Natural Sciences, 2008, 87–110.

St. Clement. *The First Epistle of Clement to the Corinthians* in *The Ante-Nicene Fathers*. vol. 1. Edited by Alexander Roberts and James Donaldson. Grand Rapids, Mich.: Eerdmans, 1987.

Clines, D. J. "Humanity as the Image of God," in *On the Way to the Postmodern: Old Testament Essays, 1967–1998*. Sheffield: Sheffield Academic Press, 1998.

Congar, Yves. "Has God Peopled the Stars?" Appendix 2 in *The Wide World My Parish: Salvation and Its Problems*. Translated by Donald Attwater. Baltimore: Helicon Press, 1961.

Congregation for the Clergy, *General Catechetical Directory* 1971; https://www.vatican.va/roman_curia/congregations/cclergy/documents/rc_con_cclergy_doc_11041971_gcat_en.html.

Congregation for the Doctrine of the Faith. "Doctrinal Commentary on the Concluding Formula of the *Professio Fidei*." http://www.ewtn.com/library/CURIA/CDFADTU.HTM.

―――. *Dominus iesus: On the unicity and salvific universality of Jesus Christ and the Church* (2000).

Connell, Francis J. "Flying Saucers and Theology," in *The Truth About Flying Saucers.* Edited by A. Michel. New York: Pyramid Books, 1967.

Consolmagno, Guy and Paul R. Mueller. *Would You Baptize an Extraterrestrial? And Other Questions from the Inbox at the Vatican Observatory.* New York: Image, 2014.

Copernicus, Nicholas. *On the Revolutions.* Edited by Jerzy Dobrzycki. Translated and commentary by Edward Rosen. Baltimore: Macmillan, 1978.

Courbet, Pierre. "*De la redemption et de la pluralité des mondes habités,*" *Cosmos,* 4th ser., 28 May 19, 1894, 208–211; 2 June 1894, 272–276.

Craig, William. "The Historical Adam." *First Things,* October 2021.

Cranfield, C. E. B. "Some Observations on Romans 8:19–21," in R. Banks, ed., *Reconciliation and Hope: Essays on Atonement and Eschatology.* Grand Rapids, Mich: Eerdmans, 1974, 224–230.

Crowe, Michael J. *The Extraterrestrial Life Debate, 1750–1900: The Idea of a Plurality of Worlds from Kant to Lowell.* Cambridge: Cambridge University Press, 1986; new ed., Mineola, N.Y.: Dover Publications, 1999.

―――. "A History of the Extraterrestrial Life Debate," *Zygon,* vol. 32, no. 2 (June 1997), 149.

―――. *The Extraterrestrial Life Debate: Antiquity to 1915: A Source Book.* Notre Dame, Ind.: University of Notre Dame Press, 2008.

Dailey, Timothy. *The Paranormal Conspiracy: The Truth About Ghosts, Aliens, and Mysterious Beings.* Minneapolis, Minn.: Chosen, 2015.

Darling, David. *The Extraterrestrial Encyclopedia: An Alphabetical Reference to All Life in the Universe.* New York: Three Rivers Press, 2000.

De Concilio, Januarius. *Harmony Between Science and Revelation* (1889).

————. "The Plurality of Worlds." *American Catholic Quarterly Review,* 9 April 1884, 193–216.

Delano, Kenneth. *Many Worlds, One God.* Hicksville, N.Y.: Exposition Press, 1977.

Delhay, P. "Antipodes," *New Catholic Encyclopedia.* New York: McGraw-Hill, 1967, vol. 1, 631–2.

Delio, Ilia. "Christ and Extraterrestrial Life." *Theology and Science,* 5:3 2007.

Denzinger, Henry. *The Sources of Catholic Dogma.* Translated by Roy J. Deferrari. 13ᵗʰ ed. Boonville, N.Y.: Preserving Christian Publications, 2009.

Denzler, Brenda. *The Lure of the Edge: Scientific Passions, Religious Beliefs, and the Pursuit of UFOs.* Los Angeles: University of California Press, 2002.

Descartes, René. *Works.*

de Vere, Aubrey. "The Death of Copernicus." *Contemporary Review* 56 1889: 421–30.

DeVries, Gerhard. *"Dissertatio academica de lunicolis,"* in Daniel Voet, *Physiologia, sive, de natura rerum libri sex, recogniti, ac notis illustrati a Gerardo De Vries … accedit hujus Dissertatio germina, altera de lumine, altera de lunicolis.* 3ʳᵈ ed. Utrecht: Trajecti ad Rhenum, 1694.

Dews, Fred. "Communication, Technology, and Extraterrestrial Life: The Advice Brookings Gave NASA About the Space Program in 1960." *Brookings Now,* Monday, 12 May 2014.

Dick, Steven J. *The Biological Universe: The Twentieth-Century Extraterrestrial Life Debate and the Limits of Science.* Cambridge: Cambridge University Press, 1996.

————, ed. *Many Worlds: The New Universe, Extraterrestrial Life & the Theological Implications.* West Conshohocken, Penn.: Templeton Press, 2000.

————. *Plurality of Worlds: The Extraterrestrial Life Debate from Democritus to Kant.* Cambridge: Cambridge University Press, 1982.

"The Divine Liturgy of the Holy Apostle and Evangelist Mark, the Disciple of the Holy Peter." *The Ante-Nicene Fathers,* vol. 7. Edited by A. Cleveland Coxe. Grand Rapids, Mich: Eerdmans, 1985.

Dolan, Richard M. and Bryce Zabel. *A.D. After Disclosure: The People's Guide to Life After Contact.* Rochester, N.Y.: Keyhole Publishing, 2010.

Donne, John. *Devotions upon Emergent Occasions.* London, 1624.

Droesser, Christopher and Hakai Magazine. "The Search for Intelligent Life Heads Underwater." *The Atlantic,* 31 October 21.

Drummond, William. *The Poetical Works of William Drummond of Hawthornden.* Edited by L. E. Kastner. Manchester: At the University Press, 1913.

Dubray, Charles. "Marin Mersenne." *The Catholic Encyclopedia.* New York: Robert Appleton Company, 1911. http://www.newadvent.org /cathen/10209b.htm.

Duhem, Pierre. *Medieval Cosmology: Theories of Infinity Place, Time, Void, and the Plurality of Worlds.* Chicago: University of Chicago Press, 1985.

Dwight, Timothy. *Theology Explained and Defended in a Series of Sermons.* 5 vols. Middletown, Conn., 1818.

Enchiridion symbolorum: definitionum et declarationum de rebus fidei et morum. Edited by Heinrich Denzinger. Rome: Herder, 1963.

Félix, Joseph. *Le progress par le Christianisme: Conférences de Notre-Dame de Paris — Anée 1863,* 2nd ed. Paris, 1864.

Fisher, C. L. and D. Fergusson. "Karl Rahner and the extra-terrestrial life debate." *Heythrop Journal* 47 2006, 275.

Fontennel, Bernard le Bovier de. *Conversations on the Plurality of Worlds* Translated by H. A. Hargreaves. Berkeley: University of California Press, 1990.

[Foster, John]. *Eclectic Review* 8 (1817), 212.

Francisco, Reginaldo. *"Possibilità di una redenzione cosmica,"* in *Origini, l'Universo, la Vita, l'intelligenza,* Edited by F. Betorla et al. Padua: Il Poligrafo, 1994.

Franklin, Benjamin. "Articles of Belief and Acts of Religion," in *Works of Benjamin Franklin, with notes and a life of the author by Jared Sparks.* Boston: Hilliard, Gray, and Company, 1840.

French, David P., ed. *Minor English Poets 1660–1780.* New York, 1967.

Friedman, Stanton T. *Top Secret/Majic: Operation Majestic-12 and the United States Government's UFO Cover-up.* 2nd ed. Boston: Da Capo Press, 2005.

Galilei, Galileo. *Dialogue Concerning the Two Chief World Systems: Ptolemaic and Copernican.* Translated by Stillman Drake. Berkeley: University of Berkeley Press, 1962.

———. "Letter on Sunspots," in *Discoveries and Opinions of Galileo.* Edited and translated by Stillman Drake. New York: Doubleday, 1957.

Garrigou-Lagrange, Réginald. *Christ the Saviour: A Commentary on the Third Part of St. Thomas' Theological Summa* (1945). http://www.documentacatholicaomnia.eu/03d/1877-1964,_Garrigou_Lagrange._R,_The_Third_Part_Of_St_Thomas'Theological_Summa,_EN.pdf.

George, Marie I. "Aquinas on Intelligent Extra-Terrestrial Life." *The Thomist* 65:2 (April 2001), 239–258.

———. *Christianity and Extraterrestrials? A Catholic Perspective.* New York: iUniverse, 2005.

Gregersen, Niels Hendrik. "Deep Incarnation: Why Evolutionary Continuity Matters in Christology." *Toronto Journal of Theology* 26:2 (2010), 179–187.

St. Gregory of Nazianzus. *First Epistle to Cledonius.*

St. Gregory of Nyssa. *In illud: Tunc et ipse filius,* in *Gregorii Nysenni Opera* III/2. Edited by Kenneth Downing. Leiden: Brill, 1986.

Hagen, John. "Nicolaus Copernicus." *The Catholic Encyclopedia.* New York: Robert Appleton Company, 1908.

Halley, Edmond. *Miscellanea curiosa.* 3rd ed. London, 1726.

Hardon, John. *God the Author of Nature and the Supernatural: Part Two: Creation as a Divine Fact.* Thesis V, http://www.therealpresence.org /archives/God/God_010.htm.

Herder, Johann Gottfried. Über die Seelenwanderung: Drei Gespräche, in Herder, *Sämtliche Werke.* Edited by Bernard Suphan Hildesheim. 1967 reprint of the Berlin 1888 original.

Hewitt, Augustine F. "Another Word on Other Worlds." *Catholic World,* 56 (October 1892), 18–26.

Hill, Nicholas. *Philosophia epucirea.* Paris, 1601; Geneva, 1619.

Hillstrom, Elizabeth L. *Testing the Spirits.* Downers Grove, Ill.: InterVarsity Press, 1995.

Huygens, Christiaan. *The Celestial Worlds Discover'd: or, Conjectures Concerning the Inhabitants, Plants, and Productions of the Worlds in the Planets.* London, 1698.

Ilive, Jacob. *Oration ... Proving I. The Plurality of Worlds. II. That this Earth is Hell. III. That the Souls of Men are the Apostate Angels. IV. That the Fire which shall punish those who shall be confined to this Globe after the Day of Judgement will be Immaterial ...* London, 1733.

St. Irenaeus. *Against Heresies.*

———. *Proof of the Apostolic Preaching.* Translated by Joseph P. Smith. New York: Newman Press, 1952.

Jaki, Stanley L. "Extraterrestrial Intelligence and Scientific Progress." Paper presented at the 1985 meeting of the History of Science Society, Bloomington, Indiana.

―――. "Extraterrestrials, or Better Be Moonstruck?" in *The Limits of a Limitless Science: And Other Essays.* Wilmington, Del: ISI Books, 2000, 150.

―――. *The Savior of Science.* Grand Rapids, Mich: W.B. Eerdmans, 2000.

Jean Paul. *Flower, Fruit, and Thorn Pieces; or, the Wedded Life, Death, and Marriage of Firmian Stanislaus Siebenkäs.* Translated by Alexander Ewing. London, 1895.

Jenkin, Robert. *The Reasonableness and Certainty of the Christian Religion.* London, 1700.

St. Jerome. Letter 124, "To Avitus," in *The Principal Works of St. Jerome,* vol. 6, *Nicene and Post-Nicene Fathers.* Second Series. Edited by Philip Schaff and Henry Wace. Grand Rapids, Mich.: Eerdmans, 1983.

St. Jerome. *The Life of Paul the Hermit.*

St. John Chrysostom. *Commentary on Colossians.*

St. John Chrysostom. *Homilies on First Corinthians.* vol. 12, *Nicene and Post-Nicene Fathers.* First Series. Edited by Philip Schaff. Grand Rapids, Mich.: Eerdmans, 1988, Homily XVII.

St. John Chrysostom. *In Gen. Sermo* II.

Kean, Leslie. *UFOs: Generals, Pilots, and Government Officials Go on the Record.* New York: Harmony Books, 2010.

Keel, John A. *Operation Trojan Horse: An exhaustive study of unidentified flying objects — revealing their source and the forces that control them.* London: Abacus, 1973.

Kelleher, Colm A. and George Knapp. *Hunt for the Skinwalker: Science Confronts the Unexplained at a Remote Ranch in Utah.* New York: Paraview, 2005.

Kent, W. "Devil," in *The Catholic Encyclopedia.* New York: Robert Appleton Company, 1908.

Kepler, Johannes. *Gesammelte Werke.*

———. *Kepler's Conversation with Galileo's Sidereal Messenger* Translated and annotated by Edward Rosen. New York: Johnson Reprint Corporation, 1965.

Kereszty, Roch A. *Jesus Christ: Fundamentals of Theology.* rev. ed. New York: St. Paul's, 2002.

Klopstock, Friedrich. *Der Messias,* in Klopstock's *Ausgewählte Werke.* Edited by K. A. Schleiden. Munich, 1962.

Koch, J. "Nicholas of Cusa." *New Catholic Encyclopedia.*

Lacatski, James T., Colm A. Kelleher, and George Knapp. *Skinwalkers at the Pentagon: An Insiders' Account of the Secret Government UFO Program.* Henderson, Nev.: RTMA, LLC, 2021.

Laframboise, T. Franche d. *"ALIEN JESUS": exogenesis, posthumanism, and the rise of the A.I. gods.* Dalton, Penn.: Mount Thabor Press, forthcoming.

Lazzari, Edmund Michael. "Would St. Thomas Baptize an Extraterrestrial?" *New Blackfriars,* vol. 99 (1082): January 1, 2018; 440–457.

Lefto, Brian. "Anselm on the Necessity of the Incarnation." *Religious Studies* 31:2 (June 1995), 167–185.

Leibniz, G. W. *Theodicy: Essay upon the Goodness of God, the Freedom of Man, and the Origin of Evil.* Translated by E. M. Haggard. New Haven, Conn.: Yale University Press, 1952.

Leitch, William. *God's Glory in the Heavens.* 3rd ed. London, 1867.

St. Leo the Great. *St. Leo the Great: Sermons.* Translated by Jane Freeland and Agnes Conway. Washington, D.C.: Catholic University of America Press, 1996.

Lewis, C. S. *The Chronicles of Narnia.* London: Geoffrey Bles, 1950–1956.

———. *Lewis: Collected Letters.* San Francisco: Harper Collins, 2007.

————. "Dogma and the Universe." in *Undeceptions: Essays on Theology and Ethics.* London: Geoffrey Bles, 1971.

————. *Out of the Silent Planet.* London: The Bodley Head, 1938.

————. *Perelandra.* London: The Bodley Head, 1943.

————. "Religion and Rocketry." *The World's Last Night and Other Essays.* New York: Harcourt Brace, 1952.

————. "The Seeing Eye." *Christian Reflections.* Grand Rapids, Mich.: Eerdmans, 1967.

————. *That Hideous Strength.* New York: Simon & Schuster, 2011.

Lewis-Kraus, Gideon. "How the Pentagon Started Taking UFOs Seriously: For decades, flying saucers were a punchline. Then the U.S. government got over the taboo." *The New Yorker,* 30 April 2021.

Locke, John. *Essay Concerning Human Understanding.*

Loeb, Avi. *Extraterrestrial: The First Sign of Intelligent Life Beyond Earth.* New York: Houghton Mifflin Harcourt, 2021.

Longenecker, Dwight. "Angels and Aliens." 1 June 2013, https://www.catholic.com/magazine/print-edition/angels-and-aliens.

Longrich, Nicholas R. "Did Neanderthals Go to War With Our Ancestors?" *BBC Future,* 2 November 2020.

Lovejoy, Arthur. *The Great Chain of Being.* Cambridge, Mass: Harvard University Press, 1936.

Maistre, Comte Joseph de. *Soirées de Saint-Pétersbourg.* Paris, n.d., 318–19. Translated by Eugene Lynch, "On Sacrifices." *The United States Catholic Magazine and Monthly Review* (1845). vol. 4, 300–305.

Marković, Zeljko. "Boscovich's *Theoria*." In Lancelot Law Whyte, ed., *Roger Joseph Boscovich.* London: Allen & Urwin, 1961.

Mascall, E. L. *Christian Theology and Natural Science.* London: Ronald Press, 1956.

Mather, Cotton. *The Christian Philosopher.* Gainesville, Fla.: Scholars Facsimiles and Reprints, 1968, facsimile reproduction of the London 1721 original.

McColley, Grant. "The Defense of Galileo of Thomas Campanella." *Smith College Studies in History,* 22, nos. 3–4 (April–July 1937).

McColley, Grant and H. W. Miller. "Saint Bonaventure, Francis Mayron, William Vorilong, and the Doctrine of a Plurality of Worlds." *Speculum* 12, no. 3 (1937), 386–89.

Melanchthon, Philip. *Initia doctrinae physicae.* Wittenberg, 1550, fol. 43.

Menshutkin, Boris. *Russia's Lomonosov: Chemist — Courtier — Physicist — Poet.* Translated by J. E. Thal, E. J. Webster, and W. C. Huntington. Princeton, N.J.: Princeton University Press, 1962.

Meynell, Alice. *The Poems of Alice Meynell.* New York: C. Scribner's Sons, 1923.

Middelton, Richard. *Clarissimi theologi Magistri* Ricardi di Mediavilla *Seraphici ord. min. convent. super quatuor libros Sententiarum Petri Lombardi quaestiones subtilissimae,* lib. 1, dist. XLIII, art. I, quaest. IV.

Mills, Marc G. and Eric W. Davis, eds. *Frontiers of Propulsion Science.* Reston, Va.: American Institute of Aeronautics and Astronautics, Inc., 2009. https://arc.aiaa.org/doi/book/10.2514/4.479953.

Milne, E. A. "The Second Law of Thermodynamics: Evolution." *Modern Cosmology and the Christian Idea of God.* Oxford: Oxford University Press, 1952.

Moigno, François. *Les splendeurs de la foi.* Paris (1877).

Monseigneur de Montignez. "Théorie chrétienne sur la pluralité des mondes." *Archives théologiques,* 9 (1865).

More, Henry. *Democritus Platonissans, or, An Essay on the Infinity of Worlds out of Platonick Principles.* Cambridge (1646).

———. *Divine Dialogues.* London (1668).

Nicholas of Cusa. *Of Learned Ignoranc.* Translated by Germain Heron. London: Routledge and Kegan Paul, 1954.

Office of the Director of National Intelligence. "Preliminary Assessment: Unidentified Aerial Phenomena." 25 June 2021.

O'Meara, Thomas F. "Christian Theology and Extraterrestrial Life." *Theological Studies* 60.1 (1995), 25.

———. *Vast Universe: Extraterrestrials and Christian Revelation.* Collegeville, Minn.: Liturgical Press, 2012.

Oresme, Nicole. *Le livre du ciel et du monde.* Edited by Albert Menut and Alexander Denomy. Translated by Albert Menut. Madison: University of Wisconsin Press, 1968.

Origen. *De Principiis.* Bk. II, ch. 3, para. 6, 273–47.

Ott, Ludwig. *Fundamentals of Catholic Dogm.,* Translated by Patrick Lynch. Charlotte, N.C.: TAN Books, reprint 1974.

Paine, Thomas. *The Age of Reason* in *Representative Selections.* Edited by Harry Hayden Clark. New York: Hill and Wang, 1961.

Paul, Erich Robert. *Science, Religion, and Mormon Cosmology.* Urbana: University of Illinois Press, 1992.

Perujo, Niceto Alonso. *La pluralidad de mundos habitados ante le fé católica. Estudio en que se examina la habitacion de los astros en relacion con los dogmas católicos, se demestrua su perfecta armonia con estos, y se refutan muchose errores de Mr. Flammarion.* Madrid (1877).

Peters, Ted, ed. *Astrotheology: Science and Theology Meet Extraterrestrial Life.* Eugene, Or.: Cascade Books, 2018.

———. "Fundamentalist Literature." *Science, Theology, and Ethics.* Burlington, Vt.: Ashgate, 2003, 129–134.

Piat, Clodius. "René Descartes," *The Catholic Encyclopedia.* New York: Robert Appleton Company, 1908. http://www.newadvent.org/cat hen/04744b.htm.

Pope Pius XII. *Humani generis* (1950).

Pohle, Joseph. *Die Sternwelten und ihre Bewohner.* 2nd ed. Cologne (1899).

Pope, Alexander. *An Essay on Man.*

Porteous, Skip. "Robertson Advocates Stoning for UFO Enthusiasts." Freedom Writer Press Release, Great Barrington, Mass. (28 July 1997).

Putz, Oliver. "Moral Apes, Human Uniqueness, and the Image of God." *Zygon* 44:3 (2009), 613–24.

Rahner, Karl. *Foundations of Christian Faith.* New York: Seabury Press, 1978.

Raible, Daniel C. "Rational Life in Outer Space?" *America: National Catholic Weekly Review* 103 (August 13, 1960), 532–35.

Redfern, Nick. *Final Events and the Secret Government Group on Demonic UFOs and the Afterlife.* New York: Anomalist Books, 2010.

Reich, Aaron. "Former Israeli space security chief says aliens exist, humanity not ready." *The Jerusalem Post,* December 10, 2020, https://www.jpost.com/omg/former-israeli-space-security-chief-says -aliens-exist-humanity-not-ready-651405.

Robbins, Peter. "Politics, Religion, and Human Nature: Practical Problems and Roadblocks on the Path toward Official UFO Acknowledgement." August 2004.

Rosenwald, Michael. "How UFOs went from joke to national security worry in Washington." *The Washington Post,* 23 May 2021.

Rossi, Paolo. "Nobility of Man and Plurality of Worlds." In Allen Debus. *Science, Medicine and Society in the Renaissance.* New York: Science History Publications, 1972, 2:131–62.

Runes, Dagobert D., ed. *The Dictionary of Philosophy.* New York: Philosophical Library.

Sagan, Carl. *The Demon-Haunted World: Science as a Candle in the Dark.* New York: Random House, 1995.

———. "UFO's: The Extraterrestrial and Other Hypotheses." In Carl Sagan and Donald Menzel, ed. *UFO's — A Scientific Debate.* Cornell: Ithaca, 1972.

Schanz, Paul. *A Christian Apology.* Translated by M. F. Glancey and V. J. Schobel. 5th ed. Ratisbon (1891).

Schmöger, Carl E. *The Life of Anne Catherine Emmerich.* Rockford, Ill.: TAN Books, rep., 1976, 2 vols.

Scientific Perspectives on Divine Action. 6 vols. Vatican City, Berkeley, Ca.: The Vatican Observatory and The Center for Theology and the Natural Sciences, 1993–2008.

Scot, Michael. *Eximii atque excellentissimi physicorum motuum cursusque siderei indagatoris* Michaelis Scoti *super auctore Sperae, cum quaestionibus diligiter emedatis, expositio confecta Illustrissimi Imperatoris Domini D. Frederici praecibus.*

Scotti, Dom Paschal. *Galileo Revisited: The Galileo Affair in Context.* San Francisco: Ignatius, 2017.

Searle, George Mary. "Are the Planets Inhabitable?" *Astronomical Society of the Pacific Publications* (1890), 165–177:169.

Secchi, Angelo. *Descrizione del nuevo osservatorio del collegio romano.* Rome (1856).

———. *Les étoiles,* v. II Paris (1879).

The Seven Ecumenical Councils. vol. 14. Edited by Philip Schaff and Henry Wace. Grand Rapids, Mich.: Eerdmans, 1986.

Sherard, R. A. "Flammarion the Astronomer." *McClure's* (2 May 1884), 569–77:569.

Sri, Edward. "Is Mary's Queenship Biblical?" https://edwardsri.com/2014/12/27/is-marys-queenship-biblical/.

Struve, Otto. "Lomonosov." *Sky and Telescope* 13 (1954), 118–20.

Swedenborg, Emanuel. *Earths in the Universe.* London: Swedenborg Society, 1970.

Teilhard de Chardin. "Fall, Redemption, and Geocentrism." *Christianity and Evolution.* New York: Harcourt, Brace, Jovanovich, 1971.

―――. *La multiplicité des mondes habités." Oeuvres* Paris: Seuil, 1969.

Thigpen, Paul. *Saints Who Saw Hell: And Other Christian Witnesses to the Fate of the Damned.* Charlotte, N.C.: TAN Books, 2019.

St. Thomas Aquinas. *Commentary on Colossians.*

―――. *Commentary on Ephesians.*

―――. *Commentary on the Letters of St. Paul to the Philippians, Colossians, Thessalonians, Timothy, Titus, and Philemon.* Edited by J. Mortsensen and E. Alarcón. Translated by F. R. Larcher. Lander, Wy.: Aquinas Institute for the Study of Sacred Doctrine, 2012.

―――. *Commentary on Romans.*

―――. *Summa Contra Gentiles.*

―――. *Summa Theologica.*

Thurston, Herbert. *The Church and Spiritualism.* London: Burns Oates, 1933.

―――. *Ghosts and Poltergeists.* Edited by J. H. Crehan. London: Burns Oates, 1953.

Tyndall, John. "The Belfast Address." In Tyndall. *Fragments of Science.* New York (1901).

Vakoch, Douglas A. "Roman Catholic Views of Extraterrestrial Intelligence: Anticipating the Future by Examining the Past." Foundation for the Future, 2000.

Valle, Jacques. *Passport to Magonia: From Folklore to Flying Saucers.* New York: Daily Grail, 2014.

van Huyssteen, Wentzel. *Alone in the World: Human Uniqueness in Science and Theology.* Grand Rapids, Mich.: Eerdmans, 2006.

Vatican Council II: The Conciliar and Post Conciliar Documents. Edited by Austin Flannery. rev. ed. Grand Rapids, Mich.: Eerdmans, 1992.

"The Vatican Ponders Extraterrestrials." *The Guardian,* 11 November 2009.

von Rennenkampff, Marik. "NASA chief Bill Nelson latest official to suggest UFOs have otherworldly origins." *The Hill,* 1 November 21.

Walker, Charlton. "Exultet," *The Catholic Encyclopedia.* New York: Robert Appleton Company, 1909.

Ward, Richard. *The Life of the Learned and Pious Dr. Henry More: Late Fellow of Christ's College in Cambridge. To Which Are Annexed Divers Philosophical Poems and Hymns.* Wheaton, Ill.: Theosophical Publishing Society, 1911.

Watts, Isaac. *Knowledge of the Heavens and the Earth Made Easy; or, The First Principles of Astronomy and Geography.* 2nd ed. London, 1728.

Whewell, William. *Of the Plurality of Worlds: A Facsimile of the First Edition of 1853; Plus Previously Published Material Excised by the Author Just Before the Book Went to Press; and Whewell's Dialogue Rebutting His Critics, reprinted from the Second Edition.* Chicago: University of Chicago Press, 2001.

Weigel, George. *Letters to a Young Catholic.* New York: Basic Books, 2004.

Weintraub, David A., ed. *Religions and Extraterrestrial Life: How Will We Deal With It?* New York: Springer, 2014.

Wesley, John. *The Works of Rev. John Wesley.* Grand Rapids, Mich: Baker Book House, 1978, reprint of the London 1878 edition.

Wiener, Leo. *Anthology of Russian Literature.* New York: G. P. Putnam, 1902.

Wiker, Benjamin. "Alien Ideas." https://www.catholicity.com/commentary/wiker/06325.html.

———. *The Darwin Myth: The Life and Lies of Charles Darwin.* Washington, D.C.: Regnery, 2009.

Wiker, Benjamin with William A. Dembski. *Moral Darwinism: How We Became Hedonists.* Westmont, Ill.: InterVarsity Press, 2002.

Wilkins, John. *Discovery of a World in the Moone* (1638).

Wilkinson, David. *Science, Religion, and the Search for Extraterrestrial Intelligence.* Oxford: Oxford University Press, 2013.

Winkler, Edwin T. "Religion and Astronomy." *Baptist Quarterly* 5 (1871), 58–74:58.

Yates, Frances. *Giordano Bruno and the Hermetic Tradition.* London: Routledge and Kegan Paul, 1964.

Yuhas, Alan. "The Pentagon Released U.F.O. Videos. Don't Hold Your Breath for a Breakthrough." *The New York Times,* 28 April 2020.

Zabel, Bryce. "The Roswell UFO Crash is on the Fast Track to Disclosure," *Trail of the Saucers,* July 2, 2021, https://medium.com/on-the -trail-of-the-saucers/roswell2021-a9e209925a66.

Pope Zachary. *Epistola XI Zacharia Papae ad Bonifacium Archiepiscopum* in the *Patrologia Latina.*

Zubek, Theodore J. "Theological Questions on Space Creatures." *The American Ecclesiastical Review* 145 (1966), 393–94.

INDEX OF
SCRIPTURAL CITATIONS

INDEX